The Lost
History of the
Canine Race

The Lost
History of the
Canine Race

Our 15,000-Year
Love Affair with Dogs

Mary Elizabeth Thurston

ANDREWS AND MCMEEL

A Universal Press Syndicate Company

Kansas City

Library of Congress Cataloging-in-Publication Data

Thurston, Mary E.
The lost history of the canine race : our 15,000-year
love affair with dogs / by Mary E. Thurston
p.   cm.
ISBN 0-8362-0548-0 (hd)
1. Dogs—History. 2. Human-animal relationships. I. Title.
SF422.5.T48   1996
304.2'7—dc20   96-11171
CIP

Attention: Schools and Businesses

Andrews and McMeel books are available at quantity
discounts with bulk purchase for educational,
business, or sales promotional use.
For information, please write to
Special Sales Department,
Andrews and McMeel, 4520 Main Street,
Kansas City, Missouri 64111.

Written on the centennial of her birth, this book is dedicated to my grandmother Vera Volz McWharter, who instilled in me an unwavering belief in the power of love—and taught me the importance of spoiling dogs.

Contents

Preface
ix

Acknowledgments
xi

One
Leaving the Garden
1

Two
The Children of Anubis
24

Three
Cave Canem
41

Four
Feudal Society,
Renaissance, and Revolution
66

Five
Class Aspirations
97

Six
Canine Empancipation
121

Seven

The Other Native Americans

146

Eight

The Dogs of War

174

Nine

Eye of the Beholder

209

Ten

The Way to a Dog's Heart

232

Eleven

Saying Good-Bye

251

Twelve

History in the Making

268

Glossary

285

Recommended Reading

291

Index

293

Preface

IN THE LAST DECADE ESPECIALLY, a wealth of quantitative and qualitative evidence has been published concerning dogs and their impact on the physical and emotional health of human beings. Science has finally confirmed what pet lovers have always suspected—that dogs are actually good for us. Studies indicate that they play a critical role in human socialization, since children who care for pets are more likely to mature into emotionally healthy adults, empowered with a strong sense of the other and the ability to empathize, skills that are essential to maintaining peace and harmony in any society. Conversely, a correlation has been found between the abuse of dogs and the abuse of people. Today, cruelty to animals is widely recognized as an indicator of serious psychological dysfunction.

Canine companionship also has been shown to lower blood pressure and prolong the lives of heart attack victims, people who live alone, and the elderly. Such revelations have opened up new avenues of employment for dogs, as four-footed therapists. Even the simple act of stroking a dog can have a profound impact on our health, enabling victims of depression and trauma to articulate the inner turmoil they experience.

The recent abundance of popular articles and other information about dogs reflects our growing appreciation of these animals, as a race of thinking, feeling beings with a multifaceted "culture" born of their interactions with people. As such, they are heirs to a rich, varied heritage reflecting their influence on modern thinking, as well as the thinking of our ancestors. In this sense, canine history not only chronicles the remarkable story of a uniquely adaptable animal, but documents the spiritual and emotional evolution of the human species as well. And it is through studying this past that our present relationships with dogs take on fuller meaning. In failing to preserve this history, we risk relinquishing the control over the future that is born of learning or knowledge. This is not to be taken lightly, since our remaining physical and spiritual ties to the natural world are in danger of being severed by habitat destruction, overpopulation, and electronic, mediated experience. For many of us, canines are our one and only link to the natural world that has shaped the human psyche for eons.

Yet whenever humanity has chosen to deny dogs their status as living, sentient creatures, it seems that their history also has been subverted. Archaeological and historical sites, artifacts, photographs, personal writings, government documents, and a host of other materials born of our relationships with dogs have been systematically ignored, trivialized, burned, buried, bulldozed, vandalized, and pulverized into garden fertilizer—or, more often than not, simply never recorded. "It's *only* dogs, after all," has been the refrain heard time and again. Conversely, it invariably has been people who treat their own dogs as members of the family who believe that canine history is important, for in knowledge of the past they find a sense of kinship with people and animals who lived centuries ago. And in the process, they acquire a new and greater appreciation for the dogs of today.

Acknowledgments

I am indebted to many generous folk, for without their help this book would have been short, indeed. Among those who have shared a unique variety of source materials are: Stephen and Iona Joseph, Gail McDonald, Curator Chryssanthy Baltoyianni, Nancy Bergendahl, Royce McWharter, Allen Sims and Lynn Carson, Jan Koler, Dr. Howard Hayes, Leslie Kopas, Geoffrey Jenkinson, Sue Schmitz, Nina Natelson, Cindy Carroccio, Donna Sadjak, Carol Clarke, James Flurchick, June Wholley, Viscount Bledisloe, Count Geoffroy de Beauffort and Countess Michelle Mommer de Beauffort, Countess Lascelles de Premio Real, David and Noelle Soren, Dr. Bill Bone, Luc Briers, Ed Martin, Jr., the Dunk family, Clifford "Doggie" Hubbard, Jerald Milanich, Bert Willemen, and Jesse Mendez. I am indebted to my friend and colleague Mike Lemish, whose unique insights and camaraderie contributed greatly to this work. And a heartfelt thank-you to Isis Johnson, Karen Fehrenbach, and the many people in Puerto Rico who are leading the fight for a new humane ethic on that island.

I am especially grateful to a legion of pet owners who live with disabled dogs and cats, for sharing their trials and triumphs. Their courage and boundless compassion are an inspiration for all of us.

Director General Duncan Green and the staff at the Dogs' Home Battersea, Leeds Castle Agent Andrew Wells and Mrs. J. Woodman all went above and beyond professional courtesy to make me feel welcome during my research in England, as did Dr. Rosalind Janssen of the Petrie Museum of Egyptian Archaeology. I owe a special debt of thanks to Theresa Fitzgerald and Simon Richards of the Central Royal Parks, who gave me permission to survey the Hyde Park Dog Cemetery, an experience I will never forget.

I also am indebted to dear friends for their infinite patience and understanding. Teenie Hefner changed the course of my life twenty years ago by teaching me the high art of artifact appreciation. And the founding members of Animal Trustees of Austin played no small part in inspiring this work—their steadfastness, courage, and compassion convinced me that one person (or one animal) *can* make a difference. Dr. Brian Stross, undoubtedly one of the most brilliant iconographers to grace the hallowed halls of anthropology, deserves credit for his years of encouragement, as does professor of art and photography Dr. Gibbs Milliken, a real Renaissance man. And a very special thank-you to Dr. Elinor Evans and Dr. William Reeder.

I am blessed to have been born into a family of free thinkers. The contributions of my mother and father to this book date back to the day they gave me a pencil, a stack of shirt cardboards to draw on, and my first animal book. Not only have they been exceptional parents, they have been exceptional friends. And my brother John, renowned for his quirky humor, saw me through some trying times in the course of this project.

I have been blessed, too, with the love and companionship of an extended family of dogs who have shared with me their innermost feelings. Brownie, Private, Pepsie, and Bill welcomed me as one of the pack when I was young, providing me a sense of belonging I could not find in the world of humans at the time. And a host of canine nieces and nephews have inspired my writing over the years, including Diamond, Muffin, Patches, Freddie, Anna, Ted, Roto, Chessie, Steiff, and little Keller.

But it was in the dark brown eyes of my own dog, Petey, that I first pondered the Lost History of the Canine Race.

The Lost
History of the
Canine Race

Kindness to all living things is the true religion.

—Buddha

One

Leaving the Garden

The earth trembled and a great rift appeared, separating the first man and woman from the rest of the animal kingdom. As the chasm grew deeper and wider, all the other creatures, afraid for their lives, returned to the forest—except for the dog, who after much consideration leapt the perilous rift to stay with the humans on the other side. His love for humanity was greater than his bond to other creatures, he explained, and he willingly forfeited his place in paradise to prove it.

—Native American folktale

WHILE AN ABUNDANCE of scattered bones indicates that people living at the end of the Ice Age were at least aware of the existence of canines, the exact circumstances under which these two species first came together is a highly speculative subject. Fragmentary material evidence in the form of bones, teeth, primitive pictorial art and sculptures, combined with more recent observations of surviving aboriginal people and dogs, have inspired scholars to construct plausible scenarios of early encounters between people and canids. Still, questions about the formative years of this relationship persist. Was it adversarial in nature, a cooperative venture centering around food procurement, something more intangible based on the emotional needs of each species, or a mixture of all three?

That the lives of these two species became intertwined early on, spanning at least sixty centuries, and have remained so to this day, is all the more remarkable because so much of our evolution occurred in vastly different environments: broken and open grasslands for canids and thick, protective forests for hominids (members of the primate family who gave rise to modern man). Yet both ultimately prevailed as mobile, intelligent, highly organized predators capable of adapting to virtually any habitat.

Our own ancestors were a physically puny lot compared with the scrappy, wild progenitors of modern dogs. Once the forebears of *Homo sapiens* moved away from the sheltering forests where they had evolved for countless generations, they were virtually defenseless against roaming predators and other perilous aspects of life on open savannas. But early hominids were endowed with several critical physical features—keen eyesight, opposable thumbs, and bipedal gait—which were the springboards for rapid intellectual development.

Stereovision (eyes facing forward) gave hominids exceptional visual acuity both close up and over great distances, which was essential to detecting hidden dangers and probably inadvertently contributed to the decline of the other senses, notably smell and hearing. This advantage was further enhanced by strengthened torso musculature and changes in skeletal structure, enabling our progenitors to stand and move about on two limbs instead of four. And with the hands freed from the task of locomotion they could be used to do the bidding of the mind—to collect naturally occurring items such as river stones or sticks, materials now reinterpreted as digging, cutting, or crushing tools. Though crude in form, such implements reflected man's emerging self-awareness and desire to effect change in the environment for his benefit, setting a trend in human thinking that continues to this day. Rather than remaining passive users or victims of the natural order, our ancestors began to envision future needs and plan accordingly. Armed with tools and the propensity to learn and adapt, humankind assumed a new way of life—in extended family units as hunter-gatherers, migrating with the seasons to prey on herds of bison, caribou, and other plentiful, large herbivores.

Writing about the cave of Lascaux in France, paleontologist Yves Coppens describes the "millions of objects of stone, bone, ivory or deer antler, weapons, implements, coloring stuffs, items of dress or offering" which tell us how prehistoric societies blossomed. "Across the whole of Europe new communities formed and cultures grew up parallel with each other, diffusing and interpenetrating . . . punctuated by all sorts of technical inventions and improvements, increasing people's comfort and raising their standard of living." Some paleoanthropologists speculate that the lives of these prehistoric hunters were similar to those led by migratory bands of Inuit (Eskimos) in more recent times, living in caves or lodges constructed of hide, bones, and rock, harvesting large animals in accordance with their seasonable availability.

British Museum zooarchaeologist Juliet Clutton-Brock points out that "a unique and paradoxical feature of man is that he is a tropical, omnivorous primate whose exceptional success as a species began to accelerate only when he became a social hunter in a subarctic environment." Early human intellectual growth occurred in surges, first when sufficient tool-making and fire-handling skills developed to support survival in semiglacial conditions at least fifteen thousand years ago. It was during this relatively recent past that humans and wolves, the likely forebears of modern dogs, first encountered one another.

The hunting of large Pleistocene mammals was time-consuming, exhausting, and dangerous, so it may be that the first encounters between humans and wolves were anything but friendly, especially if they took place over hard-earned kills. Another possibility is that as humans encroached upon canid territory, wolves gradually came to recognize them as an integral part of their domain. Attracted to butchering activities, cooking fires, rancid bones, and refuse, the animals redefined their territory to encompass human campsites and opted to follow people as they moved from region to region.

Tantalizing hints that a relationship of some sort was forming between people and wolves during this era come from La Grotte du Lazaret, a 125,000-year-old complex of Paleolithic shelters discovered in France in 1969, where wolf skulls appear to have been set at the entrance of each dwelling, leading excavators to speculate that canids already were incorporated into some aspect of human culture at this very early stage.

Sites such as this rarely offer more than a few fragmented bits of animal bone to indicate the beginnings of the human-canid relationship. It therefore is sheer speculation as to how the relationship between humans and wolves shifted from noninteractive or adversarial exchanges to something more tolerant and complex. Perhaps fear or hostile competition was replaced by admiration for the wolf's hunting prowess and tactics. Or the wolf's exceptional hearing and sense of smell that facilitates early prey detection led primitive people to attribute supernatural powers to the animals, and inspired the creation of rituals to endow human hunters with similar powers. Pleistocene people may have learned the benefits of observing wolves for behavioral cues that indicated prey was nearby, or of mimicking some of their stealthy hunting strategies.

Historical and contemporary accounts of aboriginal people are tenuous at best, but may offer some possibilities to fill in the gaps in the archaeological record. An 1870 account of Native American hunting forays on the western plains by the Reverend J.G. Wood describes how "wolves follow the hunter for weeks for offal of the beasts which he kills. They will not venture to harm him, but follow him by day at a distance of half a mile or so, and at night, when he lies down to sleep, they will couch also at a respectful distance." Realizing that wolves could remain close to prey without scaring it away, some Plains Indian hunters camouflaged themselves in wolf skins "so that when they go on all fours the head of the wolf projects just above their own head," in the process lulling bison and other herbivores into a false sense of security.

Changes in the dentition and facial structure of wolves have been touted as proof of a friendly (or at least civil) relationship between people and canids, manifesting the first signs of domestication. All kinds of domesticated mammals, from sheep and pigs to cattle and dogs, exhibit differences in their physical or behavioral makeup from their wild progenitors, alterations thought to have been triggered by interactive, multigenerational associations with people, and growing isolation from the natural selection process. At a twenty-five-thousand-year-old mammoth hunting camp in the Ukraine, for instance, some distinctive wolf skulls were found along with the butchered remains of at least 166 mammoths. The skulls were markedly different from those of average wild wolves, with many of them exhibiting foreshortened muzzles, diminished tooth size, and teeth crowding, all traits hailed as more common to domestic dogs than wolves.

But if the progenitors of domestic dogs figured heavily in the daily lives of Paleolithic hunters, as suggested by such intriguing remains, why has so little evidence been found to support the assertion that canids were integral members of Ice Age human society? All too often only small bits of canid bones and teeth are recovered, and Pleistocene pictorial art—such as the famous cave paintings at Lascaux or the more recently discovered Cosquer caves and Chauvet grotto—while depicting in meticulous detail a host of prey animals, fails to feature anything that can be definitively pointed to as a wolf or dog. It is the absence of such vital clues that continues to thwart the best efforts of zooarchaeologists—and in a sense, constitutes the beginning of the "lost history" of the canine race.

Women as Early Domesticators of the Dog

As predatory social creatures living in extended, hierarchical family units, wolves share many behavioral and cultural attributes with humans. Both were answerable to one or more leaders, who communicated through visual or vocal cues, and through this process coordinated food procurement and the care of offspring. In particular, ancient people and wolves had the inclination to share, a behavior essential to cooperative hunting and the successful rearing of offspring. Prehistoric humans carried meat home to share with those unable to assist in hunting-gathering activities, while wolves habitually swallow more food than required for their own sustenance, then return to the pack's den to regurgitate it for pups and nursing mothers.

This willingness to suppress the instinct to fend only for oneself particularly facilitated the first positive, interactive relationships between humans and canids, just as sharing was the basis for the first division of labor along gender lines in human culture, with women functioning primarily as nurturers of the next generation. Since human babies are defenseless and require constant attention, they could not be left unattended while hunting for food. Women early on assumed the task of gathering plant matter and collecting small game because the slower pace of these tasks blended more easily with the need to carry along and care for very young children. For this reason, prehistoric women might have been primarily responsible for forging the first intimate relationships with canids.

Surely some empathy was essential if humans were to communicate with animals unlike ourselves. Rather than winding up in the stew pot, orphaned or abandoned pups could have been recognized as babies, and—food resources permitting—be adopted and nurtured. It is also possible that very young (and socially imprintable) pups were abducted for religious reasons and subsequently hand-reared. That early man might have actively sought a ritualized relationship with wolves is tantalizingly hinted at by some nineteenth- and early twentieth-century accounts of Inuits who, upon discovering a wolf lair, gently removed the pups to apply a coating of oily vermilion paint (symbolic color of rebirth and eternal life) to their tiny faces, and then returned the young animals to their underground bed.

However it was that ancient people encountered young wolves, the sharing of human-procured food and shelter would have been essential to assure that such infant canids attained maturity and remained allied with the human "pack." Historical accounts of aboriginal women fostering animal infants alongside their own children lends credence to this theory. "It is not unusual, I have heard, for the Indians to bring up young bears, the women giving them milk from their own breasts," wrote Francis Galton in 1865. "The red races are fond of pets and treat them kindly; and in purchasing them there is always the unwillingness of the women and children to overcome, rather than any dispute about the price. [The bear] used to rob the women of the berries they had gathered but the loss was borne in good nature."

Inuit girls with puppies, ca. 1920.
source: Author.

An 1860 volume titled *Anecdotes of Animals* describes weight-pulling contests between Inuit sled dog teams, where the animals were "induced to exert themselves by a woman walking before them. They are particularly obedient and affectionate to women, because it is from them that they receive the only kindnesses bestowed upon them. . . . A word from a female will excite them to exertion when the blows and threats of the men only make them obstinate." And in 1920s Australia, according to Ernest Baynes, aboriginal women living along the Herbert River "find [wild] Dingo puppies and bring them up with their children. . . . They are well fed on meat and fruit, and often become an important member of the family."

True Domestication

True domestication requires the animals to remain beholden to humans and to breed easily in captivity. The human propensity for manipulating the environment may have been impetus enough to cultivate prehistoric dogs as "tools" for hunting, but evidence of the deliberate breeding of tamed wolves to "create" a new creature is elusive. Even so, domestication is not so much evolution as a form of arrested development, in the sense that animals remain physically and emotionally dependent on humans well beyond puppyhood.

Neoteny (the retention of juvenile physical and behavioral traits) could have contributed to the preferential treatment of some animals and the disposal of others. Wolves who continued to look or act like puppies into adulthood certainly would have been easier to live with because they retained a sense of kinship with people and recognized the authority of their masters, rather than running away to rejoin their wild peers. Captive-born animals exhibiting endearing or unusual traits such as soft or spotted coats, curling tails, unusually large eyes, drop ears or foreshortened babylike faces, suggest the cultivation of successive generations of increasingly neotenous wolves, eventually resulting in the emergence of a new species, known today as *Canis familiaris*—the domestic dog.

A 1906 account of the Tahl Tan Indians (inland Alaska and Canada) written by ethnographer James Teit included this rare bit of detail: "their dogs were sometimes bred for color but this was more to suit individual tastes. . . . some women liked small dogs and dogs of peculiar or pro-

This Chihuahua puppy exhibits pronounced neotenous (infantile) facial features. source: Author.

nounced colors." This is not to imply that domestication was a swift, easy process, as modern owners of tamed wolves and wolf hybrids will attest. Such animals still possess the bone-crushing strength critical to consuming large prey. Despite being socialized to humans from a tender age, they can in an instant revert to their wild ways, killing other dogs, tearing the arms off small children, or even attacking owners who have bottle-fed them from birth. In light of how difficult they can be to live with, even with the aid of modern innovations like electrical fences and shock collars, it is all the more amazing that primitive peoples persisted and succeeded in their interactions with canids.

Traditional Native American dog-keeping practices often included periodic outcrossings with wolves and a simple criterion for culling unsuitable animals. Buffalo-Bird-Woman, a Hidatsa Indian interviewed around 1924, recounted how "we gave away or killed the puppies we did not want. As a puppy grew up he sometimes developed a surly disposition. He would bite and snap at people or fight other dogs. Such a dog was killed. [We kept]

Leaving the Garden

A modern wolf hybrid.
source: Jan Koler.

puppies with large heads, wide faces and big legs." Similar methods of selection in prehistoric times could have limited the adverse effects of periodic genetic injections from wolves, resulting in animals with enhanced
strength and endurance, but lacking excessive aggressive tendencies.

Stability within the human community also was critical to the domestication process. Many animal societies are founded on the unwavering
presence of a female constituency that maintains the social cohesion necessary to the cooperative rearing of helpless offspring. These females are
the primary harbingers of learned behavior as well as the accumulated experiences of generations, all of which must be taught through demonstration if offspring are to survive and replicate. Elephants, whales, certain
primates, canids and some humans operate under matrilineal systems,
with generations of mothers, aunts, nieces, and sisters creating a protective, nurturing community for whelping mothers, while the males are either transient or of secondary importance in rearing the young.

If early dogs are indeed distinguishable from tamed wolves by virtue of pronounced fetal and juvenile traits, constituting a sort of "baby-appeal," it is tempting to speculate that a heavy female hand was involved in their creation. This is not to say that men did not play a critical role in this process, for as in the rearing of children beyond infancy, men could have assumed greater responsibility for the care and training of dogs after they were weaned. Upon maturity, canines could have been subjected to more practical criteria—a propensity for flushing game, alerting to potential dangers, or just a willingness to serve as "hot blankets" on cold nights, as so many adult Australian Dingoes do—resulting in a loose rule of thumb by which some dogs received preferential treatment in the form of food, shelter, or affection.

This Dingo puppy probably resembles the first true dogs, as they appeared in infancy. (Photo ca. 1920.)
source: Author.

Leaving the Garden

Searching for the First Dog

Because large canids such as timber wolves are so difficult to control, zooarchaeologists point to a smaller wolf subspecies once native to much of China and the Near East as the most likely progenitor of the first domestic dogs, especially because their ancient territory overlapped areas where the earliest evidence of permanent human settlements has been found. Divided into more specialized taxonomic groups such as *Canis Lupus chanco* in China and *Canis Lupus pallipes* in the Near East, these wolves occupied diverse habitats, ranging from vast stretches of lush woodlands and fertile floodplains to mountain passes and semiarid desert. Scattered throughout these areas were large, permanent water sources, notably the Tigris and Euphrates Rivers, attracting a steady stream of prey, including horses, wild pigs, goats, and sheep.

Not surprisingly, the availability of water was a draw for people, too, many of whom abandoned the hunter-gatherer lifestyle more than seven thousand years ago to establish semipermanent, and eventually permanent, planned communities. They experimented with cultivating wild grain-bearing plants native to the floodplains, and began confining and breeding sheep, goats and pigs. (Hunting continued to be an integral part of daily life but over several millennia assumed disproportionate significance as a ritualized sport.)

As the task of procuring food shifted from hunting to agriculture, the populace was inspired to fashion raw materials into specialized implements that enhanced the quality of life, such as firing clay to make ceramics, or later on, smelting ores to create metals. In this more stable communal living arrangement, where food resources were better controlled, interactions between canids and people could become more complex and in some cases, intimate, perhaps first focusing on animals who distinguished themselves by guarding the flocks (rather than attacking them) or alerting the populace to hostile intruders.

The Neolithic, as this era is called, was humanity's second great social revolution, marking the end of the free-roaming Stone Age and the beginning of the first, grounded "civilizations." Rapid human sociocultural development fueled the domestication process, probably accelerating the evolution of tamed or semitamed wolves, which became further removed

Rock art at Çatal Hüyük.
source: Drawn by author.

Rock art at Tassili-n-Ajjer.
source: Drawn by author.

from the natural selection process. Those already exhibiting a host of neotenic behavioral traits, such as the inclination to stalk but not kill livestock—the hallmark of a potential herder—or to defend their master's home—if not the master him/herself—as the epicenter of their territory, probably gave rise to the first true dogs, though the change occurred so gradually that it is impossible to pinpoint where their taxonomic classification as wolves should end, and a new *Canis familiaris* designation should begin.

Much of the evidence suggests that the emergence of the first true dogs coincides with the beginnings of domesticated livestock, a theory reinforced by the recovery of some of the oldest known depictions of dogs, in the form of rock art and crudely fashioned sculptures from sites in southwestern Asia, Iraq, Turkey, and to a lesser extent, Africa and northwest Europe (England and Denmark). Canine pictorial art such as the images found at Çatal Hüyük, an Iraqi site spread over thirty acres, suggests that dogs were an integral part of Neolithic life in the Middle East. This famous rock art features some intriguing images of people hunting deer in the company of what look like dogs with curling tails. Likewise, Algerian rock art at Tassili-n-Ajjer is highly suggestive of dogs, with one panel depicting a wild ox or wildebeest being cornered by three curly-tailed quadrupeds as a hunter with a lance moves in for the kill.

Some of the earliest known skeletal remains classified as dog come from the Neolithic site of Jarmo, situated in the foothills of the Zagros Mountains spanning Iran and Iraq. Radiocarbon-dated to 6600 B.C., the fifty-three cranial and mandibular fragments of big-boned canids suggest that they may have been descended from mountain-dwelling wolves who were larger than their brothers on the floodplain. Also recovered from Jarmo were several crude clay figurines that have been widely interpreted as depictions of curly-tailed dogs. Another site of interest is the Vlasac in Rumania's Iron Gates Gorge on the Danube River, which dates between 5400 B.C. and 4600 B.C. Unlike Jarmo, Vlasac offers no evidence of any domesticated animals *other* than dogs, nor were any items found to indicate the cultivation of grain-bearing plants. Its location in a craggy, barren mountain pass would have been unsuitable for farming or grazing, so it most likely was a hunting/fishing community, where dogs functioned as hunting assistants or sentries. Since many of the bones exhibit cut and chop marks characteristic of the butchering process, it is possible the dogs also were at times a food source themselves. Small in stature, the Vlasac dogs were quite different from the towering beasts of Zagros, suggesting that Neolithic dogs already varied in appearance, and perhaps function. Juliet Clutton-Brock speculates that by 6000 B.C. dogs were exhibiting varying coat textures and colors, different ear and tail lengths, and a broad spectrum of facial features, with some animals having more aquiline, Greyhound-like profiles while others were more square-headed and snub-nosed. This should not, however, be construed as proof of multiple breeds in the modern sense of the word, for as Clutton-Brock points out, an "examination of a population of scavenging curs associated with any single peasant community at the present day would be likely to produce all the shapes and sizes of skulls that have been found throughout the world from pre-Neolithic times."

Clutching at Straws

The quest for irrefutable evidence of the first dogs has been thwarted by several problems, the most prominent being that many Paleolithic and Neolithic sites yield little if any canid skeletal matter. Whether the bones disintegrated over the centuries or were never there to begin with simply cannot be determined. The canid remains that are recovered are usually fragmentary (sometimes only small chips a few inches in length), or lack context with human matter (tools, artwork, cooking hearths, the remains of dwellings, or human skeletal remains). For this reason it is impossible to determine their true identity, especially if they are similar to the wolf, as the very first dogs must have been.

Even La Grotte Du Lazaret, that 125,000-year-old Paleolithic camp where sensational evidence seemed to point to a budding relationship between people and canids, has been discredited since its discovery in 1969. Examining the evidence in 1980, eminent archaelogist Louis Binford concluded that the wolf skulls came from a nearby wolf den which accidentally intruded on the site, and had nothing to do with any hominid ritual.

Still, some researchers have declared isolated fragments of skeletal matter to be definitive proof of the first dogs. In *Origins of the Domestic Dog* (1985), a definitive work on canid evolution and modern zooarchaeological

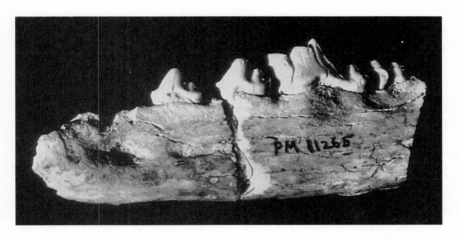

Canid mandible fragment recovered from Palegawra Cave, Iraq.
source: The Field Museum of Chicago (Negative #GEO82438).

research, Stanley Olsen of the University of Arizona cites the case of Pale-gawra Cave in northeastern Iraq, where half of a lower jawbone was dis-covered and radiocarbon-dated to be at least twelve thousand years old. While it is widely touted as the first proof of domestic dogs, scholars like Olsen feel that a three-inch bit of bone bearing a few chipped molars is shaky ground on which to base such a declaration. "If additional frag-ments of similar-sized and similar-structured individuals, even if no more complete than [this fragment] were to be recovered from the Palegawra Cave site, it would help dispel the doubts as to whether or not this speci-men has been assigned to the correct taxonomic category," Olsen says, but citing such small, isolated bits as hard proof is "really just clutching at straws in an attempt to establish the presence of the earliest domestic dog."

Citing crowded, crooked teeth or widened muzzles as evidence of neoteny (and therefore domestication) also has limited value. This was the basis on which Neolithic skeletal remains from Jericho were classified as domestic dog, but archaeologist Frederick E. Zeuner admitted that his conclusion was based on "slender evidence only, namely on size" and a de-gree of variability among the dentition of individual dogs. When Clutton-Brock conducted her own examination of the Jericho remains she concluded that they gave "no indication of evidence for domestication [since skeletal] characters cannot provide evidence for distinguishing tamed wolf from early domestic dog, and it is still doubtful how clear are the distinctions between wild and tame wolves."

Olsen pointed to the "competition among faunal workers for the 'first' domestic canid from sites the world over," resulting in a rush to label ambiguous, incomplete skeletal evidence as definitely coming from dogs, when in fact it could just as easily have come from wolves. At times the presence of any distinctive trait, no matter how slight, has inspired the creation of a new taxonomic category, resulting in a confusing plethora of unsubstantiated prehistoric breeds. Olsen hopes that future excavators "will exercise a bit more caution in assigning the name *Canis familiaris* to every scrap of wild canid that exhibits any individual variation from what they consider the norm for this species."

Bungled Bones

Potentially vital clues to the beginnings of the human-dog relationship also have been compromised by sloppy, selective excavation practices. Olsen reports that "very little attention was paid to non-human animal bones" in the past, and "some of the lack of [canine skeletal evidence] may possibly be due to selective collecting on the part of the excavators." In their quest to uncover valuable works of art, nineteenth- and early twentieth-century antiquarians routinely discarded animal bones, teeth, and other matter that could have shed light on the early stages of domestication. Even coprolites—desiccated, ancient feces—harbor potentially priceless data about the health and diet of early primitive dogs. In the 1930s, a number of Pleistocene wolf skulls were uncovered near Fairbanks, Alaska, with hydraulic mining equipment that blasted and churned the soil, pulverizing and scattering canid skeletal material, and certainly erasing any provenance it might once have had to the many human artifacts also discovered. Even today, areas suspected of harboring as yet-undiscovered prehistoric sites face imminent destruction as residential and industrial subdivisions expand, and looting is at an all-time high. In Iraq, where so much of the earliest evidence of dogs has been found, American aerial bombings during Desert Storm wreaked incalculable destruction on scores of unexcavated Neolithic sites near Baghdad.

According to Paul Bahn, a contributing editor to *Archaeology* magazine (July/August 1995), six open-air sites of European Pleistocene animal art have been discovered intact, the largest in Portugal's Côa Valley, which may be flooded and destroyed by a multimillion-dollar dam project. Discovered in 1981 along a tributary of the Douro River, it is the first open-air Ice Age art ever found. Three large, incised animal figures situated seven hundred feet up a cliff wall had been protected for millennia by a natural rock overhang. Shortly after the discovery was published, however, the images were permanently damaged by "vandals and archaeologists trying to get clearer photographs [by] chalking, scoring and painting" the depictions, dated at well over fifteen thousand years. Ultimately, the cliff depictions led to the discovery of an incredible five hundred pecked and incised animal images over an eight-mile area (most of them concentrated in a one-mile stretch). But "when the hydroelectric dam is completed in 1998, all will be irrevocably lost under more than three hundred feet of water," reported Bahn. A team of specialists from UNESCO visited the site in early 1995 and pleaded for a suspension of the reservoir project, and in 1996 the dam project was halted. But the long-term future of the engravings—and any insights into dog history that they might hold—remains uncertain.

Published archaeological monographs of excavations and artifact assemblages are becoming increasingly scarce, meaning that many sites, even after being dug up, are undocumented and essentially lost to the scientific world. Archaeologists oftentimes opt to put off the tedious task of having to write in-depth reports about their findings, especially if it entails cataloging thousands of items or coordinating a team of highly specialized researchers. Brian Fagan, another contributing editor to *Archaeology* magazine, recounted a typical instance where a "distinguished colleague" only got around to publishing one excavation report, although in the course of his long and illustrious career he had dug up dozens of sites. He died, "leaving behind nothing but sketchy field notes and a museum storeroom full of inadequately labeled artifacts. Even in retirement, he could not find the time to publish his field work [although] he was digging right up to the end." The loss to both human and dog history is incalculable.

Civilized society has entrusted archaeologists with the enormous responsibility of guarding the heritage of our species. It is a dubious honor, though, because in the process of retrieving this history, some of it is inevitably destroyed. Because of new diagnostic technologies, we know now that the exteriors of bones retrieved from Ice Age kill sites might still proffer blood samples, but in the past it was routine to scrub these bones in water with a toothbrush. Even the soil, in its undisturbed state, might harbor paper-thin layers of carbon or fossilized pollen by which bones or artifacts can be dated and the ancient seasons chronicled. The simple flick of the most well-intentioned garden trowel can destroy centuries. Archaeologists therefore have a fundamental responsibility to document each step of their work and to publish the results of their excavations in a timely fashion (or at least make the evidence known and available to others). This mandate has even been written into the Code of Professional Standards of the Archaeological Institute of America, which states it is imperative that "all research projects contain specific plans for conservation, preservation and publication from the very outset." Fagan observes that in failing to publish their findings, archaeologists may be justly criticized as being no better than looters, "a self-serving special-interest group that keeps its finds to itself."

But worst of all perhaps is that the quest for early dogs has been compromised by decades of scholarly indifference to prehistoric domesticated animals and to their presence in the archaeological record. Excavators who did bother to collect animal-related matter frequently failed to document, even through hand-scribbled notes or drawings (let alone photos), the locations of bones prior to removal. In other instances, virtually no mention of such remains was made in site reports, as evidenced by the 331-page published account of excavations at a Paleolithic site at Cape Denbigh. It offers one seven-line table and a modest paragraph on recovered animal remains, their identifications listed as "bird" and "other." Even the eminent British archaeologist Sir Mortimer Wheeler, famous for his meticulous site reports, was inclined to give animal bones short shrift—no more than a paragraph or two—because they "do not call for further comment."

According to Olsen it is "possible that canid bones were not collected because it was assumed that they represented the common, local wolves, when in actuality they might have been primitive dogs, wolves or [wolf hybrids]." Jumbled heaps of such bones, tossed into a burlap sack or box, often are hauled back to the university and, unlabeled or cataloged, placed in storage and never examined again. Other times the crated remains are handed over to undergraduate students to practice the delicate application of hand-inked catalog numbers, after which they are returned to storage and, once again, ignored.

"I have found that no single museum has adequate collections of skulls or mandibles with which to undertake an acceptable analysis," says Olsen. And due to the dwindling numbers of surviving primitive dogs, some of which are thought to have remained unchanged for six thousand years or more and could be used in comparative analyses against archaeological remains, he "sees no solution to this problem in the future."

Living Prehistory

Ancient canid remains when compared with dogs living today could shed additional light on the mystery of early domestication. In recent years an increasing amount of attention has focused on the preservation and documentation of surviving aboriginal forms of domestic dog. Many of these survived by returning to a feral state as the primitive cultures that molded them vanished in the wake of modern, industrialized society.

Among the more unusual is the New Guinea Singing Dog, a golden-colored canine native to inland Papua New Guinea. Classified as *Canis familiaris hallstromi* (after Sir Edward Hallstrom, who brought the first pair out of the southern highlands), Singing Dogs bear a striking resemblance to Australian Dingoes but are markedly smaller in stature, weighing a maximum of thirty pounds. They also possess a unique DNA triplet not found in any other canid. As with other feral canine varieties, they conform to the physical traits thought to be common to all primitive dogs (and probably prehistoric dogs)—stiff, upright ears, hard coats of uniform color, and triangular heads. Unique physical and behavioral features, particularly the distinctive, yodeling yowl for which the New Guinea Singing Dog is named, have lent further weight to their designation as a prehistoric form of domestic canine. Such dogs represent the last and perhaps oldest canine lineage in the world, unchanged in form or behavior for millennia.

Singing Dogs are thought to have been introduced into New Guinea from Australia, most likely by the first humans to settle on the island, and were an integral part of primitive village life for centuries. With the arrival of Europeans, who subsequently introduced new dog varieties, most

The author "interviews" a captive New Guinea Singing Dog who lives in the Austin Zoo (Texas).
source: Author.

Singing Dog colonies were genetically contaminated, excepting only those that lived in the most remote of villages, or that had already severed their ties to human settlements to retreat to the wildest sections of the interior. In one such undeveloped inland valley they were accidentally discovered by explorers from the outside world in 1957. Newspaper and popular magazine stories of the discovery of an idyllic "Shangri-la" in New Guinea fired the public's imagination. Two Singing Dogs were quickly captured and donated to the Taronga Zoo in Sydney, Australia, where they were touted as living relics from the Stone Age—if not the "Garden of Eden."

The discovery of these animals couldn't have come at a more critical time, since the dogs had all but vanished from traditional village life. Although the dogs' teeth, strung like a necklace, had once been a valued type of village currency, surviving natives could no longer recall what the dogs looked like, and only knew of them by faint howls echoing through the valleys at night. Over the next fifteen years a half-dozen more dogs were caught, but none have been photographed in the wild since the late seventies. Still, rumors persist that packs of the dogs roam the remote highland regions.

Zoologist I. Lehr Brisbin of the University of Georgia urged zoos to obtain and breed New Guinea Singing Dogs. "[They are] popular and well accepted by the public [and] are especially adaptable to display in a children's zoo setting," he wrote in a 1989 paper for a conference of the American Association of Zoological Parks and Aquariums. As a result, some zoological gardens in America and Europe took steps to feature aboriginal dogs in their retinues of mammals. The bulk of this captive population was descended from the lone pair in the Taronga Zoo, constituting a perilously fragile gene pool. In recent years greater effort has been made to conduct outcrossings between Taronga dogs with the last few dogs taken from the wild.

In 1991, Brisbin announced a continuing research project to sequence the genetic code of aboriginal canines, particularly the New Guinea Singing Dog, whose DNA not only harbors critical information on canid evolution (and the effects of domestication on mammalian physiology), but also has the potential to serve as a genetic "base line" for the modern canine race, from which inherited diseases and breed-specific biochemical characteristics can be documented. Also included in this ambitious project is the collection of semen samples from the Singing Dog males, to be frozen as insurance that they will not drop out of an already preciously small gene pool.

The number of captive-bred Singing Dogs increased dramatically. However, when the animals were classified as a feral form of domesticated dog, their value in the eyes of zoo administrators and curators plummeted. They became a species caught in the most vicious of purgatories—neither truly wildlife, nor "pure bred" in the modern sense. A significant number of the animals were dumped from zoo programs and onto the private market, where they wound up in roadside zoos, the founding stock for aspiring puppy mills. Still, others have been fortunate to find new lives as pampered house pets. This, in turn, has proven to be a bit of good luck for behaviorists, since observations of their conduct in a "civilized" environment are proving indispensable to ongoing aboriginal dog studies. In most respects they are no different from any other dogs—they enjoy being held, kissed, petted, and brushed, and are adept at working their way onto living room couches or into beds to snuggle with their masters.

House-trained New Guinea Singing Dogs.
source: Jan Koler.

Leaving the Garden

Despite gaps in archaeological and historical records, existing evidence suggests that the prehistoric forebears of modern dogdom were vulnerable to the duality of human nature, a key aspect of our psyche that seems to have become more pronounced over time as the relationships we form with dogs become increasingly complex and contrived. While some degree of kindness was essential in their domestication, the first dogs must have been subject to treatment that by modern standards seems cruel or at least callous. Even day-to-day survival was problematical, for the animals would have been the last in line when it came to sharing scant food sources or shelter, no matter how loyal or obedient, in some instances actually becoming a source of food themselves. Death was a constant presence in the early human experience, of course, leaving little room for excess emotional attachments. A dog whose survival depended on its ability to contribute to the well-being of humans would have been evaluated for its potential as a tool rather than as a friend. But even that was not enough to guarantee a long life, since the most subservient of dogs were subject to the discretion of their owners.

However it may have happened, a new canid life form did come into being—a creature who holds the distinct honor of being the first nonhuman being to actively seek the companionship of humans within the confines of an artificial environment. They had, as the Native American legend suggests, left the proverbial garden and were at the beginning of their journey as our most intimate and enduring companions.

Two

The Children of Anubis

WHAT WE KNOW about ancient civilizations generally offers little insight into the lives of ordinary people, since documents and histories tend to focus on prominent individuals and events. In the case of ancient Egypt, however, evidence from tomb paintings, artifacts, and texts reveals that people at all levels of society kept and loved dogs as pets and members of the family. Dogs also influenced and inspired art and language just as they do today. A number of wall paintings dating from the New

Fragment of a limestone stela depicting a dog named "Hemu-Ha," dating from the Sixteenth Dynasty (#UC14322).
source: Courtesy of the Petrie Museum of Egyptian Archaeology (University College London).

Wall relief showing a dog under his master's chair, from the
Tomb of Pabasa.
source: Drawn by author.

Kingdom (ca. 1550–1085 B.C.), for instance, depicted the deceased with his
faithful dog, usually sitting under his master's chair or assisting in a hunt,
and canines belonging to wealthy households often wore elaborately decorated neckwear, like the pink, green, and white leather collar decorated
with prancing horses and metal studs recovered from the tomb of Mai-
herperi in the Valley of the Kings.

The prevalence of dogs in ancient Egyptian daily life is reflected in
writings as well, where canine imagery is employed as a means of describing the behavior of people. As an expression of fidelity and willingness to serve, one Middle Kingdom (ca. 2130–1630 B.C.) official described
himself as "a dog who sleeps in the tent, a hound of the bed whom his

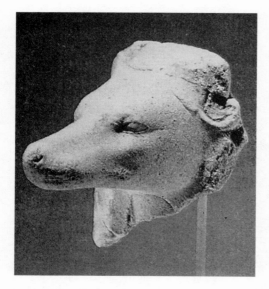

Head of an Egyptian canid, ca. 664 B.C., made of
gypsum plaster.
source: The Metropolitan Museum of Art, Rogers
Fund, 1974 (1974.264).

Hunting scene from an Egyptian tomb painting, Eighteenth Dynasty.
source: Drawn by author.

mistress loves." Conversely, the dog's cringing, servile demeanor was commonly attributed to Egypt's enemies, who once vanquished and captured were paraded before pharaoh and ordered to repeat the phrase, "We are indeed your dogs." A similar sentiment was expressed by an artisan living in the desert village of Deir-el-Medina, near present day Luxor, who complained that "the god Ptah caused me to be as a street dog." And a text dating from the New Kingdom observes that "The dog obeys the word and walks behind its master," echoing not only the place of canines but Egyptian society's subservience to the pharaoh.

Wall paintings, reliefs, and sculptures indicate that the Egyptians kept several canine varieties, some native to the Nile valley and some imported. Lean, long-legged dogs similar to modern Pharaoh and Ibizan Hounds were the preferred pets for Egyptian nobility, just as similar hounds became the preferred hunting companions of European aristocrats later on in the Middle Ages. Kept in mud-brick kennels separate from the house, they were trained and cared for by professional dog handlers who prepared the animals for recreational hunts beyond the cultivated fields. Then, while the owner looked on, the handler unleashed the hounds to bring down swift game such as wild asses, ibexes, or even rabbits, as depicted in one twelfth-century B.C. tomb painting of a hunt in the desert. Weapons in hand and the dog handler by his side, the deceased looks on in excitement while his hounds tear at the necks of their prey.

Such coursing hounds were typical of dogs in Egyptian society until the Eighteenth Dynasty (1567–1320 B.C.), when the Empire expanded northeast to the Euphrates River and south up the Nile to present-day Khartoum. The cities of Memphis and Thebes (now Luxor) became melting pots of Greek, Hittite, Babylonian, Syrian, Palestinian, Nubian, and Asian diplomats and traders. Merchants dealing in gold, spices, timber, skins, papyrus, and other goods responded to the Egyptians' fondness for pets by importing exotic canine varieties, most notably small short-legged dogs with pointed ears and "Basenjis" with tightly curled tails, both from Africa.

Paintings and figures dating from 1500–300 B.C. show small dogs sitting under the chairs of their masters, and they appear to come in a variety of colors and patterns—solid black and brown, or black-and-white speckles and large black spots. The names of these little dogs often incorporated the word *hti*, an ethnic term for natives of Africa, and one mer-

Egyptian bronze statuette of a puppy with gold collar; Eighteenth Dynasty, ca. 1350 B.C.
source: The Metropolitan Museum of Art, Rogers Fund, 1947 (48.58.1).

chant's inventory listed small dogs from Nubia and Libya as part of a tribute paid to the pharaoh. Another text from the same period testifies that Pharaoh Intef II (ca. 2150 B.C.) kept a pack of small dogs with both foreign and Egyptian names.

Massive dogs with heavy, square heads and drop ears appear in the Egyptian archaeological record beginning about 1600 B.C., shortly after the invasion of the Hyksos, thought to be Asiatic nomads who introduced the composite bow, chariot warfare, and horses into the Nile region, as well as Mastiff-like war dogs. Instead of being taught to attack other animals, these canines were encouraged from an early age to focus their aggressive tendencies on human beings, so that later on as adults they could be released on battlefields to run among the enemy's ranks, lunging and tearing at any exposed body parts. Modern Egyptologists speculate that ancient military strategists were so taken with the dogs that they quickly took steps to incorporate attack animals into their army as early as the beginning of the Middle Kingdom to be dispatched with troops stationed in the Libyan desert. Like the earlier coursing hounds, these dogs were housed in special kennels, but kept tethered on short leads to make them more aggressive and territorial. Some texts suggest that only the handler was allowed to feed and care for the dogs, thereby cultivating the animal's suspicious nature toward everyone else.

In recent decades archaeologists have translated the names of almost eighty ancient Egyptian dogs, many of them prized for their hunting or working talents, as indicated by names like Good Herdsman and Reliable. Other names reflected their appearance, such as Blackie, Ebony, or One Who Is Fashioned as an Arrow. Some were given numerical designations, such as The Fourth or The Sixth (similar to the ancient Roman names Quintus and Sextus), possibly describing their position in the litter. Grabber, Cook-pot, She of the Town, Useless, and other unusual names were likely inspired by the quirky nature of an individual animal, and expressed their master's humor or affection. These names often were prefaced or followed by *abu* or *jwjw*—ancient versions of "bow-wow" and "howler."

Ancient "Breeds"

Although iconographic evidence suggests several distinct varieties of canines, it is impossible to say that any of them were pure breeds in the modern sense. There is no evidence that ancient dog owners mated animals with a specific physical standard in mind. But Egypt's ruling class was grounded in generations of arranged marriages based on the belief that royal and common blood should not be mixed, so that practice may have been applied to dogs as well. On the other hand, medical papyri offer no evidence that the Egyptians had even a minimal knowledge of genetics, which means it is highly unlikely that breeders could exert much control over superficial physical traits such as coat color, shape of the ears, or arch of the tail. Modern breed books usually assert that Pharaoh Hounds, Ibizan Hounds, Greyhounds, Salukis, Mastiffs, and even Dachshunds are directly descended from ancient Egyptian dogs. Yet no archaeological evidence confirms genetic links between these modern dogs and those of ancient Egypt. All that can be said for certain is that today's sighthounds (also called gazehounds; lean, swift dogs bred to track prey by sight rather than smell) are descendants of progenitors imported from the Middle East in the last century.

British zooarchaeologist Juliet Clutton-Brock concedes that ancient Egyptian dogs "do look like present-day Mastiffs, together with the ancient Egyptian hunting dogs which closely resemble present-day sighthounds, [and they] appear to be two breeds that have continued more or less unchanged until the present day." But she points out that the genetic diversity inherent in a species such as *C. familiaris* can cause similar characteristics to recombine in such a way that "the same type of dog is bred in different regions or at different periods when selective breeding is carried out for the same need, this being to provide hunting, racing and guard dogs. For this reason it is difficult to determine whether the Mastiff and the Greyhound are really breeds with an unbroken line of 4,000 years."

The extraction of viable genetic material already has been successfully performed on human mummies, and deciphering the complex "code" of traits contained in DNA strands is in progress, so it may be that researchers eventually will be able to determine whether modern sighthounds are indeed descended from animals kept thousands of years ago.

Homeless and Hungry, Then as Now

Feral canines also were in abundance in ancient times, just as modern cities are overrun with homeless pets today. These pariah dogs, as they were later called by natural historians, foraged for whatever edibles they could find in the stinking heaps of refuse thrown into the streets. In times of epidemic, they facilitated the spread of fatal diseases such as cholera and bubonic plague by scavenging corpses that had been hastily buried on the outskirts of town. It appears that the Egyptians rarely went out of their way to help these animals, in part because rabies was a dreaded disease throughout the ancient world (it had already been deduced that there was a connection between dogs and this disease).

Having never been socialized to humans as puppies, most of these canine outcasts preferred the companionship of their own kind, sleeping at the edge of town during the day and roaming the streets in packs at night. In their desperation for food, they could become quite bold, even "mugging" pedestrians returning from market with groceries, or attacking livestock and leash-trained pets. Canine bodyguards and specially trained baboons were employed to restore order, helping police patrol the marketplace for transgressors, both dog and human.

The City of Dogs

The Egyptians worshiped a pantheon of gods, most of them "patron saints" of some aspect of earthly life who at times were represented by an animal or animal/human hybrid form. Thoth, the god of wisdom who invented writing, was depicted as either a baboon or ibis-headed human; Amen-Re, king of the gods during the New Kingdom, took iconographic form as a ram.

Egyptian civilization's early, formative era was characterized by the belief that only the pharaoh had an afterlife, and Old Kingdom pyramid texts invariably stress the role of dogs as the guardians of monarchs. Dogs were perceived as partners in life, death, and resurrection, associations strengthened by actually observing pariah dogs roam the mortuaries and cemeteries, and in times of plague, devouring the unburied dead. And this combination of belief and experience laid the foundation for increasingly ritualized relationships with canines, ultimately resulting in an institutionalized religious cult, the most famous of which was Anubis. Even he was preceded by an earlier dog-deity, however, having evolved from Wepwawet, the black jackal deity of Abydos on the Nile, just south of modern Luxor (ancient Thebes). There, like the pariah dogs who prowled the Valley of the Kings, he roamed the ancestral burial grounds near the dip in the western hills, where Isis supposedly found Osiris's head and "resurrected" him, assuming his powers as judge and lord of the afterlife.

Dog-headed with pointed ears and a long, sharp muzzle, Anubis was always black, the symbolic color of death. He was a second-generation deity, described by Plutarch as the product of an adulterous union between Osiris, god of the Netherworld, and his sister Nepthys. Anubis was associated with the west—where the sun dies each day, and as watchdog of the land of the dead, he was entrusted with supervising the mummification of the dead. Perhaps more important to worshipers, however, Anubis was irrevocably associated with resurrection. He was, after all, the god

Bronze dog, possibly an image of Anubis, ca. Eighteenth Dynasty (UC8194). source: Courtesy of the Petrie Museum of Egyptian Archaeology (University College London).

who escorted them to their chance for eternal life at the discretion of Osiris, who, with a host of lesser gods, listened to the souls' avowals of purity. They then passed judgment on whether the deceased merited admission to eternity by weighing the mortal's heart (thought to contain all the deeds committed in life) against the "feather of truth" on a scale, whose calibration was left to Anubis. Those who failed the test were condemned to a second and final death when their hearts were devoured by Ammit, the part-lion, part-crocodile deity. This "Judgment Day" scenario appears over and over, on tomb walls, mummiform coffins, and funerary accessories, as do depictions of Anubis directing or helping the funerary priests prepare a body.

But why worship a deity associated with death? Perhaps worship is the wrong word, since the relationship of mortal to god was more one of seeking help or favor—a bargaining (quid pro quo) in which an offering was made to the god in the hope of gaining some indulgence. In the same vein, it is doubtful that the Egyptians ever worshiped animals in the literal sense. Most gods had an animal "face" or identity—Amen with a ram, for instance, and Sobek with a crocodile. (Thus the ram-headed sphinxes that once lined the road between Karnak and Lux, temple representations of the god Amen.) Late in the New Kingdom, which ended around 1085 B.C., when ordinary people began to approach a god in person rather than through a priest, anyone who wanted to gain the attention of some deity might make an offering of a clay or bronze figurine of the animal associated with that god. Better yet, they might make an offering to the god of the creature itself in mummy form, which the god was sure to recognize.

So it was that the City of Dogs, called Hardai or Cynopolis by the Greeks, became a kind of mecca for Anubis worshipers, attracting thousands of pilgrims who came to beseech this deity for special favors on their behalf. At the peak of Anubis's popularity, Hardai was a bustling religious-commercial center, offering a wide variety of goods and services, drawing consumers from all levels of society. Naturally, the streets were filled with dogs, wandering among the shops for handouts or seeking favors from the hundreds of visiting worshipers. The temples, too, were overrun with dogs, with the city's residents supplying provisions for the care and feeding of both priests and animals.

Plutarch (A.D. 46–120) related a tale of vengeance by worshipers of the Oxyrhynchus, a Nile-dwelling fish, visited upon their Hardai neighbors. "In my day the [fish worshipers] caught a dog and ate it up as if it had been a sacrificial meat because the people of Hardai were eating the fish known as the Oxyrhynchus . . . Both sides became involved in a war and inflicted great harm on each other."

The mystical power of dogs became increasingly institutionalized in cult activities, with various canine body parts assigned miraculous healing powers. One prescription for skin eczema and infection included a topical mixture of canine feces and blood, while another called for the "leg of a hound and the hoof of an ass" as a cure for baldness. A recipe for hair removal suggested smearing menstrual blood from a dog on the area, while "the liver of a mad dog should be roasted and eaten by those who have been bitten by him. This will keep them safe from the fear of water [hydrophobia, or rabies]." Dog-bite victims were instructed to "take a tooth of that dog which did bite, putting it in a bag and so tying it to the arm," as an amulet to ward off the onset of rabies.

Life Eternal for Dogs, Too

In 1906, when Egyptologist Theodore M. Davis was lowered down a twelve-foot shaft into a tomb in the Valley of the Kings, he was "startled by seeing very near to me a yellow dog of ordinary size standing on his feet, his short tail curved over his back and his eyes open. Within a few inches of his nose sat a monkey in quite perfect condition; for an instant I thought they were alive but I soon saw they had been mummified and had been unwrapped in ancient times by robbers. . . . I'm quite sure [grave] robbers arranged the group for their amusement. The tomb of Amenhotep II being so near, it is quite possible the mummified animals were originally the king's pets."

In fact, dogs belonging to indulgent masters were routinely mummified, according to Plutarch. Pet owners shaved their bodies and heads to express their grief, just as they did on losing human members of the family. The pets of nobility received the most elaborate treatments upon death, as indicated by their carefully creased, colorful linen wrappings, sometimes arranged in ornate herringbone or striped patterns. It was routine to inter pets in their master's tombs, sometimes on a reed mat at the foot of a bed, although in a few instances dogs were actually laid out within a human sarcophagus (coffin). Other dogs were placed in custom-made cedar or limestone coffins of their own, richly decorated with hunting scenes and inscriptions—in the case of one canine reading, "the beloved of her mistress."

One exceptional account of canine interment is that of a royal guard dog named Abutiu (With Pointed Ears), who lived around 2180 B.C. The grieving pharaoh ordered a sarcophagus made for the dog, and "very much fine cloth, incense and scented oil" be used in its mummification. Abutiu was to be interred in "a tomb constructed by the crews of tomb builders" so that he might become one of the "Blessed."

In their search for treasure, nineteenth-century British excavators found cemeteries and underground vaults filled with the mummies of dogs, cats, ibexes, falcons, and other creatures. "Abd'Allatif says he saw heaps of bodies of dogs consisting of 100,000 or more," wrote antiquarian Thomas Pettigrew in 1834. The sheer abundance of these mummies tried the patience of both looters and scholars, so the artifacts became regarded as more a nuisance than a significant find. As a result, untold numbers of animal mummies were destroyed without a second thought. When British archaeologist E. Naville surveyed the cat cemetery at Tell Basta (in the southeastern Delta) around 1880, he found it had been pillaged by treasure hunters. Little remained but "heaps of white bones." About this time, too, tons of animal mummies were exported to England to be pulverized and sold as garden fertilizer. One shipment weighing in excess of nineteen tons contained an estimated 180,000 mummies, and as late as the 1950s, animal mummies could still be purchased from curio vendors in Cairo.

Even today, ancient Egyptian animal cemeteries and cult centers are imperiled by city sprawl, road construction, oil exploration, and industrial development. For example, Egyptologists are racing to retrieve artifacts from the ruins of Bubastis before the developing city of Zagazig overtakes and destroys it forever. Named after the feline goddess Bast, this ancient city once was a beacon of hope for those seeking the blessings of the patron of fertility. Infertile Muslim women from a nearby village still visit the ruins to leave ritual offerings and pray for pregnancy.

The idea of destroying thousands of animal mummies—perhaps representing a broad demographic spectrum of one of the first socially stratified canine populations—leaves modern researchers disappointed beyond words, especially since most of them were callously discarded just as the field of archaeology was evolving from a hobby for wealthy private collectors into a scholarly field of study. Fortunately, a small sampling of dogs, cats, and other Egyptian animals were retrieved from overseas shipments in the late 1800s by British Museum curators. Even wrapped in layers of linen, they are extremely fragile, and would have been destroyed in the past by scholars' efforts to study them through dissection. Until recently there has been relatively little interest in Egyptian animal mummy research, but the field of zooarchaeology is gaining acceptance at a time when new diagnostic technologies such as endoscopy and CAT (computerized axial tomography) scans are available, making it possible to conduct nonintrusive and nondestructive studies of wrapped mummies. Cats have been the primary focus of such projects to date, partly because there is a preponderance of feline-related artifacts, but assuming that ancient Egyptian animal cults were grounded in a common religious belief system, inferences can be made about canine mummies based on findings from the examination of these feline mummies.

The burials of pet dogs cannot adequately account for the hundreds of thousands of dog mummies that once existed, however, and the majority of canine mummies dating from the Graeco-Roman period (332 B.C.–A.D. 395) probably were a product of institutionalized Anubis worship. If so, most of these dogs were likely cultivated in kennel annexes to Anubis temples and may have been deliberately killed, then mummified and sold to religious pilgrims in Hardai. Embalmed canines might have been part of a larger promotional inventory featuring canine-theme jewelry, painted papyri, and figurines of bronze, ceramic, ivory, or wood, just as mass-produced Jesus posters and saintly charms are sold in evangelical theme parks today.

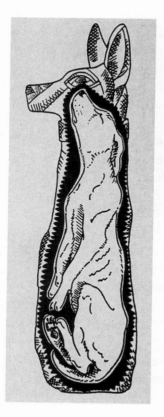

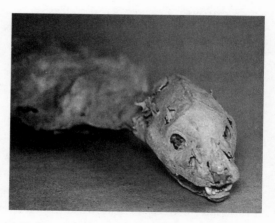

Unwrapped mummified dog, recovered by the nineteenth-century Egyptologist Sir Flinders Petrie (UC42570).
source: Courtesy of the Petrie Museum of Egyptian Archaeology (University College London).

Cutaway of a typical ancient Egyptian dog mummy.
source: Drawn by author.

X rays of surviving mummies reveal that most were preserved using only the most minimal procedures, lending further credence to the idea that they were mass-produced. After disembowelment, the bodies were packed with a mixture of sand and natron (a desiccating mixture of sodium and calcium salts), then forced into an elongated position with the forelegs extended down along either side of the rib cage and the hindquarters drawn tightly up against the base of the tail. The fur was saturated with a lacquerlike resin before wrapping with crude bandages made of scrap linen, after which they were left in hot, dry sand for several weeks to complete dehydration. A final layer of creased, dyed linen strips then was applied in decorative patterns.

Strings of faience beads sometimes were included in the fancier mummies, as were tiny fetish amulets made of colored glass or ceramic. Bronze coverings sculpted to represent the animals as they appeared in life sometimes were placed over the animals' heads, a practice inspired by human burial rituals. Such masks for cats have been recovered, and one dog mummy in the British Museum might have been accessorized in this manner, since the body is wrapped with elaborately overlapping, creased linen strips in a pattern reminiscent of "log cabin" quilts, while the head is covered with a plain, broad swatch of frayed, undyed linen. In other instances, artificial ears, eyes, and noses were fashioned from colored cloth, while facial features of the "cheapest" mummies might only have been hinted at through a hasty dab of brown or black paint.

Given the vast numbers of animals found by archaeologists, temples must have maintained veritable factories adjacent to kennels and ceremonial facilities, run by a specialized staff who manned a mummification assembly line, some gutting dogs in preparation for drying while others applied the final, decorative touches.

Most dog mummies are small, ranging from ten to eighteen inches in length, suggesting that they were immature animals (X rays of the British Museum cats show that many were kittens less than a year old). In most cases there are no signs of illness, leading Egyptologists to speculate that some animals were deliberately killed, their necks wrung or broken, victims of routine cullings at temple kennels and catteries, perhaps when the animals multiplied beyond a manageable number. The executions might have been seen as a lesser transgression than turning the animals into the streets to starve. But periodic swellings in the temple animal populations do not adequately account for the abundance of mummies. It is more likely that dogs and cats were routinely, ritualistically killed in anticipation of consumer demand, rather than in response to periodic swells in kenneled populations.

Pilgrims partaking in seasonal or annual religious festivals at Hardai might have been encouraged to pay for the interment of a temple animal as an expression of devotion to Anubis, creating a steady demand for mummies-to-go. Between periods of peak demand, temple staff would have worked to amass a backlog of mummified canines, taking care to include not only temple dogs who died of natural causes, illness, or injury, but puppies deemed nonessential to propagation (small size also made them easier to process and faster to dry, and required less preservative and wrapping materials). Until an in-depth forensic review of existing canine mummies can be conducted, however, the cause of death of these Egyptian dogs remains speculative.

At first glance, that the ancient Egyptians cast their dogs in multiple conflicting roles, ranging from cherished family members to servants, chattel, and even outcasts, seems irrational if not hypocritical. But this fragmentation within the canine population is the product of human social evolution. As a culture's socioeconomic base expands, leading to the creation of sprawling, multifunctional urban centers and stratification of the human populace according to wealth, education, and birthright, canines diversify as well. Ancient Egyptian dogs were classified in a manner similar to their owners, with a privileged minority enjoying lives of leisure and luxury. Gazehounds and Mastiffs, on the other hand, constituted an elite, in some cases "professional" working class of canines. Specially bred and trained to be sentries, soldiers, or hunting assistants, they were closely allied to the ruling class. They were assured lifetimes of shelter, care, and attention, but still were required to earn their keep. The temple dogs constituted a larger, more passive class, exploited to provide spiritual inspiration and raw material for religious commerce that promoted, at least in theory, greater respect for dogs through the worship of a dog-god. Lastly, on the bottom rung of this status ladder, were the vast numbers of pariah dogs, the impoverished underclass of Egyptian canine society.

Modern dogs living in Western society have undergone similar stratification in the last 150 years, as industrialization fueled rapid urban development, economic diversity and the emergence of a middle class. Today one portion of canine society enjoys the "good life," indulged and pampered like children. Another group, similar to the Egyptians' "professional" dogs, are well cared for but work for a living as military sentries, police assistants, emergency rescue personnel, or sporting accessories. Some canines also find themselves in less lucrative lines of work, being bred for medical laboratories, or worse, for the military to use as live targets to test new kinds of ammunition. Also as in ancient Egypt, millions of abandoned and homeless animals live a semiwild existence, scrounging for sustenance and shelter among the leavings of humans—with hundreds of thousands of them ending in municipal pounds and shelters, where they are euthanized at the rate of four animals every 1.5 seconds. Most are disposed of in public landfills or crematoriums, yet even in death a portion

Nubian servant near a garden chapel with shadoof (levered leather bucket), acccompanied by a small dog, as portrayed in a wall painting from the tomb of Ipuy in Thebes, ca. Fourteenth Dynasty.
source: The Metropolitan Museum of Art (30.4.115).

of them fulfill some human need, their bodies sold to grease-rendering plants or veterinary colleges for dissection.

Certainly the preponderance of archaeological and contemporary evidence indicates that such dichotomies are constants in human behavior, and point to the fact that despite differences in time, place, or circumstance, many practices are rooted in the emotions, experiences, and needs common to all humans and canines.

These two Egyptian mummified dogs, now in the British Museum, were among the few to escape pulverization at the turn of the century. Contrary to its "Jackal" label, the ten inch mummy on the right is probably a small domestic puppy, fitted with an ornamental head of colored linen strips. The larger dog mummy (left) may originally have been fitted with a wooden or bronze mask.
source: Copyright the British Museum.

Three

Cave Canem

Dogs are the only animals that will answer to their names and
recognize the voices of the family. . . . next to man, there is no
living creature whose memory is so retentive.

—Pliny the Elder (A.D. 23–79)

ANCIENT EGYPT did not exist in a vacuum, of course, but was contemporary with a number of other complex societies, including, during the Late Period, the seafaring Greeks and Romans. By 500 B.C the
Aegean arena (Greece and the Archipelago, western Asia Minor, Crete)
was dotted with portside towns. The Greeks had established one of the
earliest and most extensive trade routes in the then-known world, trans-

Bas-relief of a dog-cat fight from the Acropolis in Athens, ca. 510 B.C.
source: Drawn by author.

porting both raw materials and finished products. Traveling aristocrats and merchants were fascinated by the many kinds of animals they encountered throughout the Hellenistic Empire, and frequently exported wild beasts such as giraffes, lions, and hyenas back home to stock private menageries or engage in wagered battles with other, sometimes equally exotic creatures. Even the sacred domesticated cats of Egypt did not escape their notice—some were smuggled out of the country to be pitted against Greek hunting dogs, sparking one of the most enduring popular images of canines and felines—as mortal enemies.

Aristotle (384–322 B.C.) listed three "useful" types of canines by name, identifying them as "Epirotic" dogs, "Laconians," and "Molossians." Regrettably, he failed to provide any further description save to suggest that the Laconian bitches should be outcrossed with Mastiff-like Molossians in order to produce puppies that "have both the grace of their mothers and the courage of their sires." The archaeological record seems to confirm Aristotle's description of three basic dog varieties, classified according to function and the social positions of their owners, provided they had owners. Wolflike hounds were commonly employed by highland shepherds as watchdogs. Rather shaggy and large-boned, they had a reputation for savagely attacking anyone who threatened cattle, sheep, or goats.

Also throughout the Mediterranean an abundance of homeless dogs constituted the lowest rung on the canine social ladder. An integral part of the daily street scene in most towns and colonies (except for Athens, where a law sparked in part by the fear of rabies banned all dogs from the city), they fended for themselves, subsisting on whatever edibles could be scavenged from the garbage of households, shops, and seaside docks where fishermen cleaned their catches.

But "common" dogs, like people, fare poorly in most historical and archaeological records, and it was the canines of the elite who were immortalized in classical art and writings. Coveted by rich, adventuresome men for their ability to pursue swift game such as rabbits or deer, then tear them to pieces, Laconians were among the most highly prized animals. Possibly bred from Egyptian exports, these lithe hunting dogs enjoyed the rewards of being coveted companions to the affluent. The annual festival of Artemis (goddess of the chase), for instance, was celebrated by sacrificing calves, goats, or sheep, after which both dogs and masters partook of the roasted flesh in a great feast. Garlands of flowers were lavished on at-

Sixth-century B.C. Corinthian (Grecian) vase.
source: Drawn by author.

tending canines, giving rise to the enduring custom of draping winning racing Greyhounds with ribbons and roses. And to honor Maleatas (god of the hunt), sportsmen made pilgrimages to the holy sanctuary situated on a hill outside Epidaurus (Epidauros or Epidauras) called Kynortion, the "Mountain of the Rising Dog," where sacrifices were made to solicit good luck for the hunt and blessings for their hounds.

Lower-class dogs rarely enjoyed the gastronomic privileges accorded the Laconians. Instead they were one of the more popular sacrificial animals in classical Greece, perhaps because they were accessible to even the poorest citizens. July 25 marked the Kunophontes—a sanctioned "massacre of dogs" intended to appease the gods and head off violent summer storms or droughts. Hundreds of dogs perished under the knife on sacrificial altars on this bloody holiday, many of them puppies or homeless street curs. Doubly unlucky were black-coated dogs, the preferred sacrificial fodder for purification rituals and special appeals to the gods. Seeking to possess the fierce tenacity of dogs in battle, Spartan youths routinely killed black puppies to honor Ares, the god of war. Black puppy sacrifices also were made to Hecate, Queen of Hades and goddess of death. Also in her name adult black dogs were slain at crossroads to insure safe journeys, and killed to purify households after childbirth or to exorcise restless ghosts. In the province of Boeotia, one particularly grisly rite involved chopping a dog in two and walking between the halves.

The tradition of sacrificing puppies persisted well into the Christian era, as indicated by recent excavations along the Tiber River just north of modern Rome, where an ancient Roman cemetery dating between A.D. 300 and A.D. 450 was discovered. So far the graves of forty-seven infants and children have been found, who are thought to have perished in an outbreak of malaria. Scattered among the infants' graves were the skeletal remains of numerous dogs, most of them less than six months of age. Four of the animals were virtually intact, but various body parts were missing from the rest, affirming accounts by Pliny the Elder that puppies often were thought to absorb illness like a sponge, after which they—and the disease—could be "disposed" of. One puppy grave contained only a head, and four others included the skulls but lacked lower mandibles. The graves of three other puppies, on the other hand, had mandibles but no crania. And one puppy skeleton lacked a head altogether.

Religious cults were not the only ones to siphon animals from the homeless dog pool. The eminent Greek physician Claudius Galenus, or Galen (A.D. 129–199) would routinely dispatch apprentices to corral trusting street dogs to participate in his anatomical investigations, because he regarded canine physiology as "near to man." Before audiences of students and practitioners, Galen would slit open the belly of a live—and conscious—animal to demonstrate the peristaltic movement of the gastrointestinal tract, constituting one of the earliest written accounts of scientific vivisection (the practice was revived with enthusiasm by nineteenth-century medical researchers).

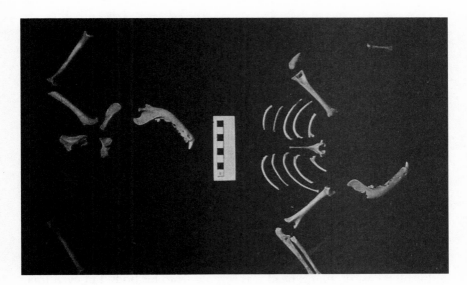

This puppy skeleton was uncovered during the recent excavation of the Roman infant cemetery of Lugnano in Teverina, Italy (near Rome). The animal was chopped in half as part of a curing ceremony. The remains of other puppies found here show no cut marks, and forensic experts theorize the animals were torn apart by hand.
source: Noelle Soren.

Still, dogs and horses were the only creatures the Greeks regarded with even a modicum of sentimentality, and many prominent individuals publicly expressed their respect or affection for canines. Nicknamed "The Dog," philosopher Diogenes (412–323 B.C.) was one of the few to openly praise canines as brave, faithful creatures who bore no false shame or modesty, and had only the humblest of needs. Testimony to the fact that at least a few dogs succeeded in touching the hearts of their masters is that they were buried with honors befitting a person, including tombstones. One reads:

> Thou passest on the path, if happily thou dost mark this monument,
> Laugh not, I pray thee,
> Though it is a dog's grave, tears fell for me,
> and the dust was heaped above me by a master's hand,
> who likewise engraved these words upon my tomb.

Some owners grew so emotionally attached to their dogs that they ceased perceiving of the animals as servants or tools, but rather regarded them as colleagues. Writing around A.D. 200, Aelian recounted an Athenian who took his dog with him to the Battle of Marathon, after which the canine "received the reward of heroism—the reward being to be seen in public along with the heroes."

Perhaps the most famous classical dog lover was Alexander the Great (356–323 B.C.), who owned several Molossian-type hounds from India. According to an account by Ailtonos, Alexander was shocked by a brutal demonstration of canine strength put on for his benefit by an Indian nobleman, who pitted one dog against a lion, then proceeded to amputate various parts of the canine's body, beginning with the tail and moving on to a leg. "This was done but the dog held to his grip more tenaciously, as if the dismembered limb was not his own. The remaining legs were cut off in succession, but even this did not in the least make him relax the vigor of his bite. Last of all, his head was severed from his body, but even then his teeth were seen hanging onto the part [of the lion] he had first gripped. The Indian, seeing the King's vexation, gave him four dogs similar to the one that was killed [and] joy at the possession of the four dogs soon obliterated from mind [Alexander's] sorrow for the other."

Alexander also owned a Molossian named Peritas, reputed to have killed single-handedly in sporting matches a lion and an elephant. Grief-stricken at her death, he led a formal funeral procession to her grave, erected a large stone monument on the site and ordered nearby residents to celebrate her memory in annual festivities.

There also is the famous legend of Odysseus's aging hound Argus, considered one of the great tributes to canine fidelity. According to Homer, Argus was abused and cast aside during his master's ten-year absence after the battle of Troy (1184 B.C.), relegated to "the deep dung of mules that lay heaped up before the doors." Upon hearing the voice of the long-lost King, the feeble Argus began "wagging his tail and dropped both ears, but nearer to his master he had no longer the strength to come. Odysseus glanced away, wiping a tear. As for Argus, black death descended on him that same hour he saw Odysseus again, in the twentieth year of his age."

The courage of the Molossians sometimes touched the hearts of an entire populace, as in the account of fifty dogs who patrolled the perimeter of Corinth, which one night was the object of a surprise attack. While the soldiers slept, the dogs alone defended the citadel, fighting valiantly until all were killed save one. Impressed by the canines' devotion, the citizens erected a marble tribute to the forty-nine dogs who died protecting their town, and Sorter, the lone survivor, was given a pension for life and an engraved silver collar that read, "To Sorter, defender and savior of Corinth, placed under the protection of his friends."

But little evidence exists indicating that most Greeks kept dogs simply for companionship. Writings and depictions seem to focus instead on the animal's capacity to serve tangible human needs, procuring game and protecting property. This lack of inspired writings celebrating the affection of a master for his dog leaves us with very few names of classical canines, unlike the dozens of endearing terms bestowed on Egyptian dogs.

Even insights into the relationships between the wealthy and their dogs run the risk of being stilted or embellished, and are limited by a scarcity of realistic, depictional artifacts. The famous Hellenistic red-and-black ceramic pictorial vases exhibit "a continuous repetition of the same themes, almost *ad nauseam*—the labors of Herakles, the Exploits of Theseus, the Rape of Europa and the many episodes of a complicated mythology," observes anthropologist A. Houghton Brodrick, "but not many pictures showing us how the people really lived." Brodrick adds that many of the so-called Greek sculptures that fill museums are in fact Roman, executed by a people fundamentally different in their experiences and outlook from their classical predecessors.

The Dogs of Rome

By 30 B.C., the Roman Empire supplanted and absorbed classical Greek society, encompassing not only Egypt but vast territories in Syria, Asia Minor, North Africa, Europe as far north as modern Denmark, and even the British Isles. Interlinked through trade and intermittent war, isolated colonies blossomed into sprawling city-states—magnets for mingling new ideas and technologies, expanding the material and philosophical cultures of all communities involved. Accordingly, the role of dogs in the civilized Western world also grew in significance and complexity.

The network of Hellenistic settlements laid out by the Greeks were both peaceably absorbed and forcibly taken over by the Romans. Struggling colonies grew into thriving commercial centers, dominated by a substantial merchant class, ranging from small family-owned and operated shops to international export companies. Now upwardly mobile moguls patterned their own lifestyles after the Emperor's court in Rome, at least to the best of their financial abilities. Some owned sprawling country villas or fashionable, multistoried townhomes, vying with one another to have the best clothing, jewelry, carriages, food, wine, and animals money could buy. In this newly affluent environment, many dogs were valued not only as tools but also as "ego adjuncts," a trend that would echo through the centuries to come.

At its height, Rome was a veritable melting pot of both domesticated animals and people. As always there were dogs of "lowly" birth, relegated to life on the streets as undesirables, although a lucky minority probably found favor with sympathetic housewives, street merchants, and shop owners, assigned the task of greeting houseguests or customers, keeping stray dogs at bay, or barking an alarm during the night.

Roman bronze figurine of a starving dog devouring a hare, recovered from Aix-en-Provence.
source: Copyright the British Museum.

Roman bronze "howling" dog figurine.
source: The British Museum.

At the same time, "exotic" dogs continued to arrive from Northern Europe, Africa, and the Middle East. Outcrossed with one another as well as with the more primitive, Neolithic canines still residing in rural parts of Southern Europe, they gave rise to a plethora of new varieties: giant "Mastiffs," Spitzes, chubby, Beagle-like canines, curly-coated "Poodles," pocket-sized lapdogs, and a large constituency of mild-mannered, midsized hounds with upright and drop ears, square muzzles, foreshortened faces, or coats of differing colors, lengths, and textures.

This pageant of Roman hound varieties exhibited appearances and behaviors often approximating those of modern breeds, and constituted a substantial, canine professional working class. The most famous among them was the war-trained "Molossus" (Molossian, Molussus, Molassian Hound), possibly descended from the legion of giant war dogs who accompanied Xerxes, King of Persia, when he invaded Greece in 480 B.C. (Ultimately, the animals may have been the progeny of the Asian war dogs brought to Egypt by the Hyksos in 1600 B.C.)

Weighing well in excess of one hundred pounds, the Molossus was death incarnate, capable of surprising speed and sufficient strength to knock or drag an armed man off his horse, disembowel and dismember him. Indeed, many of the dogs functioned as public executioners, deliberately starved for several days before being set loose in Rome's gory Circus to attack and devour unarmed prisoners as cheering crowds looked on. According to the first-century observer Polyen, these "hefty fighting dogs [were] responsible for preventing all contact between besiegers and besieged, by intercepting all messengers and uncovering all messages." Sustained by special requisitions of oxen and their every need tended to by their personal handlers, battalions of the dogs were assigned to trouble spots all along the Roman front in North Africa and the Near East, and were instrumental in the acquisition of new territories. Blondus, a Roman military essayist, believed these canines should be "a terrifying enemy to everyone except his master, so much so that he will not allow himself to be stroked even by those he knows best, but threatens everybody alike with the fulminations of his teeth, and always looks at everybody as though he is burning with anger."

The Romans weren't the only ones to employ aggressive canines on the battlefield, however. The Roman Consul General Gaius Marius (ca.

157–86 B.C.), for instance, had to overcome a battalion of snarling, snapping dogs at the battle of Vercellae—led by a team of Cimbri women handlers, no less—who delayed the advance of Roman troops for several hours. And the lanky hounds of the Celts (Western Europe and Britain) often proved an equal match for the Molossus. Two days after a battle against the Celts in Gaul, "barbarian'" dogs still held the Romans at bay, blocking them from confiscating their masters' chariots and goods. Dressed in spiked collars and protective, jointed metal or quilted cloaks capable of deflecting arrows, the nimble dogs wreaked chaos on battlefields, tearing at foot-bound soldiers, slashing the legs of horses, and keeping the Molossus occupied.

One Roman poet referred to "the British hound that brings the bull's head to the ground," a dog that greatly impressed military officials when they arrived in Britannia. An official was soon assigned to Winchester expressly to canvass the land for the best specimens of this dog, which then were exported to Rome. There, in the circus arena, four were set against one lion, three against a bear, and one against an armed gladiator, for duels to the death.

With a long tradition of handling war dogs, the Celts injected their own ideas about dog care, training, and breeding into Graeco-Roman culture. Roman military strategists were quick to adopt the same kind of accessories for their own legion of dogs. Celtic canine training drills virtually identical to those used by modern military establishments encouraged the dogs' aggressive tendencies. According to Blondus, in one exercise a man was "fitted out with a coat of thick skin, which the dog will not be able to bite through. The dog is then spurred on against the man, upon which the man in the skin runs away and then allows himself to be caught and, falling down on the ground in front of the dog, to be bitten."

In civilian life, the Molossus found steady employment as prestigious bodyguards for prominent citizens and senators, patrolling the grounds of rural estates or escorting them on journeys into town. They were kept tethered outside the doors of fashionable, wall-enclosed city homes, where they doubled as emblems of their masculine masters' affluence, clout, and to no less an extent, personal virility. Some households in Pompeii featured mosaics of a snarling dog straining at the end of a short chain with the words *cave canem*—"beware the dog."

Pompeiian house mosaic of a Molossus, reading *"Cave canem"* ("Beware the dog"). source: Drawn by author after mosaic in the National Museum of Archaeology, Naples.

Roman identification tag worn by a dog or human slave, ca. fourth-century A.D. It reads, "Hold me, lest I flee, and return me to my master Viventius on the estate of Callistus," probably near Rome. source: Copyright the British Museum.

After their integration into the Roman Empire, the Celts contributed a more "sporting" philosophy to the dominant dog culture, one that endures to this day. Rather than seek bloody, final resolution to the hunt at all costs (even to the point of penning or tying up the quarry), the Celts, wrote the Roman observer Arrian, "do not hunt in order to capture the game, but to watch their dogs perform with ability and speed. If the hare

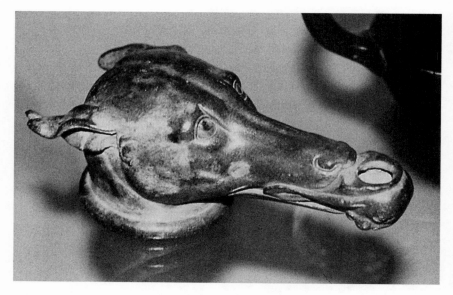

Roman bronze lamp of a Greyhound-like dog with a hare in its mouth, ca. first-century A.D.
source: Copyright the British Museum.

should escape their pursuit, they recall their dogs and rejoice sincerely in the luck or superiority of the adversary." The Emperor Julius Caesar (100–44 B.C.) reputedly placed high value on Celtic hunting dogs, which when outcrossed with canines who protected livestock, gave rise to gentler retrievers and pointers. Also making their debut during this era were the possible forerunners of terriers—small, feisty dogs called "vestigators," who eagerly ran small game to earth.

Some of the "soft-mouthed" Celtic hunting dogs exhibited a highly specialized propensity for fetching wounded game and returning it to their owners intact. Even the bloodhoundlike Segusii, while reportedly slower than other dogs, had an infallible talent for tracking scent trails and refraining from immediately killing the animals. Pliny the Elder wrote glowingly of such dogs in the first century, reporting that they "discover and trace out the tracks of the animal, leading by the leash the sportsman who accompanies it straight up to the prey. And as soon as ever it has perceived it, how silent it is and how secret but significant is the indication which it gives, first by the tail and afterward by the nose."

Diverse canine appearances and temperaments certainly made dog ownership appealing to a wider range of people. Not surprisingly, there was plenty of advice to be had on the selection and purchase of dogs, some of it rather obvious, such as the admonishments of one first-century essayist to buy only sheepdogs from shepherds, rather than from butchers or hunters, since "butchers' dogs often attack livestock and the huntsmen's dogs, at the sight of a hare or a fox, too easily remember they once were hunting dogs." Roman essayist Columella offered his own criteria for selecting working dogs in a treatise on agriculture penned around A.D. 70:

> A dog which is to guard cattle ought not to be as lean and swift of foot as one which pursues deer and stags and the swiftest animals, nor so fat and heavily built as the dog which guards the farm and granary. But he must, nevertheless, be strong and to a certain extent prompt to act, since the purpose for which he is acquired is to pick quarrels and to fight and also to move quickly. He has to repel the stealthy lurking of the wolf, to follow the wild beast as he escapes with his prey and to make him drop it and bring it back again. Therefore a dog of a rather long, slim build is better able to deal with these emergencies than one which is short or even squarely built.

In a culture where most animals were killed either for food or for amusement, it is interesting to note that quite a few Graeco-Romans were touched by the "human" quality of the canine personality. Unlike other, more emotionally detached domesticated animals, writers frequently remarked on the dogs' desire to be in the company of people at all costs, even if it endangered their lives. Pliny cited several accounts of canine courage and fidelity, praising one anonymous dog for thwarting a roadside robbery of his master as he journeyed alone through open country on the back of a mule. And Senator Caelius, "while lying sick at Placentia was surprised by armed men, but received not a wound from them until they had first killed his dog."

The extraordinary behavior of one grieving canine was witnessed by dozens of people who turned out for the execution of Titius Sebanius and his slaves. According to Pliny, "it was impossible to drive away a dog that belonged to them in prison, nor could it be forced away from the body, which had been cast down the Gemitorian steps; but it stood there howling in the presence of vast multitudes of people. Someone threw a piece of bread to it [and] the animal carried it to the mouth of its master. Afterwards, when the body was thrown into the Tiber, the dog swam into the river and endeavored to raise it out of the water . . . quite a throng of people collected to witness this instance of an animal's fidelity."

Even in this relatively inhumane society, the bond between human and canine sometimes transcended the mundane master-slave relationship to something more respectful and loving, as hinted at by Pliny's description of hunting dogs, who despite being "worn out with old age, blind and feeble, are carried by the huntsman in his arms, being still able to point to the coverts where the game is concealed, by snuffing with their muzzles at the wind." This is among the first written evidence of people making the emotional decision to care for working animals even after they had been permanently crippled by physical disabilities.

The Healing Lick

The uncertainty, discomfort, and danger associated with practical Roman medicine was incentive enough to seek out alternatives, though this was not entirely motivated by an aversion to doctors. Deities were an integral part of the human experience, so present in everyday imagery that soliciting divine intervention was the preferred recourse for curing ailments. Rational medicine worked hand in hand with religious ideology, and the worship of healing deities evolved parallel to science. Physicians and priests were inclined to regard themselves as the mortal instruments through which the gods could work their magic if so inclined—nowhere is this more apparent than in the Hippocratic Oath itself, first penned in the fifth century B.C. to read, "I swear by Apollo the healer." The belief that dogs could cure predates Roman culture and in fact was an offshoot of Greek mythology surrounding Apollo, sun-god and supreme healer. Since the dog was sacred to Apollo, canines were associated with his image and eventually they too were imbued with curative powers.

As the Roman Empire absorbed classical Greek society, however, the perception of dogs as sacrificial fodder was supplanted by the idea that canines who cured should be nurtured rather than killed. Now ailing citizens sought the services of a temple "cynotherapist," or healing dog, who would diagnose and relieve their suffering, provided appropriate offerings had been made to Asklepios, the Graeco-Roman god of healing. Often depicted as a bearded, grandfatherly figure in a simple, belted tunic with a snake-entwined staff, he may have been inspired by a real-life physician who lived in northern Greece about the fifth century B.C. At some time after his death, Asklepios the doctor was elevated to Asklepios the demigod, son of Apollo and a mortal woman. Then, as stories of his curative powers spread and multiplied, he was promoted to the rank of a full deity. Under Roman rule he eclipsed his immortal father to become the paramount god of healing.

The cult of Asklepios was one of the most prosperous, lasting well over a thousand years. Healing "sanctuaries"—temple complexes built in his name—thrived throughout Europe and the Mediterranean, chief among them being in the city-state of Epidaurus (described earlier as a pilgrimage site for Greek hunters). High priests received written appeals from regions hundreds or even thousands of miles away requesting assistance in establishing "branch" temples. In this way, Asklepian imagery and lore were slowly incorporated into an already existing pantheon of gods native to other communities.

The Asklepieions were people-friendly complexes, open to anyone seeking a cure. Temples generally contained one or more large public halls where sacrifices and mass celebrations could be staged, supplemented by wings with smaller, private chambers. As with the cult of Anubis, followers were encouraged to make their appeals directly to the gods; priests played the secondary role of advising or assisting worshipers, often by offering interpretations of the supplicant's dreams or personal experiences. Accordingly, the Asklepieions also featured "abatons"—dormitories where worshipers spent the night after a day of meditations, prayers, and purification rites. Reclining on settees, cots, or even the hard stone floor, they sought "incubation," a temple sleep through which Asklepios could effect a complete cure, or at least offer a prescription. It wasn't always easy to interpret these dreams, since Asklepios might appear in nonhuman form, including that of a dog, to relay a message so cryptic or bizarre as to require deciphering by a priest, who then prescribed drugs or exercise and diet regimens.

Supplementing incubations were real-life temple dogs, whose status as healers had survived the transition from Apollo to Asklepios. Small or medium in size, the gentle canines walked or lay among worshipers, doing the bidding of Asklepios by licking afflicted body parts. (In a similar vein, wealthy women clutched tiny lapdogs resembling spitzes and terriers to their stomachs in the belief that they prevented minor aches and pains—sparking a feminine association with small dogs that has lasted into modern times.)

In an ancient version of consumer endorsement, satisfied worshipers were encouraged to leave their testimonies on flagstones and metal platters to be prominently displayed in the temple. "Thuson of Hermione, a blind boy, had his eyes licked by one of the dogs about the temple and departed cured," reads one Epidaurian slab. Similarly, a boy from Aegina "had a growth on the neck. When he came to the god, one of the sacred dogs healed him, while he was awake, with his tongue." In gratitude, offerings of garlands, sacrificial animals, coinage, ceramic and metal dog figurines, and likenesses of formerly afflicted body parts were left at the altars, instilling confidence in future temple visitors (and probably fund-

Roman bronze dog figurine, possibly depicting a cynotherapist, recovered from the temple complex at Lydney Park, Gloucestershire, England.
source: Courtesy of the Lydney Park Estate.

ing temple expansions). Not to be forgotten, some of the dogs also received their own thank-yous from grateful clients, in the form of honey-sweetened cakes or other morsels.

Such a temple was unearthed in 1932 at Lydney Park in Gloucestershire, England, by the eminent antiquarian Mortimer Wheeler (who later served as a lieutenant colonel during and after World War II, assigned to safeguard classical ruins from excavators sent by Stalin to collect spoils for a planned national museum). Here, Asklepios and his cynotherapists were integrated into the resident "barbaric" belief system to create the Romano-Celtic healing cult of Nodens. The sanctuary featured a number of private "bungalows" separate from the communal abaton abutting the temple. At its height around A.D. 400, it is thought to have been popular as a resort/health spa, since it offered mosaic sunken baths fed by thermal springs, saunas, and artificially heated sleeping quarters. An abundance of canine figurines, notably one four-inch-long recumbent "greyhound" stunningly executed in bronze, suggests that dogs were an integral part of this cult. It is tempting to imagine them at their work, perhaps licking the exposed parts of visitors languishing in the healing waters.

Sixty years after excavation, the site's artifact assemblage is reposited in a private museum in Gloucestershire, and the famous bronze dog is proudly featured at the tops of Lydney Park tourist fliers, serving as an impromptu mascot.

A letter published in the April 1989 issue of The *Lancet* (a British medical journal) recounted the case of a middle-aged woman who went to Kings College Hospital in London for examination of a lesion on her leg, which was diagnosed as malignant melanoma. According to Drs. Hywell Williams and Andres Pembroke, she first became aware of the problem mole because her dog, a female Doberman pinscher–Border Collie mix, "frequently spent several minutes a day sniffing [it] intently, even through trousers." The strange ritual culminated several months later when the dog attempted to bite off the growth as the woman wore shorts, convincing her to seek "further medical advice." Doctors concluded that "the dog may have saved her owner's life by prompting her to seek treatment when the lesion was still at a curable stage."

The incident inspired Florida dermatologist Dr. Armand Cognetta and retired police dog handler Duane Pickel to launch a two-year training project with a seven-year-old Schnauzer named George, who first learned to locate vialed skin cancer samples hidden around the house. Then he progressed to identifying melanoma scrapings from a lineup of normal cell samples, which he did correctly nine times out of ten. Next, cancer samples were hidden under bandages on a volunteer, and George found them five out of seven times.

With their superior sense of smell, dogs may be able to distinguish a protein configuration unique to malignancies. Given the many ways the human body sheds cells daily, canines might prove useful in diagnosing other forms of cancer at an early, treatable stage, particularly in poor countries where technologically advanced diagnostic equipment is unavailable.

Did the Graeco-Roman cynotherapists really cure people? They might have, especially if the ailment was psychosomatic. Today the cuddling of pets has been shown to lower blood pressure and stimulate the production of brain endorphins. And as so adroitly demonstrated by George, some ancient canines might have displayed a propensity for locating injuries or abnormal growths, after which priests or physicians could have stepped in to perform minor surgery—after all, the ancient Romans were highly skilled in the manufacture of scalpels, forceps, and other medical equipment. Furthermore, a recent chemical analysis of canine saliva shows it to possess antibacterial properties, albeit minor. In the ancient world, where antiseptic practices were unknown, having a dog lick an infected area might have been one of the less dangerous prescriptions.

Watchdogs of the Gods

Keeping holy sanctuaries well stocked with dogs had other advantages, not the least of which was deterrence to theft. Altars glittering with bronze, silver, and gold thank-you offerings were an irresistible target for burglars. One thief in the Asklepieia of Athens was caught in the act by a healing dog, who after trying unsuccessfully to alert temple attendants to the break-in, opted to follow the criminal back to his home. The theft eventually was noticed by the priests, and a search led by the dog resulted in the culprit's capture. To mark the occasion, a special decree was passed stating that the dog be rewarded with food at the public's expense, and that the priests of Asklepios should tend to his needs for the rest of his life, even when he could no longer work as a cynotherapist.

Quite a few cults were quick to catch on to the idea of using dogs as temple sentries, and other Graeco-Roman gods became absentee pet owners. However, these dogs differed considerably from the cuddly, kissing canines of Asklepios. Often they were allowed to pass their own canine judgments on new supplicants, or functioned as four-footed temple "bouncers," doling out punishments for unbecoming worshiper conduct. For instance, the Sicilian temple of Hephaestus (god of subterranean fire) at Etna was filled with dogs who reportedly ingratiated themselves only to worshipers with pure hearts and honorable intentions, but bit the hands of those who were corrupt. And in some instances, the dogs actually were allowed to chase followers away from the temples, certainly a questionable public relations move. The temple of the Sicilian war god Adranus also supported a legion of "sacred" dogs, said to number at least a thousand. During the day they were mild-mannered animal ambassadors, partaking in temple rites and greeting new visitors at the entrance to the shrine. After a day of drinking in the god's honor, staggering worshipers could enjoy a canine escort back to their homes—unless they became rowdy, in which case the dogs ripped their clothing to shreds. In a Roman shrine for Diana, dogs killed a man as he attempted to rape a woman worshiping this goddess of chastity. Even the canines of Dionysus, lord of wine and fertility, were reputed to savagely attack anyone who interfered with the musicians employed at his temple.

The Mark of Anubis

With their own mythology in tow, Greeks visiting the Nile valley were equally impressed with Egyptian gods, so much so that they blended these deities with their own. Anubis, the dog-headed guide of the dead and calibrator of the scale of truth, was identified with Hermes, the Greek conductor of the dead to Hades (known to the Romans as Mercury), resulting in the birth of Hermanubis. Commonly known as Latrador, meaning "The Barker," he was depicted on bas-reliefs, glyptographs (engraved gems), and coins. Like Anubis, Hermanubis had a dog's head but presented

Hermanubis bronze figurine.
source: Copyright the British Museum.

a friendlier, more "domesticated" de-
meanor, often resembling the short-eared coursing hounds of Graeco-
Roman sportsmen. Instead of the Egyptian-style pleated kilt, he wore a
short Roman toga, accessorized with a heavy woolen cloak slung over one
shoulder and winged sandals on his feet. Echoing images of Asklepios, he
also carried a snake-entwined staff in one hand, while in the other he bore
a blossoming palm branch, the symbol of triumph and rebirth.

The Egyptian funerary god had been softened by Hermes's reputation as a benevolent protector. When souls followed the path of the plan-
ets in search of heaven, it was Hermanubis who now escorted and assisted
them, for he possessed special words to overcome opposing spirits and pass
through locked gates. In time, he even gained a reputation as the protector of pregnant women and sympathizer of men hoping to win the love of
women.

The cult of Hermanubis not only endured but thrived, with thousands of worshipers journeying annually to his Alexandrian sanctuary, called the Anoubeion, one of the most prestigious temples in the empire. Its feast days were legendary, with supplicants partaking in "hecatombs"—animal sacrifices sometimes consisting of one hundred or more oxen. Solid gold ingots were offered up to Hermanubis, as well as gold libation bowls and silver likenesses of the god. And like the temples of Anubis and Asklepios, the sanctuary of Hermanubis was filled with dogs, revered by the public not so much as healers but simply as his earthly representatives.

Playing on the role of Hermes as a divine messenger, Hermanubis became the designated protector of Isis, the Egyptian goddess of fertility and love, now transformed in Graeco-Roman culture into the mother of the Earth itself. Annual ceremonies were held in her honor throughout the empire, marked with sacrifices, parades, processions, the singing of hymns, and feasts that lasted till dawn. Life-size likenesses of both deities were paraded before the public, perfumed, coiffed, and dressed in real clothing (much like the Virgin Mary, carved and costumed in effigy, is paraded before supplicants on religious holidays throughout Catholic Latin America to this day).

Roman philosopher and humorist Lucius Apuleius (A.D. 124–170) described a joint ceremony honoring both Isis and Hermanubis that commenced after sunset. Singing youths, pipes, flutes, and trumpets heralded a grand procession of women dressed in white, sprinkling herbs, balm, and ointments, followed by bearers of mirrors and ivory combs to coiff the goddess. A throng of men came behind these holy hairdressers, carrying oil lamps, torches, and candles, then the priests of both cults, who bore relics, portable shrines, or icons. A painted wooden likeness of Hermanubis towered over the parade, "messenger of the gods, supernal and infernal, his dog's head and neck rearing on high, displaying alternately a face as black as night and one golden as the day . . . he bore the caduceus [serpent-entwined staff] and in his right hand waved a green palm branch aloft." The colors noted by Apuleius symbolized the duality of Hermanubis—as a symbol of death and decay, and a patron of man's resurrection. Hence the two-tone face, with darkness implying death, and gold, the color of the sun, suggesting life.

Such solemn proceedings were not without their lighter moments, as evidenced by an account of the Emperor Commodus (A.D. 161–192), who with ceremonially shaven head, had the honor of being sole porter of the dog-god's likeness. In the course of the march, however, the top-heavy Hermanubis repeatedly toppled forward, its muzzle knocking the backs of the priests' heads, much to everyone's embarrassment (or amusement, knowing human nature).

Canine Resurrection

Like Christ, Asklepios was a kindly healer, and despite the Gnostics' efforts to discredit him as a pagan "destroyer of souls," people were loathe to discount his centuries-long record of working miraculous cures. It was this attractive power of the Asklepian faith, not just blasphemous pagan rites, that inspired such overwhelming fear and hatred in the early Gnostics. Under the command of the converted and zealous Emperor Constantine (A.D. 306–377), the Asklepieions at Aigia and Cilicia were razed because, according to the Roman observer Eusebius, Asklepios "distracted" too many people from "the true savior." As Christianity gained in popularity, the decline of Asklepian temples was hastened by a campaign of vandalism by early Christians, who systematically defaced paintings, sculptures, and public altars throughout the empire, while adopting many of the pagan temple rites to meet the growing need for rituals in their own church.

History fails to tell us the fate of the healing dogs who resided at these temples, but given the wrath of the early Christian zealots, they may have been killed outright or at least driven from their homes into the streets. The cult of Asklepios maintained a tenuous existence for a time in remote areas of the empire (such as Lydney Park), but worshipers continued to be hounded for practicing their beliefs. The influence of this divine healer and patron of doctors was not entirely eclipsed, however. Christian churches were erected on many Asklepian sites, including Epidaurus, Corinth, and Rome, in some instances continuing under the mantle of healing centers, with one Christian basilica at Athens built on the remains of the Asklepieia dedicated to the memory of "doctor saints."

The legacy of the cynotherapists also has prevailed and found new life in the Christian era, first as the dog who licked the sores of the diseased beggar Lazarus, whom Christ resurrected from the grave. Later on in thir-

Painted Spanish wood figurine of St. Roch, ca. 1500.
source: Courtesy of the Board of Trustees of the Victoria and Albert Museum.

teenth-century Europe, when the "Black Death" (bubonic plague) gripped the land, a monk named Roch traveled throughout Languedoc with his dog to comfort ailing peasants, until he contracted the disease himself. As Roch lay under a tree near death, his dog wandered to a nearby castle, helped itself to a loaf of bread before an astonished lord, and left. The theft was repeated several days in a row, until out of curiosity the nobleman followed the animal back to the prostrate monk, where he witnessed the dog drop the bread and tenderly lick his master's plague sores. So moved was the man by this scene, he forsook his wealth and entered the Church. Today "St. Roch and his dog" is an enduring proverbial reference to two inseparable companions.

Surprisingly, Hermanubis managed to elude most of the Gnostics' wrath by metamorphosing into a more acceptable, Christian form, eventually reemerging as St. Christopher. In the formative years of Christianity, supplicants even experimented with the notion of merging Hermanubis with Christ, drawing the dog-headed god with outstretched arms in the form of a cross, or in the case of one likeness scratched on the wall of a Roman house, holding a crucifix before a worshiper—for like Asklepios, he, too, was similar to Christ in the sense that he was an integral part of resurrection myth and imagery. Also like Christ—and mortal dogs—Hermanubis embodied the ethic of unquestioning acceptance. His transformation may have been sparked with the Gnostic tale of a giant, pagan man who carried an incognito Christ Child through torrential waters to safety. Literally meaning "Christ-bearer," Christopher was immortalized in text as the protector, servant, and, in essence, "dog" of the Lord, making it fairly easy to graft the tale onto Hermanubis lore, paving the way to cast him as a saint. Still dog-headed, the former Hermanubis now clutched spears, swords, and crucifixes, tools of the trade for any soldier of Christ.

Even in the Greek Orthodox church, where St. Christopher was never identified as a carrier of the Christ Child, other hints of Hermanubis linger. Oral tradition holds that Christopher once was a handsome Roman soldier, who because of his beauty was in constant trouble with both sexes. One day he prayed aloud that he might be made ugly in order to be delivered from such troubles, upon which he immediately grew the head of a dog. Incorporating various aspects of this myth, a sixth-century Irish legend tells of a holy man in the final years of the Roman Empire, who was tortured for refusing to partake in a sacrifice to pagan gods. When interrogated, the man replied, "I am Christian. 'Reprobus' was my name before I believed, but 'Christopher' has been my name since my baptism. My face shows that I am of the race of dog-heads," apparently referring to his strangely deformed head. Miraculously cured of the speech impediment associated with his "canine" visage, the man was executed by the Emperor for preaching about Christ, sparking the beginning of Rome's unsuccessful genocidal campaign against the Christians.

As the curtain rang down on pagan Graeco-Roman culture, the followers of Hermanubis quietly ensured his rebirth in the new empire, and in the process unwittingly perpetuated an iconographic "chain" stretching back three thousand years or more to Wepwawet, the Egyptian guardian of the dead. Just as the timeless role of mortal dogs seems to be to assist mortal men, the repeated resurrection of the dog god—as Anubis, then Hermanubis under the Romans, and finally as St. Christopher among the Christians—may reflect a deep-seated need for a canine protector or companion into the next life as well. One eighteenth-century Greek Orthodox hymn unwittingly paid homage to the immortal dog-headed champion of human souls in this way:

> St. Christopher,
> Dog-headed,
> Valiant in faith
> Fervent in prayer.
> Thou soldier of Christ
> Raised to sanctification
> O victorious Christopher
> Feared by the king of idols
> And glorified by the songs of Angels
> Thou paragon of martyrs.

Four

Feudal Society, Renaissance, and Revolution

B Y A.D. 400, the Romans had become both economically and geo-graphically overextended, no longer able to sustain the burden of a large military force, which eventually buckled in the wake of warring Germanic tribes pooled in the fringe provinces. Ultimately, though, it was the humble flea that dealt the final death blow to the great empire.

Hopping a ride on the rats that frequented merchant vessels traveling from Egypt to Europe in A.D. 540, fleas infected with a deadly bacillus took advantage of Rome's well-developed infrastructure to spread bubonic plague from the Nile valley to the far corners of Western Europe. Because everybody was afflicted with fleas—always had been—no one, rich or poor, prominent or insignificant, was spared. Historians estimate the mortality rate rose as high as 95 percent in many regions. Entire families, some with lineages stretching back before the time of Christ, were completely wiped out, leaving critical voids in aristocratic society. People were dying faster than they could be buried. When graveyards filled to overflowing, bodies were thrown into the rivers or were simply dragged out of the house and left in the street, where they could remain for days before a cart happened by on its way to one of the many common interment pits.

Famine and lawlessness ensued, with people waylaying one another for even the smallest crust of bread. In the end, entire communities lay deserted and soon were reabsorbed into the wilderness. Fifty years and twenty-five million deaths later, the plague subsided as abruptly as it appeared because the population was so depleted that the epidemic lost the critical mass necessary to sustain a catastrophe. Taking advantage of the social and political upheaval, Anglo-Saxons, Franks, and Visigoths cemented their tenuous holds on former Roman provinces, establishing their own independent kingdoms and laying the foundation for a feudal socioeconomic structure. These new medieval settlements were quick to incorporate key elements of the Roman network of aquifers, roads, and bridges over critical mountain passes, not to mention a variety of stone structures.

It was easy for the populace to believe that the great disaster was supernatural in origin, a notion the now-institutionalized Catholic Church did nothing to dispel as it rushed to fill the social and political void left by the epidemic, proclaiming itself "doctor to the soul *and* the body," in the words of historian Charles Panati, author of *Panati's Extraordinary Endings of Practically Anything and Everybody* (1989). The Church claimed the plague was a divine reprimand sent by Christ himself to humble the human race. Earlier Graeco-Roman theories that disease was spread by pathogenic agents were branded heresy, effectively bringing empirical investigations and scientific dialogues to a halt. Bewildered and demoralized, lord and layman alike accepted the holy declaration, paving the way for the Church to proclaim itself the sole authority on God's plans.

By A.D. 700, papal power had surpassed that of the state and Catholicism was securely entrenched in the psychological, political, and economic fabric of independent kingdoms throughout the Western world. The churches were perceived as the "castles" of God, giving many clerics a social rank equal to aristocrats. Ultimately, the decisions this new papal-hierocratic government made over the next millennia proved to have as profound an impact on the culture of dogs as it did on humans.

Cult of the Hunt

During and immediately following the height of the contagion, dogs were left ownerless and homeless by the hundreds. While people, cattle, sheep, cats, and even poultry succumbed to the epidemic, the canine race, with its inborn resistance to the plague bacillus, was subject to a rising tide of superstitions and paranoia. Desperate for food, many dogs resorted to scavenging corpses, and packs of feral hounds roamed the hamlets each night, their snarling and yapping playing on the imagination of a populace already convinced that the apocalypse was at hand.

Although compassion for both beast and man was in short supply after the plague, a lucky canine minority continued to live secure lives as companions to people with sufficient political and financial clout to access precious caches of food for animals. Under the feudal socioeconomic system of the Middle Ages, in which an elite minority was supported by the toils of an underclass majority, vast tracts of forest land harboring precious natural resources such as timber, medicinal herbs, and culinary delicacies (honey, truffles, berries) were appropriated by kings throughout Europe, who then parceled out the acreage to favored subjects in exchange for services, goods, or money. "Venery," or hunting, quickly evolved into a highly specialized, ritualized activity. It was removed from the common realm and elevated to the status of a sport, reserved for an idle, privileged few. A wide workforce was needed to manufacture and maintain the trappings and accessories of a noble hunter, who required the finest in lances, crossbows, arrows, oliphants (trumpets), and saddlery. Since dogs rivaled horses as the more important sporting accessories, the services of a professional "huntsman," renowned for his expertise in the care and training of the dogs, was mandatory. Henry I of England (1068–1135) employed no fewer than four huntsmen to tend to a kennel containing several hundred dogs.

By this time, considering that even the longest of Roman dog lineages were probably shattered by decades of plague and encounters with "bar-

"Dog boys" tended to the needs of aristocratic hunting hounds under the watchful eye of a professional huntsman (left).

source: Drawn by the author after a fifteenth-century French illustration by Gaston Phoébus.

barian" canines who had accompanied Germanic invaders, the majority of medieval hounds were likely of mixed blood, but performance was more important than breeding. They were loosely defined according to their size or propensity for a certain type of game. "Brachets," for instance, identified nimble, medium-sized dogs who were adept at chasing small game such as rabbits. (During the Renaissance such canines would give rise to the diminutive Italian Greyhound.) By contrast, "Levriers" (alternatively called Greyhounds in England, though they should not be confused with the modern purebred dogs of the same name) were larger and more robust, and were capable of killing a large stag while the master, beaming with pride, watched the spectacle from atop his horse.

Venturing out shortly after dawn on a typical day's hunt, the lord was accompanied by a caravan of servants, among them the professional "huntsman," who was expected to orchestrate a fruitful (or at least entertaining) chase. With one or two leashed hounds in hand, he cautiously advanced on foot to search for evidence of deer or other game that could be tracked or herded back toward the hunting party. The discovery of droppings, broken branches, or hoofprints was marked by a quick burst of one-pitched notes on the oliphant, signaling assistant dog handlers in the rear to release the pack. The chase continued, often for hours, until the hounds brought the quarry to bay, at which time the lord was invited to deal the death blow with a lance or well-placed arrow. Or he could leave the animal to fight a losing battle with the dogs.

Some huntsmen collaborated with falconers, training birds of prey to work with the smaller Brachets in a sport called "hawking at the brook." Canine and falcon were taught to work as a team, a slow process that began with having the animals dine together in the hope that a bond could be fostered. Once training was complete, the duo were escorted to a riverbank and while the lord watched, the dog was released to startle the waterfowl. Circling overhead, the falcon struck, sending ducks, swans, or storks plummeting to earth for the dog to retrieve.

The assistance of Molossus-like "Alaunts" was required for the pursuit of dangerous game, notably wild boar. Such hunts were risky for all involved. Armed with razor-sharp teeth, boars weighing several hundred pounds could suddenly pivot to slash their pursuers, and dogs, horses, and people frequently met tragic ends. "The boar slays a man with one strike, as with a knife," observed Edward the Duke of York in his treatise titled *The Master of the Game.* "Some have seen him slit a man from knee up to breast." Inexperienced young lords could be more dangerous than the quarry they sought. Rustling through the underbrush, huntsmen and dogs were sometimes mistaken for game by an overeager nobleman, triggering a deadly rain of arrows. Even the lord himself could accidentally be killed, as was the case with William Rufus, the son of William the Conqueror, who after a hearty breakfast on August 1, 1100, rode out to the forest with friends in search of game. A stag bolted out of the underbrush to run between the horses, and without a second thought, one of his friends fired off an arrow—which ricocheted off the deer's back and impaled the prince, killing him instantly. Understandably, then, the huntsman who could make a chase come off without a hitch was highly sought after. In a few great households he even held the rank of knight.

High-ranking church officials also became hunting and dog enthusiasts, despite their vows of poverty. Abbott Samson of Bury St. Edmunds obtained the King's blessing in the twelfth century to enclose "many parks, which he replenished with beasts of the chase, keeping huntsmen with dogs," according to Jocelin of Brakelon. Clerics with no land of their own simply made use of a neighboring nobleman's estate, with or without his consent. When the Earl of Arundel (Hugh d'Aubigny) learned that the Archbishop of Canterbury routinely trespassed on his land to hunt deer, the cleric's hounds were surreptitiously confiscated. An enraged archbishop retaliated by excommunicating the earl, who then was unable to attend the coronation of Queen Eleanor. By the thirteenth century, reports of vicars converting their churches into barnyards, stables, and kennels were so widespread that the Archbishop of Canterbury (John Peckham) was compelled to issue a decree ordering all parish priests to conduct public services at least four times a year.

The Gauge of Privilege

The exclusive nature of hunting culture did little to endear aristocrats to their subjects. Peasants paid a heavy price for poaching, even if they were only fishing or trapping rabbits to supplement meager diets of bread and boiled onions. Penalties ranged from blindings with a hot poker to years of imprisonment, fines, the confiscation of property and material goods. The lord's poaching edict applied to canine commoners as well. Any dogs not belonging to the royal kennel were subject to execution on the spot, even when accompanied by a human and on a leash. Exceptions sometimes were made for puppies or lapdogs, thought to be incapable of catching game, but all canines had to be small enough to pass through a "dog gauge," a calibrated wooden or metal hoop. Large dogs who herded swine or worked as beasts of burden and belonged to peasants had to be surgically hobbled, a process in which the animal's forefoot was placed on a thick wooden block so a mallet-driven chisel could neatly sever three of the four toes.

The term "cur" derives from the medieval practice of requiring lower-class dogs to have their tails docked so they could be distinguished from hounds belonging to aristocrats. Such canines were first described as "courtalt," then "curtal," and finally "curs." Francis I of France apparently was not much of a dog lover, for he issued an unusually cruel mandate that "all dogs belonging to peasant or farmer must wear, attached to their necks, a heavy block of wood, the weight and bulkiness of which will stem their ardor whenever they move away from their homes. If despite this precaution they take to hunting on royal land they will be punished *in situ* immediately by pure and simple hamstringing."

Relations between the upper and lower classes only worsened when new game preserves were established, an act that sometimes took farms, churches, or even whole communities. Residents were simply ordered to vacate the premises, sometimes with no compensation or provision for re-location. Yet they were still expected to meet tribute (tax) deadlines! Writing of one such eviction in the twelfth century, Florence of Worcester reminisced that "in former times this tract of land was thickly planted with churches, but by command of King William the Elder, the people were ex-pelled, the houses half-ruined, the churches pulled down and the land made a habitation for wild beasts only."

Assigned to uphold hunting laws and to apprehend transgressors were the "verderers" or "foresters"—medieval game wardens with the author-ity to search any and all premises or persons for evidence of poaching. Usually freeholders or the second-born sons of knights seeking to make their own fortunes, verderers were inclined to abuse the powers of their of-

A verderer and his tracking dog.
source: Drawn by the author after a fifteenth-century French illustration by Gaston Phoébus.

fice for personal gain. They chopped down trees, grazed their livestock in the royal forest, and routinely hunted the very game they were entrusted with protecting. Others were known to take bribes or extort goods and services from the peasants in exchange for not arresting a suspected poacher. Understandably, they were despised by the working class. Upon meeting a verderer, one unusually cocky farmer openly declared, "I would rather go to my plow than serve in an office such as yours." Peasants often united to thwart these investigators, feigning ignorance though they knew a poacher's identity, or supplying false information. So it is probably no coincidence that the legend of Robin Hood, the selfless poacher who squatted on royal land and stole from the rich to help the poor, first appeared in the thirteenth century.

Every effort was made to deny the public's access to hunting accessories as well, particularly dogs bred for sport. To stake a pack of such distinctive hounds outside one's thatched cottage would have been regarded as the height of stupidity—the medieval equivalent to parking a fleet of red Jaguars outside a trailer home—and a sure way to attract the attention of the authorities. Nets, traps, arrows, deer hides, even the tip of an antler was sufficient to drag a man away in chains. The punishment for possessing such accessories sometimes was to watch them being chopped up with an ax—dogs included.

Experienced poachers therefore enlisted the help of sympathizers, who out of friendship or in exchange for a portion of the kill would deny any knowledge of criminal activities or the whereabouts of illegal dogs. In the thirteenth century, Robert Bacon, the parson of Easton, discreetly kept a poacher and hounds on the church payroll to supplement his dinner fare. At one point the man was caught and imprisoned for taking a deer near Rockingham Castle, but he eventually was released on bond, whereupon he unexpectedly died. Bacon, however, was still expected to appear in court to answer charges leveled by the arresting officer, Sir John Lovet, who was rumored to accept bribes—at the trial, Lovet unexpectedly withdrew the charge, saying that he had mistakenly identified a sheep as a deer, so Bacon was acquitted.

Some poachers escaped punishment by openly claiming to be church employees. As such, their bosses argued, they were entitled to exemption from the law. In 1255, Gervais of Dene, a "servant" of John of Crakehall, the Archdeacon of Bedford (and later treasurer to the King), was freed from prison after just such an argument was made and the arresting foresters were threatened with excommunication. The power to excommunicate so emboldened some church officials, in fact, that they openly joined poachers in their employ for illegal forays into the forest. In 1272, one such cleric killed eight deer and left the head of a buck impaled on a pole in a clearing, its mouth wedged open with a wooden spindle to create a ghoulish, mocking grin, an act "in great contempt of the lord king and his foresters," according to court documents.

In May of 1246, three verderers assigned to Rockingham Forest were tipped off that poachers were planning to infiltrate the "lawn of Beanfield for the purpose of doing evil to the venison of the lord king." According to court documents, an ambush was arranged by officers "William, Matthew and Roger." The offenders appeared at dusk, in the company of "five greyhounds, one of which was white, another black, the third fallow, a fourth black spotted." The dogs were immediately seized, "but the fifth Greyhound, which was tawny, escaped." The poachers also eluded capture, stopping only long enough to release a few well-aimed arrows, killing Matthew. The next day a house-to-house search for the missing hound was launched with the aim of discovering the identity of the murderers. From the start the investigation was derailed at every turn by witnesses who denied all knowledge of the incident. After several false leads, the dog was discovered with the Abbot of Pipewell, who claimed it belonged to one "Simon of Kivelsworthy." Because of the social prominence of the good cleric, Simon was only asked to pay a fine of half a mark. Matthew's killers were never identified.

As in any breeding project, there must have been some canine "castoffs" from lordly kennels, which if not killed outright, wound up being covertly sold by castle servants to the populace at large, a theory that would go far to account for the persistent presence of Greyhounds in peasant communities despite the strictest of royal edicts. Perish the thought that the working class was capable of breeding their own gazehounds from a few illegally obtained dogs, let alone canines as competent as those in the service of the King. In 1570, Dr. Johannes Caius (John Cay, Key, Kaze, or Kees) of Cambridge University would identify a Greyhound bred by the lower class as the "Thief Dog," who at "his master's commands goes out at night and follow[s] up the rabbits without barking. By the scent borne in his face, he catches while coursing as many as his master allows."

With the chase playing such a pivotal role in European culture, the lord and his dogs inspired an enduring body of "flying huntsmen" lore—the "Wild Hunt" of ethereal hunters and spirit dogs who flew through the forests and over the moors in an eternal chase, their passage marked by the deafening sounds of ghostly hoofbeats, shouts, and barking. Tales of a phantom huntsman actually predate the Middle Ages, having originated with the myth of Woden, a Germano-Celtic storm god who rushed across the night skies in the company of a large pack of hounds, whose infernal howls split linen as it hung on the line. Hedges were crushed, wagons overturned, and thatched roofs peeled from the rafters when Woden passed by, hot on the trail of spectral wild boars (or as some tales recount, women). Sometimes he and his dogs descended to earth long enough to enter cottages and empty peasant larders, even gobbling up the fireplace ashes. When one serf asked for compensation after his larder was emptied by this spectral party, Woden returned dragging a dead dog and instructed the trembling peasant to throw the carcass into the hearth. This he did, whereupon the skin burst open and gold coins tumbled out.

In the new Christian era, the Wild Hunt assumed a more malevolent air as Woden the immortal pagan was replaced by a mortal sinner, condemned to ride the storms for all eternity. Now the horses of the Wild Hunt were said to be the souls of women who had been intimate with priests. One Basque version of the tale recounted how an abbot who enjoyed the chase interrupted the Holy Sacrament and bolted out the door of the church to follow his hounds, who had picked up the scent of a hare. For this sacrilege, the man was condemned after his death to an eternal chase across the plains, never to rest, and never to catch his quarry. And the Huntsman of Normandy was rumored to be Satan himself, leading a galloping troupe of nuns and monks, who in life had fornicated without repentance.

In one instance the Huntsman was a woman, known in life as Fru Gode. "The chase is better than heaven!" she shouted one day as she rode with her daughters (twenty-one in all). No sooner had she uttered the words of heresy than her children were transformed into dogs and Gode ascended to the clouds, where she and her daughters have been hunting ever since.

In Welsh lore, the Wild Hunt is a death omen. Led by Annwn, the King of Hell, demonic hounds fly to the houses of the terminally ill to whine, pant, and scratch outside doors and windows until the soul departs. These *Cwn annwn* ("Dogs of Hell"), also known as *Cwn y Wybr* ("Dogs of the Sky") exhibited symbolic color dualities reminiscent of those in Graeco-Roman times: the appearance of white dogs at one's door implied the soul would be escorted to heaven, while the presence of black dogs meant the soul was doomed to eternal torment.

The Flowering of Canine Culture

The fourteenth century marked the beginning of a "golden age" for the breeding of dogs. During the Renaissance (approximately 1300–1600) the hunt became increasingly complex and lavish, and noblemen vied against one another to own the fastest, strongest, most talented dogs. The goal was to create one's own, personalized canine variety, unique to a particular family or estate, just like a vintage wine.

Medieval dog varieties became more distinctive and uniform in appearance, and for the first time there were probable, easily recognizable progenitors for modern Mastiffs and Greyhounds. A substantial class of retrievers was fashioned from dogs collected on Holy Crusades to the Middle East or from animals who, beginning around A.D. 800, had accompanied the Moors into Spain (hence the name "Spaniel"). Also featured with increasing frequency from the fourteenth century onward in sculptures, paintings, and tapestries were endearing miniature "lap dogs"—tiny Spaniels, Terriers, and hounds—apparently kept and bred for no other purpose save companionship.

Typical of the new sporting breeds was the Hound of St. Hubert, created by monks at the Abbey of St. Hubert at Mouzon in the Ardennes (who may have drawn on surviving Roman Segusiis for early breeding stock). These dogs had soft, pendulous ears and somber, gentle countenances accentuated by furrows and loose folds of skin. Compared to the Levrier and Alaunt, it was not a particularly swift or muscular breed, but possessed exceptional endurance and determination, while remaining surprisingly obedient. It had a nose capable of finding virtually anything—the canine equivalent of gold. Legend has it that as early as A.D. 800 the monastery began sending six of their finest young dogs to the King of France every year in lieu of tribute, who in turn gave the pups to close friends and favored associates. Ultimately this dog, and many other hounds like it, were just as coveted (if not more so) for their potential as fashionable status symbols as for their hunting talents.

The manner in which humans related to canines also became more complex. Now many noblemen developed genuine friendships with their dogs, and were inclined to great public displays of affection. Hounds of all shapes and sizes became an integral part of elite family life, and great care was taken to immortalize their unique likenesses in family portraits. Lords routinely presented themselves for holy services with one or more beloved dogs in tow, an act that offended some chaplains, who attempted to put an end to the practice by declaring that animals were not welcomed in the house of God. Aristocrats retaliated by refusing to enter the church, choosing instead to remain in the outer courtyard with their pets (if they showed up at all). Apparently fearful that this could be the start of a more serious rebellion, some clerics began conducting services on the outer steps of the churches, giving rise to the enduring custom of issuing a formal blessing over hunting dogs every year on the third of November during the Mass of St. Hubert (patron saint of hunters).

Next to noble people, no one enjoyed more of life's pleasures than noble dogs, who were sustained on slabs of venison or grain-fattened beef and wore collars made of gold-embroidered silk velvet or precious metals. Nothing was too good for their dogs, not even the lord's bed, much to the chagrin of one English steward who blamed the animals for a perpetual mess in the castle, its floors littered with "an ancient collection of beer, grease, bones, spittle, excrement of dogs and everything that is nasty." The very notion of indulging dogs in such a manner—in essence elevating them to the status of human aristocrats—was difficult for the working class to understand. To watch a lord spend the equivalent of a year's wages on a dog collar was in their eyes the height of decadence—and arrogance.

The role of women in Renaissance dog culture is not nearly so well documented as that of men, yet paintings and writings indicate that they, too, enjoyed canine companionship, albeit in the form of pint-sized dogs who lent themselves to the arduous task of being constantly kissed and cuddled. The smaller or more babylike in appearance, the more popular these animals were with women. The *Boke of St. Albans* (1486), attributed to Juliana Barnes (Berners), the prioress of Sopwell, indicates that she was one of the few to believe that small, dainty canines performed a task equal in merit to the talents of men's hounds, as "laydes poppees that bere awaye the flees." By contrast, Johannes Caius, who published the first book devoted exclusively to dogs in England, was critical of ladies who "bore [small dogs] in their bosoms, fed them at the table, nursed them in their laps and let them lick their lips as they rode in wagons." He admitted in a letter to a colleague, however, that such dogs might have some redeeming value as cynotherapists. Calling them "Rubbing Dogs" or "Comforters," he observed that "[they] will relieve indigestion if pressed against the stomach or moved up and down the breast of a sick person." In general, though, he thought that such dainty dogs had no function save "to satisfy the delicateness of dainty dames and wanton women's wits." Adorned with ribbons, jewels, and even lace doll's clothing, these "spaniel gentles" were "instruments of folly for them to play and dally withal."

Caius was just the first of a long line of male commentators who looked askance at the woman-dog relationship. Many such observations

Two women with a tiny lapdog, ca. 1800.
source: Author.

seem tinged with jealousy—physicians advised husbands to do away with their wives' little dogs, hinting that their affection for the animals was immoral, "unnatural," and compromised the desire to produce children (according to Caius, such pets distracted women from "more commendable exercises").

An avid horsewoman and huntress, Queen Christina of Sweden (1626–89) was quite fond of a dashing wolfhound named Caesar, who according to one observer "always sat with her at church. Having been lamed he was left alone one Sunday, but leaping from the window he hobbled to the cathedral and rent the air with cries for admission. They were heard by the Queen. Soon Caesar appeared. Christina's finger pointed to her feet. The dog reposed there like a stone effigy." And Catherine the Great (1729–96) sparked a clerical uproar by consecrating an entire cemetery to the memory of her beloved hound, Zemire, then opening its gates to both humans and animals.

Eighteenth-century satirist Sébastien Mercier sufficiently understood the depth of the bond between woman and canine to caution his male readers: "Step on the paw of a little dog, and you have lost the esteem of the woman; she may pretend otherwise, but she will never forgive you."

To keep such "useless" animals was viewed by some men as the height of excess, spawning an interesting but obscure body of folktales describing magic lapdogs, among them a fairy spaniel who fulfilled the wishes of whomever it served. By squeezing its tiny paw, one could cause gold, pearls, and precious gems to fall to the ground.

Canine Conquistadors

As in earlier times, stocky dogs were still employed as sentries or attack animals, with some actually receiving "wages" for their service in the form of dried meat or loaves of bread. Day and night they walked estate perimeters or sat atop castle parapets, sniffing the wind and listening for any disturbance beyond the walls. (The skulls of eighteen such guard dogs, dating between the fourteenth and sixteenth centuries, were discovered during modern excavations at the Tower of London.) As the Renaissance progressed, however, pitting such dogs in wagered battles to the death against bulls, bears, lions, and an occasional man became increasingly pop-

Fairy spaniel whose paw produces jewels, as featured in "The Little Dog," from
La Fontaine's *Tales and Novels*; 1884 Paris edition.
source: Author.

ular as a form of entertainment, much as the Molossus was featured in the infamous circus of Rome.

Such fun and games found a new, even more evil purpose in sixteenth-century Spain as a means of conquering the New World. Financially strained from fighting and finally defeating the Moors (at Granada in 1492), the Spanish monarchs embarked on a new crusade of sorts, to plunder the New World in search of gold. At the same time, by imposing a tyrannical feudal system on the natives and forcing them to abandon their wild, "sinful" ways, the path would be cleared for missionaries to convert the heathen to the true word of God, and to expand the Catholic empire. Armed for war, the conquistadors were accompanied by cavalry regiments and platoons of foot soldiers. Levriers and Alaunts were pressed into service with unprecedented zeal as instruments of subjugation, in what would later be labeled one of the most sadistic campaigns in human history.

The first "dogging" took place in 1494 when Christopher Columbus debarked for freshwater on the island of Jamaica, where he was met by a band of ceremonially painted Indians. Assuming they were hostile, he ordered his soldiers to release a volley of arrows and then a large dog, which fatally mauled a half-dozen natives within a matter of minutes. In 1495, in what is thought to have been the first pitched battle between Indians and Europeans, twenty hounds were unleashed on natives attempting to pull down a large outdoor crucifix erected at Vega Real in Hispaniola (Haiti). Friar Bartolomé de las Casas witnessed the scene and recorded that the dogs knocked Indians to the ground, then tore out their throats or intestines—he attributed their success to the fact that human skin was thinner and therefore much easier to tear than the hides of deer and boar, on which the canines had been trained. News of this victory convinced even the most skeptical of Spanish strategists that dogs were essential to New World conquest, so with the blessings of the throne, Archdeacon Fonseca ordered another, larger pack of hounds be shipped to Hispaniola to "protect" supplies and personnel.

The conquistadors demanded exorbitant gold tributes from subjugated natives throughout the Caribbean, and rather than face being thrown to the dogs for failure to pay, many committed suicide. Mothers killed their own children and then hung themselves. Some even attempted to bury themselves alive. Others fled into the forest but were mercilessly tracked down and dismembered by the dogs. Hoping to deter the Span-

A Puerto Rican Indian dogging illustrated in *Opmerkelyke zee-togten tot nader Ontdekking der West-Indize . . . in da jaaren 1508 en 1509* by Antonio de Herrera y Tordesillas (1706 Dutch translation of the Spanish).
source: Benson Latin American Collection, University of Texas at Austin.

A sick Indian mother, unable to escape the Spanish, hangs herself. A child, suspended from her waist, is thrown to the dogs. A chaplain (left) administers last rites, while three "grim reapers" are shown in the background leading dogs. From *Narratio regionum indicarum per hispanos quosdam devastatarum verissima* by Bartolomé de las Casas (1598 translation of the 1552 Spanish edition).
source: Benson Latin American Collection, University of Texas at Austin.

ish, many native communities ceased planting crops—the worst mistake they could have made, for once the conquistadors had depleted wildlife populations, the natives themselves were eyed as a source of food for the dogs. Parents watched in horror as Spanish dogs consumed their children, while soldiers stationed in Cuba herded small convoys of chained Indians, setting one free whenever food was needed for the hounds, the idea being that the chase would help hone their canines' killer instincts. Las Casas even described marketplaces where portions of human flesh could be purchased like so many hams or briskets. Legs, arms, and whole quarters of human beings hung on metal hooks, with some peddlers even offering roasted children as a delicacy for both dogs and Spaniards. Soldiers hag-

Open market in the Caribbean displaying sectioned Indian bodies for sale.
source: Benson Latin American Collection, University of Texas at Austin.

gled for flesh to feed the dogs, promising it would be replaced when they
had time to kill another native.

Converting to Christianity was no guarantee of safety. All Indians, regardless of faith, were expected to submit to the will of their new lords,
toiling every waking moment to satisfy the Spanish thirst for gold. Church
officials back home were inclined to either overlook reports of doggings or
else explain the practice as a necessary evil if the "savages" were ever to
see the error of their pagan ways. Canines worked with brutal efficiency,
dealing out divine retribution to those suspected of sodomy, homosexu-
ality, or bestiality, not to mention the greatest sin of all—heresy.

Some clerics stationed in the New World were genuinely appalled by
the doggings, but were afraid to challenge the military. A few, like Las
Casas, did muster the courage to write home about the atrocities, and as
a result several commanders were deported back to Spain, but only to be
replaced by other, equally corrupt or sadistic officers. More often than not,

Typical New World battle scene of Spanish dogs being loosed on native forces. Watching from the harbor are four missionaries. (The castle symbolizes Spain or the Catholic Church.) From *Twee opermerkylke [sic] scheeps-togten afgevaerdigd naar de West-Indien . . . jaar 1502,* by Antonio de Herrera y Tordesillas (1706 Dutch translation of the Spanish). source: Benson Latin American Collection, University of Texas at Austin.

chaplains stepped in only after the dogs had finished, ministering last rites over torn bits of bodies or touring the gallows to offer last-minute absolution to victims. Upon learning from a pious friar that heaven would be filled with "good" Spaniards, one rebel cacique (chief) who was about to be hung declined last rites, saying he would rather die as a pagan.

Perhaps the most infamous of the canine conquistadors was Becerrillo, the legendary terror of Borinquén (Puerto Rico). A strikingly ugly, battle-scarred dog with smoldering, bloodshot eyes surrounded by a black mask of fur, he sometimes was identified as a "Lebrel" (Greyhound). This term was carelessly applied to most any dog with a penchant for bloody chase, however, and most engravings of Becerrillo suggest that he was in actuality a Mastiff-Greyhound mix. Even his name, literally "Little Bull Calf," hints that he might have been a stout mongrel dog, as were so many Spanish hounds of this era.

Reputed to come from the kennels of Diego Columbus, the brother of Christopher, Becerrillo first endeared himself to his human colleagues in the village of Aguada by defending Diego de Salazar (who was nude and armed only with a saber) having been rousted from bed by rebel caciques conspiring to reclaim the island. Soon Becerrillo was enjoying a reputation among both Indians and Christians as an unusually cunning and ruthless animal, and the Spanish accurately credited him with playing as significant a role in the conquest of Borinquén as a full one third of the cavaliers stationed there. So highly valued was Becerrillo that he wore a finely crafted, spiked collar and was jealously guarded by soldiers, who feared that he might be murdered by the natives. Before going into battle, Becerrillo was wrapped in an *escaupil* (cotton-padded cloak similar to quilted woolen ones first fashioned for ancient Celtic war dogs), and was generously rewarded for his bloody work with one and a half times the pay of a crossbowman, plus a share of slaves, gold, food, or other spoils (entrusted to his human caretaker).

The soldiers believed Becerrillo was a true *perro sabio*—a learned dog capable of making fine distinctions between between friend and foe, Christian and pagan. One moment he could be quite affectionate, soliciting a friendly pat on the head, only to suddenly become a raging monster at the sight of a native. It was said that he could pursue a quarry into the midst of a large crowd, clamp his jaws around the culprit's wrist, and return him or her with hardly a scratch to the authorities. At the least hint of resistance, however, the fugitive was instantly killed.

During lulls in the fighting with natives, boredom tempted many Spanish officers to dog Indians simply for sport, much as a deer might be run down in the forests of Europe. One anecdote relates how a mischievous Captain Diego de Salazar handed an old Indian woman a piece of paper and ordered her to deliver it to the governor. As she shuffled down the street, Becerrillo was unleashed. Seeing the animal bearing down on her, the woman dropped to her knees and in her own language pleaded, "Oh, my Lord Dog, I am on my way to bear this message to Christians. I beseech thee, my Lord Dog, do me no harm." Much to the surprise of everyone, Becerrillo stopped in mid-stride, and after sniffing the trembling, prostrate form, lifted his leg, hosed the woman down with urine, then calmly walked away. The soldiers were stunned. Surely such behavior was a manifestation of heavenly intervention. Juan Ponce de León, Becerrillo's owner, ordered the woman freed, since in his opinion the charity of a dog should never outshine that of a Christian.

Becerrillo's reign of terror came to a sudden end near Caparra in 1514 when two Indians attempted to kidnap Sancho de Arango, a captain under Ponce de León. Becerrillo thwarted the ambush and chased the natives

Becerrillo and the old woman, from Herrera's *Opmerkelyke* (1706).
source: Benson Latin American Collection, University of Texas at Austin.

into the surf. Slowed by the water and without his protective cloak, he took several poisoned arrows in the ribs, but still managed to catch and kill one of his attackers before returning to shore. His wounds were drained and cauterized, thereby saving the dog from the feverish madness that usually ensued from such toxic projectiles, but he died soon afterward. A secret funeral service befitting a human was held for Becerrillo, then under the cover of night, the soldiers buried him in an unmarked forest grave. Officers reasoned that it was critical that the natives be kept from learning of his death, for to them, Becerrillo was invincible—perhaps even Satan himself—and the mere mention of his name was enough to strike fear into the hearts of even the most defiant pagan.

The "Familiars"

Back on the other side of the Atlantic, dogs who became too "cozy" with their masters were increasingly subject to persecution at the hands of religious zealots and angry peasants. Negative canine myths and superstitions first sparked by the devastation of the plague of A.D. 540 only worsened in the ensuing centuries as plague returned several times more, each time taking devout Christians with the same eagerness it took sinners. When prayer had failed to stem the tide of deaths, the Church pointed to an outside, malevolent force, and the populace was encouraged to seek out any and all suspected agents of Satan living within their midst—both human and animal. Tales of ghost-dogs—ethereal, malevolent creatures who preyed on unsuspecting mortals—were common, as was the belief that Satan and his minions walked the earth in the guise of dogs. As long ago all things pagan had been labeled demonic, dogs—after centuries of affiliation with pagan temples and deities—were ideal scapegoats during the era of witch-hunters.

Sworn to further Satan's infernal plan, witches and warlocks were said to enlist the assistance of "dog familiars"—demons in canine form who offered advice or performed malicious errands, and anyone suspected of harboring such an entity was tortured until they confessed. Afterward, these unfortunates were drowned, drawn and quartered (hung and disemboweled simultaneously), boiled or burned at the stake as church "investigators" read last rites and the mob cheered, confident that their community had been purged of evil.

Dog-familiars from the English pamphlet "The Discovery of
Witches" by Matthew Hopkins, London, 1647.
source: Copyright the British Museum.

Women and their dogs often were the focus of this hysterical persecution. Spinsters and widows who lived alone with only a dog for companionship were naturally inclined to treat their pets as surrogate children
or spouses, talking to them as they would another person. But too often
such innocuous conversations were misconstrued as proof that a neigh-
bor was dabbling in the black arts. After Elizabeth Clark, a seventeenth-
century English "witch," confessed under torture to having carnal relations
with Satan on a regular basis and to suckling a short-legged, spotted
demon-spaniel named Jarmara, she and her dog were executed. The same
fate befell Alison Device and her brother James, both arrested and killed
for keeping company with dog-familiars—James's dog, Dandy, was tried

and convicted of killing four people on his own. The names of other dogs have been preserved in such ecclesiastical records, including a little brown canine named Ball, and a Greyhound called Vinegar Tom. Condemned heretics usually were portrayed in engravings with exaggerated, demonic features, bearing little or no resemblance to actual animals or people.

Nor was aristocratic birth any guarantee that one's relationship with a dog would be above suspicion. One of the more notorious dog-familiars of this era was a large white poodle named Boye, belonging to the German-born Prince Rupert, who obtained the animal from Lord Arundel while he was imprisoned in Austria. After his release the dog accompanied him to England to assist his uncle King Charles I (1600–49) in conflicts with the Puritans. During a meeting with the King and his military strategists, Rupert repeatedly turned to kiss Boye, who was seated at his side in a chair of his own, and Charles himself became so entranced by Boye's charm and good manners that he encouraged the animal on subsequent visits to sit in the royal chair. In time Boye became a regular visitor to the palace, and when not rolling on the floor with the royal children, enjoyed the privilege of receiving tidbits from the King's own dinner plate. Charles even insisted that the dog accompany him to church services. Ultimately, Boye's seemingly extraordinary ability to interact with people would spark an enduring image of the Poodle as a "learned dog."

But the spectacle of a sparkling white dog, ears flapping in the wind as he galloped before the Royalist army, was hard for the Puritans to overlook, and noting how Rupert always emerged from battle with nary a scratch, they concluded that Boye was a familiar. A "Popish profane Dog, more than halfe a divell. . . . whelped in Lap-land where . . . none but divells and sorcerers live," was how the unknown author of one Puritan pamphlet described Boye, calling for his death "by poyson and extempore prayer." It also was rumored that Boye could make himself invisible and change the course of bullets in mid-air, thereby making "Mr. Prince Rupert shott-free." Boye followed his master into the hottest part of the battle at Marston Moor in 1644, where he finally was killed. Perhaps because they were demoralized by the death of their mascot, the luck of the Royalists took a turn for the worse, while the Puritans celebrated Boye's death in "A Dog's Elegy" (alternatively titled "Rupert's Tears"), which included a mocking invitation:

Feudal Society, Renaissance, and Revolution

The death of Boye, portrayed as a black, monstrous creature. Prince Rupert also is shown, with the ears of a demon. From "A Dog's Elegy," drawn after a Puritan pamphlet printed in London in 1644.
source: Drawn by author.

> Sad cavaliers Rupert invites you all
> That doe survive, to his Dog's Funerall,
> Close mourners are the witch, Pope and Devill,
> That much lament your late befallen evill.

Let Them Eat Dog Biscuits

Like their father, the sons of Charles I also had a soft spot for dogs, but as adults preferred the smaller breeds typically associated with women. Caught in a violent storm at sea, James II (1633–1701), an ardent admirer of Italian Greyhounds, exclaimed "Save my dogs!" when he heard that the ship might go down. His elder brother, Charles II (1630–85), preferred to shower his affections on a troupe of small spaniels (popularly thought of today as the Cavalier King Charles Spaniel). Obviously disgusted by the sight of the commander in chief down on his hands and knees, Secretary of the Admiralty Samuel Pepys noted "the silliness of the King playing with his dog, all the while not minding his business," adding that the monarch even "suffered the bitches to [birth and] nurse their puppies" in the royal bedchamber, which "rendered it very offensive and made the whole court nasty and stinking."

The beloved Great Dane of the Prince of Condé (1621–86) always attended military strategy meetings with the advisers of King Louis XVI. "Well gentlemen, having heard all you have to say, we will take the advice of a veteran," Condé would say before turning to ask his dog which plan he favored. The somber canine then typically descended from its chair and offered a paw to one of the advisers. In one instance, though, he simply walked out of the room. Taking this to mean than none of the advice was sound, Condé remarked, "I agree with the dog."

Surely Frederick the Great (1712–86) was one of the more sentimental male dog lovers of the preindustrial era, keeping as many as thirteen Italian Greyhounds at one time and lavishing them with every luxury imaginable. The King of Prussia christened members of his diminutive pack as Diana, Pax, Pan, Madame de Pompadour (after the mistress of King Louis XV), and Amoretto. Biche was his favorite, and he frequently signed the dog's name on letters penned to his sister Wilhelmine. She responded in kind under the moniker of her pug, "Folichon." Apparently the dogs accompanied Frederick on military campaigns, for Biche was captured by the Austrians at Soör in 1745. The dog eventually was sent back to the palace, where it ran down the hall and burst into his master's private chambers, leaping on a table and kissing an overjoyed Frederick. The death of Biche in the palace concert hall in 1752 was said to have emotionally devastated the King.

Thirty-four years later as he lay dying of a respiratory illness, Frederick awoke in the night to see one of his Italian Greyhounds shivering from the cold, and mustered sufficient strength to call a valet to cover the dog with a blanket, after which he relapsed into a fit of coughing. Before he died he left orders that he be buried in the palace lawn in a special mausoleum situated to overlook the graves of eleven of his dogs, each one marked by a simple sandstone marker bearing the animal's name (one unknown dog, perhaps the last one he owned, was laid to rest inside the royal crypt). Instead, Frederick was entombed beside his father in Potsdam's Garrison church, where he lay until 1945, when the threat of the advancing

Bronze of Frederick II and two
of his Italian Greyhounds.
source: Stiftung PreuBische Schlösser
und Gärten Berlin-Brandenburg.

Mausoleum of Frederick II with
dog graves in foreground.
source: Stiftung PreuBische Schlösser
und Gärten Berlin-Brandenburg.

Russian army forced his exhumation and concealment in a salt mine near Bernterode. Transferred to St. Elizabeth's Church in Marburg, and in 1952, to Hohenzollern castle near Stuttgart, the royal remains were finally returned to the palace called Sanssouci ("No Tears") in 1991, 205 years after his death, and laid to rest with his canine family.

Many a king and queen went to the chopping block with only their dogs for comfort. Before a crowd of three hundred spectators, just moments after Mary, Queen of Scots, was decapitated in 1587, one witness reported that the executioner "espied her little dog which had crept under her clothes [and] which could not be gotten forth but by force." Legend has it the dog pined for its mistress, refused to eat and eventually died. Even Charles I, fast friend of Boye and victim of the Puritan rebellion, was said to go to the guillotine in 1649 with only a miniature hound for company. And Alexandre Dumas wrote in *Chevalier of the Red House* that Jet, Marie Antoinette's dog, ruined the loyalists' plot to free her by tunneling into the compound where she was imprisoned by the Revolutionary Tribunal. It might have worked, but the dog's acute hearing detected the digging. His barking alerted the guards, who discovered the incomplete tunnel, and afterward, "Jet was taken from his mistress [and] she shed bitter tears at the separation."

In the eyes of an oppressed peasantry, "useless" animals who were treated with greater respect than most people were the pinnacle of selfish extravagance. Ministers to the French crown agreed and in 1770 levied a heavy dog tax—not against the aristocracy—but against the lower class, arguing that like their peasant owners, peasant dogs were dirty, ill-mannered, harbored disease, and siphoned off the nation's precious bread supply. Taxes on common dogs only added to the simmering resentment against the aristocracy, and to no less an extent, the dogs of the elite. In the days following the overthrow of the French monarchy, life for aristocratic dogs was perilous at best, and many a beribboned or bejeweled dog of "blue blood" was stripped of its decadent accessories, then stomped, stoned, beaten, or bayoneted after their owners were beheaded. Lap dogs paid a heavy price for their intimate alliances with women, for at the Place de Grève, toy spaniels, terriers, and hounds were rounded up and burned alive en masse "for a crime that morality prevents us from naming," wrote an observer. In 1918, the tradition of executing luxury dogs was briefly re-

Russian empress Alexandra with a
Japanese Spaniel in 1899, two decades
before the Romanovs, including
Jimmy the family dog, would be
executed.
source: Author.

vived—Jimmy, the spaniel of Alexandra, the last Empress of Russia, was
dispatched with a blow to the head from a rifle butt after the Romanov
family was gunned down.

Surely it was one of the great paradoxes of the Christian era that compassion for animals was not only viewed as a luxury, but as a sin. Catholic,
Puritan, and Protestant clerics alike reiterated that humanity was god's
"aristocracy," appointed to oversee creation and the animal serfdom it contained. People who "lowered" themselves to the level of the beasts, or elevated animals to the station of people by loving or acknowledging them
as conscious beings were going against the will of God in a most dangerous way. The eighteenth-century Anglican Reverend James Granger was
disgusted by the sight of grown men and women expressing affection for
animals, and considered "mentions of dogs and horses from the pulpit a
prostitution of the dignity" of the clergy. Yet despite the disapproval of society, the first concern of many aristocrats was for the safety of their dogs.
If it was impossible to take the animals with them as they fled the persecution, lords and ladies arranged to leave their pets behind in the care of

rational, kindly commoners, their ears cropped and tails or toes docked to disguise them as curs. Alaunts probably contributed to the creation of hardier varieties of cart dogs, while the Levriers certainly added to foundation stock for middle-class sporting dogs, the best known being the Whippet, also called the "poor man's racehorse."

The fall of Louis XVI and the declaration of the new French Republic in 1789 spelled an end to the hunt as an exclusive privilege of an aristocratic few in France, and served as a warning bell for other feudal nations—that social reforms were well past due. For the first time in a thousand years, the right to hunt was once again returned to the masses, who were quick to obtain or breed hounds of their own. Scorn for the trappings of affluence was quickly replaced with admiration and covetousness, and in the coming century, the working class would once again find itself pounding on the gates of elite society, this time demanding equal consideration in the world of dogs.

This overfed hound was the favorite pet of Augustus the Strong (ca. 1700). Carved from a solid piece of ivory standing approximately four inches in height, the animal is seated on an elaborate cushion carved in low relief, and wears a jewel-encrusted collar.
source: With the kind permission of the Trustees of the Leeds Castle Foundation.

Five

Class Aspirations

The world has been advancing in science, in living conditions, in
wealth—advancing in everything. Smart breeders . . . are breeding dogs to fit the times. They are keeping up with the styles.

—Oscar H. Schultheis,
Dogs and Their Care (1930)

S WEEPING SOCIAL and economic reforms in the last years of the
eighteenth century began to take hold in industrialized Europe and
America, dramatically altering the lives of both people and dogs. Lured by
tales of high-paying factory jobs and inexpensive housing, emancipated
peasants relocated in bustling cities like Paris and London, or left Europe
altogether for a new life in New York, ultimately giving rise to a large
urban middle class with sufficient financial and political clout to petition
for sweeping social and economic reforms, including labor unions, child
labor laws, and public education, spelling doom for rigid feudal socioeconomic systems. Manufacturers produced a wealth of new consumer goods
for a populace with disposable income beyond that required for food and
shelter. As the standard of living rose, people grew more confident about
the ability to improve the quality of their own lives, as well as that of society as a whole.

For centuries the natural world had been humankind's greatest an-
tagonist, a merciless force bringing plague, drought, and other calamities
on God-fearing people and laying waste to entire nations. But as scientific
discoveries and technological innovations promised to eliminate the haz-

ards of everyday life, that began to change. Ambitious explorers—the Victorian equivalent of astronauts—charted the far corners of the globe, collecting all kinds of biological "curiosities," which were unveiled at zoos and museums amid great flurries of publicity. The works of naturalist Charles Darwin were widely read and discussed—with weeklies like the *Illustrated London News* posting public lectures on fossils, evolution, and newly discovered animals.

Despite scientific revelations about evolution and natural selection, a hierarchy in which humans were the divinely appointed "lords" of creation persisted, as laid out by the Church in earlier centuries. Naturally, animals who could be subjugated to meet the needs of society received preferential treatment. As explained by one cleric, "good" animals could be easily defined as "those whose services are most required, as if conscious that they were ordained to be subject to man's dominion, yield to it without reluctance."

Inexpensive books and magazines on natural history and zoology, particularly those featuring dogs, were favorite items with this newly empowered, literate populace, as evidenced by Thomas Bewick's illustrated work, *A General History of Quadrupeds*, which sold out immediately and was reissued in eight subsequent editions. The popularity of Bewick's book did not go unnoticed by other enterprising naturalists, who quickly produced a plethora of easy-to-read, illustrated zoological treatises. Publishers and booksellers specializing exclusively in works on animals, many for children, flourished in big cities, as did portable public libraries.

"The mind of the dog is undeniably as perfect as an animal's mind can be," remarked Alfred Brehm, the popular nineteenth-century American naturalist and children's author. "Of no other brute creature can it so appropriately be said that the only human quality he lacks is that of speech." But Victorian dog enthusiasts argued that the "ennoblement" of *Canis* was far from finished. To establish true and lasting perfection, further cullings of the dog populace were critical to enhancing the best attributes of the species. It was the most fitting of rewards for a "dumb" (i.e., mute) creature whose unwavering devotion had lent so much to civilization. In the hands of educated Victorians, ancient concepts of hierarchy and social order found new life in the modern republic, as a means of elevating the canine race to unprecedented heights of physical and moral perfection—

Cover illustration for Alfred Brehm's *Life of Animals*, a subscription naturalist magazine for children, in 1895.
source: Author.

and in the process honoring the divine perfection of humanity, the dogs' creator and overlord. Just as handcrafted goods were supplanted by mass-produced, machine-made articles, hailed for their uniformity of size and quality, so too were dogs now targeted for standardization. The "fancy"—the selective breeding and keeping of dogs—began to take shape as a popular form of recreation, not just for the aristocracy, but for the middle class as it aspired to ever greater social prominence, gentility, and prosperity.

In the 1908 catalog for the British Museum's sensational exhibit of the world's domesticated animals, featuring masterfully taxidermied horses, cattle, sheep, goats, rabbits, rats, mice, ferrets, Guinea pigs, pigeons, ducks, chickens, and even a few house cats, zoologist Ernst Haeckel observed that "wild animals, one year after another, appear approximately in the same form," while domesticated animals display great changes, because "the perfection attained by breeders in the art of selection enables them to produce entirely new forms in a short time."

Outshining them all and drawing the biggest crowds were the dogs, their personalities suggested with artful subtlety through a cocked ear, a panting grin, a pose on a parlor pillow, or a time-worn collar still buckled around the neck. In life they were celebrities, hailed by the press as

British Museum of Natural History's domesticated-animal exhibit as it appeared in 1900.
Dogs are displayed in center case.
source: The British Museum of Natural History.

canine aristocrats. In death, they celebrated civilization's growing sense of mastery over nature. To the adoring public, dog breeders were artists who wielded mastery in the medium of living flesh just as others did in clay or oils, and the hallowed natural history hall had become their gallery. Despite the social and political upheavals of the late eighteenth century, certain varieties of canines, notably those who assisted in sport hunting, persisted as cultural fixtures in nineteenth-century aristocratic life, thereby perpetuating the image of dog breeding as a leisurely pursuit for the privileged.

Human Reforms, Canine Reforms

Applying taxonomic classifications first laid out by Renaissance enthusiasts such as Gaston Phoébus and Johannes Caius, dogs continued to be categorized more according to function than physical type in the first decades of the nineteenth century. "Beast Dog," "Coach Dog," and "Ver-

Middle-class Victorian sportsmen, ca. 1860.
source: Author.

min Dog" were a few of the simple terms applied to a wide variety of dogs—even the Mastiff, a name today associated with a specific breed, defined any number of big dogs, making the task of tracing specific breed origins difficult if not impossible. Now that gave way to the notion that controlled breeding was central to the entire process of creating a new canine empire composed of superior individuals. The quest to eliminate cosmetic physical differences in dogs of the same variety was all-consuming, inspiring a new definition of the very term "breed," now applied to animals of like appearance rather than function. In theory, the more closely related the sire and dam were, the more uniform in appearance their offspring would be. The application of such principles, as guided by written (and frequently revised) checklists of physical features embodying an imagined ideal for each canine variety, was the first step in the realization of a new, "civilized" canine society.

Fanciers welcomed the imposition of human social concepts on the canine race as an improvement on nature; the further removed from their wild origins dogs became, the better off they would be. Not only would

Dog breeds featured in the 1806 edition of Thomas Bewick's *A General History of Quadrupeds.*
source: Author.

their health and beauty improve, but their morals and intellect as well—just as a heathen savage, once bathed, clothed, educated, and Christianized, made for an "improved" human. With few exceptions, the less a dog resembled its wild, wolfish progenitor the more ennobled it was believed to be.

"No one would plant weeds in a flower garden, [so] why have mongrels as pets?" queried George Taylor, author of *Man's Friend the Dog* (1891). In his expert opinion, mixed breeds were "mischief loving," and had "dirty tendencies." Victorian dog expert Gordon Stables echoed the same sentiment. "Nobody who is now anybody can afford to be followed about by a mongrel dog," he wrote, reflecting middle-class dreams of the good life. The Rolls-Royces of the companion animal world, papered pure breeds were an integral part of the fantasy. Every workingman daydreamed of becoming a well-heeled squire, whiling away his days riding "blooded" horses over miles of rolling estate in the company of refined colleagues and hounds after "royal" game like deer or boar. For women, elegant or dandified animals, such as those associated with courtiers of the Renaissance, complemented visions of the perfect home, family, and personal fashion. By 1860 consumer demand for companion animals had become so great that street vendors could turn a steady profit offering dogs, cats,

Field Sports and Manly Pastimes periodical ca. 1837.
source: Author.

monkeys, and birds to the exclusion of all other wares, and grocers ped-
dled a growing array of grooming accessories, health tonics, shampoos,
and prepackaged edibles for pets.

Status by Association

Predictably, canines already in possession of lengthy, closed lineages
patterned after the human aristocracy were the perfect candidates for establishing the new hierarchy, and for marketing dog ownership as a glam-
orous, exclusive hobby, for despite the emergence of a more democratic
form of government in Britain, the monarchy still figured heavily in the
underlying psychology of English society. Upheld as a fair but iron-willed
matriarch, Queen Victoria was regarded with affection by much of the
working populace, who followed royal activities through the newspapers.
Nothing about the Queen was too trivial to report—when and what she
ate, what she wore, and not surprisingly, what kind of company she kept,
both human and animal. Her penchant for dogs was well known, as was

Queen Victoria and one of her dogs.
source: Author.

the fact that the royal kennel was a veritable zoo, housing everything from Fox and Staghounds to tiny Pomeranians. A writer for *Lloyd's Weekly* remarked that the Queen had a particular fondness for Collies, especially one named "Sharp, [who has] all his meals with his mistress, being seldom away from her"—though the dog was notorious for biting servants and visitors.

Monarchs, like dogs, were selectively "bred" through carefully arranged marriages, and were viewed as the harbingers of a superior moral code. Accordingly, people in both high and low places strove to pattern their own conduct after that of the royal family. Victorian consumers emulated the aristocracy by acquiring the material trappings of affluence and, indirectly, gentility and exclusivity. As a result, Queen Victoria's affinity for dogs blended with middle-class fantasies of status, and fueled the market for pedigreed animals.

Not everyone celebrated the public's growing interest in well-bred dogs. Clinging to traditional class separations in the deepening sea of public empowerment, many "pedigreed" people considered it the height of impertinence that the peasantry would insinuate themselves in the hallowed world of blue-blooded dogs. As important as the ownership of the "right dog" had become to the social mobility–minded working class, aristocrats rationalized that it was even more critical for the breeding of these animals to remain in the hands of nobility, lest impeccable canine lineages be soiled by profiteers.

Elite kennels maintained private registries, barring all dogs save those sired in equally illustrious kennels. "A breeder does not seek to make great profits," sniffed Charles Burkett in *Our Domesticated Animals* (1907), implying that fanciers who depended on stud fees or puppy sales to cover the costs of maintaining a kennel would never produce quality animals. "If a high-bred dog is desired, one on whom the eye can rest with pleasure, then the purchaser must apply to some well-known kennels." James Brierly of Mossley Hall was typical of many lordly fanciers. Fearing contamination of his dogs' family tree, he was careful to confirm that the Earl of Berby's Bloodhound bitch was truly of "pure" blood, the product of "principles of keeping the breed to themselves," before he proposed mating her with one of his animals of similar, exclusive descent. Pug breeders also defended their decision to maintain a closed, private studbook, and even refused to participate in the first dog shows to feature classes for nonsporting breeds. To pit such animals against those of the middle class not only demeaned and devalued the breed, but diminished the social standing of the elite breeders as well.

The Breeder's Art

Despite such snubs, middle-class breeders remained enthralled by the prospect of rubbing shoulders with society's finest. Aristocrats were warmly received no matter how rudely they behaved, since their presence at shows guaranteed media coverage, which in turn fueled consumer demand for pedigreed dogs. Limited supply and unlimited demand, compounded by rumors of family lineages as lengthy as any king's, meant that upper-class animals' social and monetary value skyrocketed. It is little wonder, then, that "pure" bred dogs were so eagerly embraced by the middle class as a means of elevating their own status, if only by indirect association. Stud fees and puppy sales boomed as thousands clamored to purchase Collies, Spaniels, Retrievers, Poodles, and Pomeranians, despite Brehm's admonishment that "only well-disposed human beings can bring up dogs properly." Likewise, Burkett conceded that these noble dogs "may very well be the product of inbreeding," but that "the lines of the body are beautiful, the expression intelligent. A dog which has no blood cannot be noble. We baptize him with the name of 'street cur.'" Taking such advice to heart, the mistress of one Blenheim Spaniel in the 1860s not only took pains to avoid interacting with "common" people, but strove to prevent her pet from coming in contact with "vulgar dogs."

Middle-class enthusiasts would eventually overwhelm and supplant aristocrats in positions of power within the fancy. But in an effort to perpetuate an aura of glamour, systematized methods for documenting ancestry (patterned after human class distinctions grounded in lineage) became even more important. As class lines continued to blur, ever stricter guidelines for canine registration were imposed in an effort to exclude not only certain animals, but certain people as well, notably foreigners and the lower class. The dream of a canine hierarchy became increasingly complex and convoluted, with dogs being repeatedly recategorized or split into more specialized groups as the number of pet owners swelled. Increasingly, the dogs were defined by physical appearance alone. To the casual observer, the breed standards appeared stable and firmly grounded in deference to the animals' noble heritage; but in truth they were more the product of imagination than scientific principle, setting a precedent for the arbitrary alteration of dogs, even those who previously had remained largely unchanged for centuries.

Dog shows were routinely conducted prior to 1850, but these were informal competitions, concerned mostly with hunting dogs. Sponsored by local tavern owners who saw such "doggie proclivities" as a boon to business, the events often lasted well into the night, with participants serving simultaneously as exhibitors, spectators, and judges. "Of course there is much drinking over the event," remarked American fancier George Taylor in 1872. Rational discussions gave way to shouts and raucous laughter as ale consumption increased and efforts to reach a consensus on the best dog became more difficult. Victorian Collie breeder Hugh Dalziel recalled that founding members of the institutionalized fancy found the casual tone of these competitions contradictory to their own, more dignified ideas of a canine exhibition, and admitted that "it is felt to be inconvenient . . . to trace the pedigree too curiously, lest the low origin be found inconsistent with existing pride."

The idea of putting the growing array of registered animals on display in more structured public competitions was first proposed in an 1857 editorial in the British periodical *Stream*, and in the summer of 1859, the first formal British dog show was held at Newcastle-on-Tyne, featuring sixty hounds divided into two broad classes for Pointers and Setters. Newspapers hailed it a success, so a second show was quickly scheduled in Redcar. It, too, was so popular with the press and public that it was repeated the following year in Birmingham.

In theory, rewarding dogs who conformed to a tighter set of physical parameters would steer breeders in a more sensible, scientific direction and hasten the dogs' evolution into an "improved" form. Human nature being what it is, though, judges couldn't help rewarding dogs who appealed to their personal preferences for a certain coat color or texture, slightly larger and smaller builds, the point of a nose, or the curve of a tail. When such dogs garnered top honors, fanciers revised or scrapped their written standards, and purged their kennels of "old-fashioned" animals. The gene pools for each breed were sharply curtailed, as fanciers mated canine grandfathers and granddaughters, or even sons and mothers, in an attempt to "fix" the same cosmetic feature in their own stock.

Show arenas glittered, but backstage kennels often were cramped and filthy. Provided the dogs survived arduous journeys in feces-filled crates aboard drafty railroad boxcars, they were at peril from poor ventilation and sanitation in the convention hall. Dogfights of unbelievable ferocity resulted in injuries to both canine and human competitors, a serious hazard in an era with no rabies vaccine. Newspapers made light of these incidents, with one reporter for the *Illustrated London News* (1860) casually

Front page of the *Illustrated London News* featuring dogs at the Birmingham Show in 1860.
source: Author.

remarking that although the dogs "had occasionally a battle royal among themselves, we heard only a rumor of one man having been bitten."

The sheer number of spectators taxed exhibit halls to the limit. Audiences often disrupted proceedings by booing exhibitors or shouting insults at the judges. Backstage spectators were equally troublesome, crowding in until there was barely space between cages to accommodate "one crinoline," and unwittingly spreading canine diseases as they petted one animal after another. Like a wildfire, distemper swept through the show circuit or was taken back home to the kennels, cutting down whole litters of promising young puppies or abruptly ending the careers of proven champions—some of whom wound up in the British Museum of Natural History.

Favoritism was rife. In one instance in 1863, dogs were led into the ring with the names of their owners prominently attached to the collars, rather than anonymous numbers. In an effort to save time, overworked judges sometimes arbitrarily combined classes, judging Retrievers against Setters. Playing on popular prejudices against immigrants, dogs from other countries were lumped together in a "Foreign Dog" class without discrimination as to breed. On several occasions, author and show judge Charles

Backstage at a turn-of-the-century French dog show. Open holding pens facilitated public access to the dogs, as well as theft and vandalism.
source: Author.

Henry Lane was pressured by show committees to insure that Queen Victoria's dogs received first prize. He refused, explaining that he felt certain that his judgment would "have been approved by Her Majesty if the circumstances be known at the Palace."

The fancy outwardly touted itself as the very model of gentility, while in actuality exhibitors could be quite deceptive. Much of the judges' time was consumed in the search for "fakers"—dogs with flaws deliberately disguised by plucking, dying, clipping, or even surgery. Handlers obstructed one another in the ring or attempted to distract judges with derisive gos-

Cartoon parody of a dog show from Lytton's *Toy Dogs*, 1911.
source: Author.

sip about fellow exhibitors. Breeders of toy dogs kept their prize animals padlocked in cages throughout the entire event for fear they might be vandalized, poisoned, or stolen (if not by a fellow breeder, then a sticky-fingered spectator). Ink was splashed on unattended dogs or huge clumps of their hair were cut out. (Twentieth-century Pekingese breeder and author Rumer S. Godden would later recall in her 1977 book *Butterfly Lions* how at least one prizewinning dog was slipped a piece of candy laced with poison. At another show she barely managed to foil an assassination attempt on her own animal by a mysterious man with a hypodermic syringe.)

Even the most highly respected breeder was not above padding his or her wallet by selling or standing at stud animals of dubious parentage, as evidenced in the late 1800s by a wave of complaints of black, curly-coated Retriever puppies with docked tails being passed off as Standard Poodles. By 1870, poor sportsmanship and corruption threatened to end the fancy. The looming public relations disaster helped inspire the establishment of the British Kennel Club in 1873 (and the American Kennel Club in 1884), to function not only as a registry but also as a union of sorts, lobbying on behalf of the breeding industry, and orchestrating a monopolistic series of interlocking shows through which members had to work their way toward champion standing. The new registration and membership guidelines were not enthusiastically embraced by everyone. Unscrupulous breeders and sellers aside, legitimate exhibitors from all classes complained that the fancy had strayed from its true mission to create healthier, and thereby superior, animals. The best interests of the dogs had been compromised by obsessions with trophies and acclaim, not to mention the spectacle of profits to be made from fleeting consumer fads for certain breeds.

At first these grumblings were confined to small circles of aristocratic fanciers, including the outspoken Baroness Judith Neville Lytton, who was one of the few to openly criticize the notion that pedigree implied a superior creature. An English Toy Spaniel enthusiast, she decried the inflated monetary value assigned to pure breeds and argued that it encouraged the propagation of inferior animals with exaggerated or unhealthy features. In her 1911 treatise, *Toy Dogs,* Lytton accused the British fancy of doing more harm than good, citing the new snub noses, stocky builds, coat colors, and inherited "idiocy" in Spaniels. Lytton believed these so-called refinements were in fact flaws, cultivated to appeal to jaded judges and buyers.

Punch cartoon, "Dog Fashions for 1889."
source: Author.

Male exhibitors and their hounds at a dog show around the turn of the century.
source: Author.

Class Aspirations

Reminiscing about dog days at the tavern, aging sportsmen grumbled about the stuffiness of the new shows and the growing participation of women, and like Lytton, worried that the working instincts of hunting dogs were being undermined by the fancy's preoccupation with looks. Noting the breeding of hounds for softer coats and daintier features as early as 1860, the *Illustrated London News* remarked that "the stamp of the old English setter which we remember twenty or thirty years ago seems to have very much departed, [and] many of the Clumbers [are] out of condition." Such dogs were forgeries, Lytton asserted, their pedigrees and registration papers worthless, the Kennel Clubs' claims of bettering the canine race a lie.

In an attempt to deflect the choir of critics, apologists for the fancy pointed their fingers at a vaguely defined, anonymous group of "irresponsible dealers, [who] show for the purpose of winning the money prizes," according to Burkett.

East Meets West

In its ignorance and arrogance, the fancy very nearly fumbled the greatest canine discovery of the nineteenth century—the Pekingese, one of the oldest and most dramatically altered breeds in the world.

Stout little canines with compressed noses, called "Happa" or "Hahbah" dogs, were coveted as early as 1000 B.C. by the Chinese Imperial court, which demanded the dogs as tribute from the southern provinces. By 500 B.C. they were sufficiently popular for Confucius to advise frugal readers that "the torn chariot umbrella," a very small swatch of cloth, was sufficient "to cover the dear house dog in his grave." Around the same time another eyewitness recorded that after a day's hunting, large hounds ran alongside the chariots, but small, pampered canines with distinctive "short mouths" were allowed to ride inside the cart with their aristocratic masters. Other accounts described the same square-mouthed animals as "under-the-table" dogs, standing no more than eight inches at the shoulder.

The long-haired Maltese, a dog already miniaturized in the Roman era, also is credited as having assisted in the creation of the Pekingese. Such canines could have found their way to China in ancient times via the many overland trade routes, perhaps as part of a larger cargo of fine textiles and perfumed oils. All that is known for certain is that two dogs (a male and female) matching the description of "Melitaei," (Roman Malteses) were formally presented to the Emperor Kou Tzü around A.D. 620 as a gift from the Holy Roman Emperor in Byzantium.

Quite a few Chinese emperors enjoyed lavishing small dogs with every indulgence. The Emperor Ling Ti, who ruled from A.D. 168 to 190, was so smitten with one Imperial pooch that he presented the animal with an official literary hat—an ancient version of the Nobel prize—which stood over eight inches high and was ten inches from brim to brim, effectively concealing the whole dog. Likewise, the other palace dogs were officially promoted to the court position of viceroys, with the bitches assuming the rank of their wives (suggesting that royal dog breeding already had begun). "This had the effect of likening high officials to dogs and was bad practice," complained one observer at the time.

It cannot be said with certainty that these early dogs were Pekingeses in the modern sense of the word, but descriptions seem remarkably uniform from the second century to the nineteenth century, with numerous accounts describing diminutive royal dogs, some with long fur, but all with "square mouths." By A.D. 700—as Europe struggled to recover from its first encounter with the plague—the Imperial court had isolated the palace dogs from canines in the outside world, and set about breeding for evermore aesthetically pleasing pets.

"They all have long histories," the Empress Dowager Tzu-tsi reportedly once told her lady-in-waiting. And it was under her direction in the latter half of the nineteenth century—while England's institutionalized fancy was still in its infancy—that canine neoteny was elevated to a high art. An elite complement of eunuchs entrusted to care for the Pekingese received specific orders from Her Imperial Highness on which dogs should be mated, but were equally inclined to experiment on their own in hopes of producing unusual colors or features, thereby winning the royal favor. Where breeding failed, more drastic measures succeeded. Puppies were confined to small wire cages to stunt their growth. The tail tips of newborns were bitten off to create a more "lion-like" look as the fur grew long, and there were numerous cosmetic techniques for cultivating a more flattened facial profile—tender young noses were crushed with the whack of a stick, or puppies were fed on flat plates and encouraged to bite tightly stretched pigskin.

Consisting of stacked bamboo cages in a high-walled courtyard, the Imperial kennel was subject to periodic reviews by the Empress. An otherwise-unidentified Princess Der-ling witnessed several of these inspections and reported that:

> If Her Majesty wished to examine one of the dogs closer she would indicate which one and the eunuch would hold the animal up for her inspection. Then she would say, "Its hind legs are not of the right length," or "Its body is too long." Whenever she commented thus on any dog, especially the puppies, it was a decree of exile—for it meant the dog had to be taken away.

What became of the rejects is a subject of speculation. Certainly many were immediately dispatched by a blow to the head, but in some instances, eunuchs secreted the dogs away rather than put them to death, and they occasionally turned up on the black market. Commoners caught possessing such dogs were subject to execution. Even the servants and deliverymen who linked the Forbidden City to the outside world were commanded to avert their eyes should they encounter a Pekingese on the palace grounds.

The Pekingese was one of the best kept secrets of the world until 1860, when French and British troops embroiled in the second Opium War stormed the Summer Palace in the Forbidden City shortly after the royal family fled the compound. The Empress left behind an assortment of treasures, including a number of Pekingeses. Some of the dogs wound up in the hands of street merchants, and may have been marketed as culinary delicacies. Others were carried away by the soldiers. The Empress returned in 1861 to reestablish civil order, but she was never able to fully regain her canine monopoly, and an untold number of Pekes now circulated in the outside world, hopelessly lost and beyond the influence of the Imperial court. Despite decrees banning their sale to commoners and "barbarians" (outsiders), the Pekingese made its debut in the Western world a year after the war officially ended. Many lived out their lives in quiet obscurity as regimental pets or ship mascots, their names and personal stories forever lost.

The few dogs who were identified were those who wound up in the possession of Britain's high society. The first known Peke, christened Lootie, was presented to Queen Victoria in 1861 by Captain Hart Dunne, who had bought the dog from a profiteering eunuch in Peking. "It should be treated as a pet, not a curiosity," he wrote in a letter of introduction for the animal, but a curiosity is exactly what Lootie became. Rather than hailing her as canine royalty or an innocent victim of a horrible war, the *Ladies' Home Journal* and the *Illustrated News* depicted Lootie as some sort of zoological freak—just one of many oddities to come from the heathen East. Victoria apparently expressed only passing interest in Lootie, perhaps because she was constantly deluged with gift-dogs from subjects seeking notoriety. Lootie was soon relocated from Buckingam Palace to the kennel at Windsor Castle, where an unsympathetic kennel master expected the dog to hold its own against a rabble of hounds, many of them quite large by comparison. "Her Majesty already has a dog which remains in Her room," the palace spokesman informed a disappointed Dunne, who remarked, "I only hoped it would be made more or less a pet of the Royal Family. . . . If it is not made much of it will die." Someone, perhaps a softhearted assistant dog handler, must have "made much of" the little dog, because she wound up living another eleven years. No photos of Lootie are known to exist, but a likeness was painted by a student of the famous animal artist Sir Edwin Landseer.

Schlorff, a red-brindle female Pekingese, was already several years old when she to came live with Admiral Lord John Hay, and thrived eighteen more years. Hay obtained a second female, named Hytien, which he gave to his sister, the Duchess of Wellington. Around the same time, two other females were obtained by the Duchess of Richmond and Gordon. And Mrs. Loftus Allen, the wife of a wealthy merchant captain, personally traveled to China in search of Pekes, but came away empty-handed. Her husband had better luck, ultimately locating four dogs. Captain Allen stumbled on the first in a Shanghai taxidermy shop, sitting in a cage, and felt compelled to purchase it on the spot, for no other reason than he feared it was about to be killed and mounted. Three other dogs were subsequently acquired through a "friend of a friend" who knew a palace eunuch. Back in England, two of these three animals, dubbed Pekin Prince and Pekin Princess, were stolen and never heard of again. It was fortunate indeed that these few animals were removed from China when they were, as the Manchu Dynasty would be stripped of its power and wealth by 1911. The Imperial kennel—in operation for more than a thousand years—was dismantled.

By the 1890s there were quite a few canine "Eves" standing ready to birth the first generation of foreign-born Pekingeses; now all that was needed was an "Adam." Therefore, the accidental discovery of the little male Ah Cum, who along with a female called Mimosa had made his way to England concealed in a crate of live Japanese deer, was the most unbelievable of coincidences. Walking in London one day, Lady Algernon Gordon-Lennox (the sister of the Duchess of Richmond and Gordon) just happened to catch a glimpse of the canine couple as they trotted around a street corner. Abandoning all notions of propriety, she ran after their human escorts and immediately negotiated for stud services, marking the beginning of an illustrious Pekingese lineage that in the years to come would be jealously guarded by the heirs of Lady Algernon.

A second, larger, chestnut-colored male dog named Glanbrane Boxer arrived in Britain in 1900. Unlike the lost lineages of so many imported Pekes, Boxer was a certified "palace dog" (and the last Peke known to leave China), having been personally presented by Prince Ch'ing to Major J.H. Gwynne of the 23rd Welsh Fusiliers. Boxer's imperial connections provided the final impetus for the breed's legitimization, for in the same year, Crufts Dog Show eagerly designated a special class for the breed, despite the entry of only one dog.

The Pekingese was a public relations jackpot. Shows were packed to the rafters with spectators hoping to glimpse this rarest of dogs, made all the more endearing by a surprising propensity for obedience trials, traditionally dominated by hounds bred for the hunt. At one show, delectable morsels were brought into the ring and placed before the dogs, which then were tested for their ability to leave the plates untouched for four minutes. The audience held its breath as a teacup-sized Beeswing, the lone Pekingese in the group, sat through the first two minutes, then ever so slowly rose into a begging posture and remained there until the time elapsed. The performance brought down the house and Beeswing walked away with first prize. Unknown to the public at the time, the show committee barred the Pekingese from future obedience competitions—

An English-born Peke named "Dimple II," 1913. source: Author.

Beeswing's performance had put the hunting dogs and their owners in an embarrassing light.

The Pekingese had risen above its reputation as a freak to actually rival Old World breeds, including Standard Poodles and even the Cavalier King Charles Spaniel, as high-dollar fixtures of Edwardian society. Illustrated volumes of Peke poetry and Peke "autobiographies" sold out as soon as they hit the shelves. Lithographs of anthropomorphized Pekes, dressed in silken Mandarin robes, sipping tea, smoking opium pipes, or chasing butterflies in an idyllic still-life of oriental kitsch were extremely popular, as were studio photos of Asian men and women, dressed as though they just stepped out of the Forbidden City, ministering to small herds of the dogs. Indeed, the Pekingese itself became kitsch, as the dogs paraded about the show ring in hats and dolls' dresses. Such overtly infantile displays, and the fact that the majority of early breeders were women, inspired an enduring albeit undeserved image of the breed as effeminate and fussy, the snappy cynotherapists of matronly, overbred hypochondriacs.

Given how dramatically different in appearance the Pekingese is from its prehistoric, wolfish progenitor, one is hard-pressed to imagine how a

Contrived photo of Pekes in the
company of a Chinese manser-
vant. English, ca. 1918.
source: Author.

dog like Ah Cum, the breed's partiarch and savior, could be viewed with an
eye for further "improvement." Still, over the last century fanciers have
made their own, distinctive mark on the breed. The round skull so characteristic of Ah Cum, today derogatorily called an "apple head," was
phased out for a tabletop cranium that enhanced ever-rounder and larger
eyes. The legs have been shortened, the dogs now sport floor-length hair
worthy of Rapunzel, and most startling of all, the nostrils are now perfectly aligned with the forehead, if not slightly behind it, when viewed in

profile. By comparison, Ah Cum, with his one-inch muzzle, looks like a Greyhound.

But such beauty comes at a high price. Today's Pekes may suffer a number of congenital health problems caused by extreme inbreeding, including breathing difficulties, tooth loss, and inguinal hernias (a life-threatening protrusion of the gut into the groin). Even an innocent tumble down the stairs is sufficient to literally knock the eyes out of their now overly recessed sockets.

On the advent of the twenty-first century, the British Museum's collection of domesticated animals has been broken up and integrated into larger mammal collections. Ah Cum and his taxidermied canine colleagues have been removed to make room for state-of-the-art dioramas and interactive videos, and relegated to the Walter Rothschild Zoological Museum in the tiny town of Tring (an hour's drive northeast of London). A dignified-looking Ah Cum now stands among a towering crowd of English Sheepdogs, Collies, and Bulldogs in an illuminated glass case lining one side of a darkened corridor among Edwardian displays of Galápagos Tortoises and Tigers. Their showring triumphs have been obscured by successive generations of ever-more "improved" dogs, but they enjoy a more enduring sort of fame—as symbols of the power to manipulate and the power to purchase.

Paradoxically, the imposition of a rigid feudalistic hierarchy on dogs by the working class was a perfect reflection of the well-ordered social ranking they so desperately wanted to buck. With the advent of the modern era in the late 1800s, the creation of new breeds, and the arbitrary alteration of old ones such as the Pekingese, not only perpetuated medieval notions of rank and privilege, but through indirect association, concepts of human worth.

Six

Canine Emancipation

There is implanted by Nature in the heart of man a noble and excellent affection of mercy, extending even to the brute animals
which by Divine appointment are subjected to his dominion. The
more noble the mind the more enlarged is this affection. Narrow
and degenerate minds think that such things do not pertain to
them, but the nobler part of mankind is affected by sympathy.

—Lord Bacon,
Plea for Mercy to Animals (1874)

THE FEUDAL SOCIOECONOMIC system set in place in Europe during
the Middle Ages dictated an individual's rank from the moment of
birth, with little regard for personal aspirations or abilities, leaving preindustrial society sharply divided between a minority of "haves" and a huge
majority of "have-nots." Believing that it was their right by birth and divine appointment, wealthy land-owning families with managed lineages
depended on the toil of the land-poor to support their lavish, leisurely
lifestyles, an arrangement that was rarely questioned, and indeed was accepted as the way things ought to be. And if it was acceptable for the upper
class to exploit the people beneath them, what could be wrong with the
underclass doing same to dogs?

"The most useful conquest achieved by man is the domestication of
the dog," proclaimed one author in 1865, reflecting the Victorian philosophy that good or worthwhile creatures were those who could be induced
to serve or amuse humankind. In a sense, canines living with the peasantry

formed a body of laborers even lower on the social ladder than their masters. The peasant dog "fancy," if it can be called that, was a practical kind, with a simple emphasis on endurance and obedience. Since the fifteenth century, the working class had perpetuated several canine varieties, but because of their association with the lowest level of society, peasant dogs were rejected by the elite Victorian dog fancy as improperly bred, or worse, not bred at all.

In addition to the more familiar array of herding dogs such as Collies (which, because of their exceptional aptitude for following complex verbal and visual commands, were regarded as a "step up" from other peasant breeds, a professional working class of dogs), historical documents and firsthand accounts indicate that substantial populations of small dogs specialized in turning cooking spits, butter churns, or cider presses, while mild-mannered, Mastiff-like hounds hauled cargo and passenger wagons. Struggling farmers and merchants would have found it advantageous to employ such dogs—certainly they were cheaper than human laborers, plus there were no laws dictating how they were to be compensated for their services. Moreover, dogs reproduced frequently and easily compared to other beasts of burden, and could be sustained for next to nothing on leavings from the dinner table.

Poultry and joints of meat traditionally were roasted over roaring kitchen fires on horizontal, revolving spits, a tedious process requiring vast quantities of firewood and constant attention, lest the meat burn unevenly. Many busy kitchens featured permanently installed treadmills connected to the hearth spit, which were turned for hours on end by small dogs, the "lucky" ones working in tag-teams of two or more. Four broad spokes braced a flat wooden rim that doubled as running track, much like the suspended wheels now provided for pet hamsters. Chefs preferred a distinctive class of long-bodied, short-legged canines recognized by Johannes Caius in 1576 as "Turnspetes." And turned the spits is what they did, "by a small wheel, walking round it and making it turn evenly," in such a manner that "no cook or servant could do it more cleverly." (He also noted that Turnspits were common fixtures in street circuses, having been "taught to dance to the drums and to the lyre.")

Considering that they often turned roasts and hams weighing thirty pounds or more, the dogs were surprisingly small, standing less than ten inches at the shoulder. Descriptions of Turnspits are remarkably similar

Turnspit wheel.
source: Abergavenny
Museum, Wales.

from century to century, and no less consistent in physical type than many of the preindustrial standards written for hounds kept by the aristocracy (and now popularly recognized as pure breeds). Carl Linnaeus, the famous Swedish naturalist, recognized Turnspits in 1756, reporting that there were long- and short-haired varieties, both characteristically sporting grizzled or spotted coats, as well as distinctively crooked legs. Writing in 1866, George R. Jesse described what are likely the same "little bandy legged dogs" as bluish gray in color with black spots. Even the eminent Thomas Bewick was inclined to acknowledge the Turnspit as a breed in his *A General History of Quadrupeds,* and added that the dogs frequently had eyes of differing colors—"the iris of one eye black, and the other white."

Like the human underclass who worked long hours with little or no pay, Turnspits often were kept to their wheels for hours at a time without water, despite the popular folk belief that hydrophobia (rabies) could be brought on by heat exhaustion and dehydration. Moralistic tales were told and retold of "lazy" Turnspits who attempted to shirk their kitchen duties, only to be exposed cowering under a chair or in the corner of a darkened pantry by an irate and sometimes violent cook, or in some instances betrayed by a canine comrade. "[They] are enclosed in a wheel from which they cannot escape. . . . If they are lazy [one puts] into the wheel a hot coal as a stimulant to their feet," the Reverend Henry Crow wrote in 1822.

An off-duty Turnspit stands under a kitchen table.
source: Author.

Turnspits frequently were taken to church to serve as foot warmers. When the Bishop of Gloucester held a service in Bath Abbey, a lesson was read from the Book of Ezekiel that included verses from the tenth chapter, which referred to "wheels" and the "animals that control them." Like a pet that dives under the bed at the mere whisper of the word "bath," the Turnspits cued in on the words, and according to one witness "clapt their Tails between their Legs and ran out of the Church." (Another version of the story relates that the good bishop gave a passionate sermon on the horrors of hell and shouted the words "fire" and "roasting on a spit," effectively sparking a canine stampede.)

Large, docile dogs also were expected to earn their keep by carrying packages or pulling wagons for farmers and merchants. A "coarse hound" was what Caius called such dogs as the "Tyncker's Curre [Tinker's Cur]," trained to "beare bigge budgettes [satchels] fraught with tooles . . . mettall meete to mend kettles, porrige pottes, skellets . . . and other such like trumpery requisite for their loytering trade." In later centuries, these likely progenitors of modern Newfoundlands, Appenzell Mountain Dogs, and

Greater Swiss Mountain Dogs were loosely lumped together in a class simply identified as "cart dog," also known in French-speaking regions as the "Matîn." In parts of Belgium and Holland, however, the cart dogs were so prevalent that a special breed called the Belgische Rekel was widely recognized as the most suited for this arduous work. It was famous for its exceptional strength and endurance, despite a rather long-legged, lanky appearance. Owners frequently docked the dogs' tails to prevent entanglement in harness trappings (though the practice just as easily could have been an outgrowth of the medieval tradition of mutilating peasant dogs). And for a short time in the eighteenth century, it was customary to amputate their ears in the belief that this kept their vision clear. But the practice was abandoned when it was discovered that rain and snow caused sores and even deafness.

The idea of employing canines as beasts of burden was not unique to Europe. Cart dogs also were commonplace throughout Canada. In 1824, for example, a force of two thousand Newfoundlands living near the lake of St. John toiled around the clock during the summer months hauling cartloads of fish from the docks to packing sheds and markets. In the winter months, smaller teams of the same dogs were harnessed to timber or postal sleds and were said to willingly traverse miles of trail without the supervision of a master. After delivery, the dogs would beat a hasty retreat home for a reward of smoked fish.

Hell for Dumb Animals

The streets of New York, London, Brussels, and Amsterdam were clogged with dog carts each Saturday, driven or led by farmers, fishermen, butchers, bakers, and merchants delivering groceries and wares to fashionable townhomes, or sifting through curbside trash heaps for linen and cotton rags to sell to papermakers. "Indeed it is astonishing to see what a disproportionately large load [they] can pull," one turn-of-the-century author remarked. Tales of Trekhond trios hitched to four-hundred-pound-plus cartloads, running at a steady trot for miles without signs of weariness, were common. For demonstration purposes, individual dogs could be induced to tow as much as four hundred pounds without any help from their masters or other animals.

Just as an abused child is at risk of becoming an adult abuser, those on

Flemish milk cart with trio of Belgische Rekels.
source: Author.

Dutch carter and his dog.
source: Author.

Canine Emancipation

A single Belgian Trekhond and milk cart on routine town deliveries.
source: Author.

the lowest rung of the social ladder often were inclined to vent their frustrations on their animals. In an era when other dogs were finding new lives as cherished members of human families, Turnspits and cart dogs lived much as they had in feudal times, often being overworked, underfed, and abused. But cruelty was (and is) an integral part of any economic system that relied on animals for power and profit, and the lives of many Victorian working dogs were not exempt from the savage whippings, ill-fitting harnesses, excessive burdens, and water deprivation that plagued other beasts of burden. In the case of Turnspits, most acts of cruelty occurred offstage—behind closed kitchen doors. But cart-dog abuse was part of everyday life in preindustrialized cities, one of many street scenes replayed daily in which animals were flogged, clubbed, burned, stabbed, and even sliced with knives when they tired or weakened on the job. Such cruel displays drew little if any reaction from a population that believed animals were the property of their masters.

"England is the hell for dumb animals," wrote a journalist around 1820. He was one of a growing number of writers and civic leaders who questioned the brutal exploitation of dogs, such as the English cleric William Drummond, who wrote that he regretted living in a country where "the duties of morality and religion have such eloquent advocates, [while] so little attention is paid to the relentless abuse of animals." The growing cacophony of criticisms, backed by national educational programs and charity-organized campaigns to discourage sadistic behavior, heralded a new era of public awareness regarding the treatment of working animals. By 1850, numerous published treatises were decrying cruelty to animals as immoral, and calling for a new ethic of empathy and compassion. Hard-line traditionalists countered that the brutal treatment of animals was a reaffirmation of society's masculine character and, according to one English Prime Minister, "inspired courage and produced a nobleness of sentiment and elevation of mind."

But the public was becoming more vocal on the subject of human slavery and child labor, and a new social consciousness based on the principle that members of even the lowest social class were entitled to certain fundamental rights soon was extended to working animals as well. Popular art and literature, particularly works for children, expounded a gentler, more sentimental view of nature and its uncorrupted innocence. As these depictions became more prevalent, businesses with a vested interest in animal labor (particularly dogs) desperately tried to cast humane proponents as extremists or even traitors. By 1860 it was clear they were losing the battle.

Canines long associated with the lower class found an exceptionally sympathetic champion in Sir Edwin Landseer, the wildly popular Victorian animal painter and portraitist of the Queen's dogs. In the early 1800s he was famous for his glorified depictions of mortal combat between stags and hounds, but in the latter half of his life, his depictions became more romantic and sentimental as he came to detest cruelty to animals. An outspoken critic of the cropping of dogs' ears and dog fights, he was hailed as an influential champion—if not unofficial patriarch—of the English humane movement. For unlike earlier artists such as George Stubbs, who stressed anatomical accuracy to the exclusion of virtually all other qualities, Landseer stressed the less tangible aspects of the animal, emphasizing personalities and depicting them as motivated by emotions common to humans, including joy, love, anger, and grief. His portraits expressed the unspoken feelings of all people, common and otherwise, who had ever formed an intimate bond with an animal. As one art critic remarked, Landseer's paintings were not of "mere animals—you see them not only alive but you see their biography and know what they do, and if the expression be allowed, what they think."

Canine Emancipation

The commissioned works of Landseer were reproduced as steel engravings and sold individually or in bound sets, making his dog portraits affordable and accessible to the public. Printed by the thousands, these popularized images encouraged the underclass "to abandon their callous indifference for the virtue of tenderness as a means of self-ennoblement and spiritual elevation," according to the Reverend James Macaulay, author of *Plea for Mercy to Animals* (1874), who credited Landseer and other artists with "arresting the attention and touching the feelings of the lower classes."

Often unnoticed at the time, many of Landseer's dog renderings doubled as social commentary on the human class structure, by juxtaposing plump, pampered canines and starving street dogs. In the process, he bolstered his popularity with the working class, and as the idea that animals could think and feel gained acceptance, the overworking of animals became widely recognized as the height of bad taste—and "poor breeding."

Mass-produced steel engraving of Sir Edwin Landseer's *Jack in Office.*
source: Author.

Noble Causes and Characters

Animal protection organizations such as the Dogs' Home Battersea and the Royal Society for the Prevention of Cruelty to Animals (RSPCA) were legitimized and empowered by Queen Victoria's public declarations of support, triggering an avalanche of elite patronage and participation. Having lost the battle to monopolize the breeding of dogs, the upper class attempted to "up the ante" by turning to charitable animal endeavors as a means of distinguishing themselves from the rabble of middle-class fanciers.

Countless committees for civic-minded high-society women appeared after 1850, such as the one created in conjunction with the RSPCA under the leadership of Baroness Burdett Coutts. This committee orchestrated the erection of public drinking fountains for animals and the donation of five hundred leather bound books (illustrated by Landseer) to be awarded to children as prizes for essays on the importance of kindness to animals. As Victorian children's author Eleanor Fenn pointed out, "nothing could more effectually tend to infuse benevolence than the teaching of little ones early to consider every part of nature as imbued with feeling." It was especially important to *teach* benevolence because it did not come naturally, especially to boys, who according to Fenn were indoctrinated into a masculine society rife with an archaic definition of virility that condoned brutality and ridiculed tenderness. Opportunities to demonstrate empathy for animals were occasions to exercise self-control, a critical skill if one was to rise above a common background.

As the 1800s progressed, the correlation of animal cruelty with unacceptable behavior toward fellow humans became more widely accepted, with the mastery of all such base urges as the ultimate goal. Former French cavalry officer General Grammot described neglected and abused animals as a fixture of nineteenth-century life, and commented that "the spectacle of suffering encourages cruelty, that the child accustomed to bloody pastimes or witnessing cruelty will become a dangerous man, that the vicious carter [cart driver] is latent in the child."

In theory and rhetoric, it was unacceptable for anyone to be cruel, no matter what their social rank. But aristocratic activists and the media selectively focused their attention on the underclass as the major perpetrator of crimes against animals. The mistreatment of dogs, the "noblest" of

Alms Giving, by G. Doré, 1871.
source: Author.

Public drinking fountain for
people and animals, English,
ca. 1870.
source: Author.

Caricature of a man harnessed to a wagon, part of an English children's lesson on the
importance of kindness to animals, ca. 1870.
source: Author.

creatures next to man, was a perfect example of their "lack of breeding." Animal welfare periodicals featured articles detailing the savage treatment of dogs in the hands of lower-class carters, yet artfully dodged any suggestion that aristocrats might also be perpetrators of cruelty. According to the Reverend James Macaulay, similar criticisms leveled at ladies and gentlemen who partook of fox hunts and pigeon shoots, or whipped race-horses and dogs, were "for the present tabooed" because some of the keenest sportsmen were "warm friends and liberal supporters of the RSPCA."

Beginning in 1830, the RSPCA began lobbying Parliament to ban the use of dogs as draft animals. Lord Ellenborough believed that lower-income families should be exempt from prosecution, while RSPCA advocates such as Lord Brougham countered that "nothing could be more shocking or disgusting than to see the practice of great, heavy men being drawn by dogs. . . . Indeed, I have seen, near the place where their Lordships assemble, all sorts of articles drawn by small dogs who could scarcely get on." Brougham also expressed concerns for the public's health and safety, since "the increase of hydrophobia is attributable to the overheated state of [cart] dogs, prevented as they are from having free access to water, and we have frequently seen these dogs fastened to vehicles panting and foaming with exertion beyond their strength."

Arguments over the proposed legislation dragged on for years until finally in 1839, despite the protestations of breeders and merchants, England passed the first Dog Cart Nuisance Law, prohibiting draft dogs within fifteen miles of London's busy Charing Cross station. Organized lobbying efforts to undermine or revoke the law did not stop, however. RSPCA documents recount how "the costermongers of [London] have got up a petition to Parliament stating that their kindness to their dogs is well known, and that their trade will be knocked up under the New Police Act, as they cannot afford to keep horses." A *Times* editorial in 1843 painted a bleak picture of the draft dogs' fate, suggesting that if activists had their way thousands of Matîns would die horribly from abandonment: "What is to become of the canine labor which is to be thus suddenly displaced from its legitimate channel? Are out-of-work mastiffs to crowd our crossings and hang disconsolately about the corners of our butchers' shops, like coach-men thrown out of employ by the railroads? Or is the more frightful alternative [of killing cart dogs] to be adopted? Why condemn to dissolute idleness or indiscriminate extinction whole generations of respectable quadrupeds? . . . Will the Thames itself contain the puppies, merged in it under this new stimulus to canine infanticide?"

Despite the alarmist rhetoric, the Dog Cart Nuisance Law was progressively strengthened by amendments granting the police greater power to apprehend offenders without warrants. Penalties also became increasingly severe, with one abusive merchant sentenced to a month's hard labor. Finally, on January 1, 1855, England distinguished itself from the rest of Europe by enacting the first nationwide ban on dog carts. The authors of the bill said they "could not see why dogs in the country should be treated worse than those in the metropolis," and called the sight of dogs straining in harnesses "offensive to humanity."

News of the British ban inspired restrictive legislation in the United States. After an impassioned argument by American Society for the Prevention of Cruelty to Animals (ASPCA) president Henry Bergh in 1866, New York State passed a law requiring all cart dogs to be licensed and registered with municipal authorities. It fell short of Bergh's hope for a total ban on dog exploitation in such capacities, but shortly after its passage "a large collection of carts [were] seen in the City Hall Park with one, two or three lolling, panting, fatigued dogs each, their owners having been arrested either for failure to take out licenses or to muzzle the dogs. A procession of six carts, escorted by a squad of police [was even] seen coming down Fifth Avenue."

Inspired by his success with the cart-dog issue, Bergh next devoted his efforts to the abolition of dog treadmills. He saw a Turnspit slaving away on a cider press in the window of a New York City saloon in 1874, where "the underside of [his] collar had chafed a raw sore. . . . He panted and frequently tried to stop, but was so tied that he had to keep on running or choke." The proprietor was arrested and subsequently appealed his case before the state supreme court, but lost and had to pay a fine of twenty-five dollars. Bergh was notorious for storming into saloons that exhibited treadmill dogs and shouting down proprietors when they tried to defend their actions. The merchants "could not see how it was any of [my] business how they worked their cider mill," Bergh later recalled. "What was a dog good for anyhow if he wasn't put to something? Was he only fit to be patted on his head?"

On at least two occasions, Bergh revisited New York businesses convicted of Turnspit abuse, only to find the dogs replaced with goats, small donkeys, or in one instance, African-American children. As with other city jobs held by children, wages were low or nonexistent and hazardous work conditions resulted in many becoming permanently maimed or killed (only ten years earlier African slaves had been put to turning sugar presses in the South, often to the point of exhaustion). To see the ease with which dogs and children could be interchanged for this dangerous work incensed animal lovers like Bergh, who had long ago concluded that the menial employment of dogs was simply another form of slavery.

After the enactment of anticruelty laws in America and England, humane advocates then set their sights on the continued use of draft dogs on the Continent. The RSPCA Ladies' Committee drafted a declaration in 1870 calling for the abolition of "dog traction" in Belgium and was backed by Bergh, who in a letter to the Belgium's Société Royal Protectrice des Animaux, pointed out that "the dog is not adapted by nature for use as a beast of burden." Lobbying was equally strong for the continued use of Rekels, however. Belgium's National Federation for the Breeding of Draft Dogs retorted that "the dog in harness renders such precious services that

Turnspit donkey, ca. 1870.
source: Author.

never will any authority dare to suppress its current use. A disastrous economic revolution would be the consequence. Penury and poverty would enter thousands of homes where a relative affluence is apparent now." Forty years would pass before a total ban on cart dogs in Belgium would be enacted in 1910. Even then activists complained that the law was gutted by grandfather clauses and exemptions for those whose livelihoods depended on cart dogs. Proponents countered that new dog licensing fees and mandatory inspections would insure humane treatment for cart dogs, in essence endowing the animals with their own set of laborers' rights, including entitlements to rest periods, adequate shelter, fresh water, and regular meals. All carts, wagons, and harness trappings had to meet strict design and safety guidelines and could not be overburdened with people or goods. Belgian police conducted roadside inspections of dog carts on their way to market, issuing citations for the slightest infraction. Substantial penalties and licensing fees, combined with intimidating bureaucracy, further discouraged the use of cart dogs, yet they endured as the preferred mode of transport for many Flemish and Dutch dairymen and merchants until World War I.

Fleeing the German invasion of Belgium in World War I, this Flemish family resorts to using a small German Shepherd as a draft animal.
source: Author.

One of the
Belgian
Dog-drawn
Machine Guns
Off to the Front.
13

© BY THE INTERNATIONAL NEWS SERVICE, N.Y.

Belgian carabineer with machine-gun-toting Trekhonds.
source: Author.

With the German invasion of Belgium in 1914, cart-dog ordinances were suspended and hundreds of Matîns were confiscated by the military, leaving civilians to search out any and all dogs large enough to wear a harness, and whether they had a propensity for draft work or not, hitch them to carts laden with children and luggage in a mass exodus for the border. Meanwhile, the Army hastily retrained its new regiment of Rekels for the front, pulling machine guns, small cannons, ammunition, ambulances, cauldrons of slop in messenger dog camps, and even paddy wagons.

"They take weapons right up to the firing line without a sign of fear and lie down in the midst of shot and shell," Kate Sanborn gushed in *Educated Dogs of Today* (1916), apparently unaware that many Rekels were abandoned in the line of fire, trapped in their harnesses when the carts became stuck in seas of mud. Other times the handler was killed as well as one of the two dogs, leaving the surviving dog to the mercy of the enemy. In some cases entire platoons were machine-gunned within the first few minutes of being called into action. Walter A. Dyer's account of the life of

Paddy wagon pulled by dogs, ca. 1900–1915.
source: Author.

a fictional Rekel in *Pierrot: Dog of Belgium* (1915) contains a riveting description of what it must have been like at the front for many of these canines:

> They were turned about and obliged to stand facing away from the tumult of battle as the machine guns began to rattle directly behind them. Two of the dogs started wildly off, their guns bumping and careening behind them. Other dogs reared and snarled, and it was all the men could do to prevent a stampede. A speeding bullet caught one spotted young dog [as he trotted] close by his mate, and he fell dead at Pierrot's feet. The carabineers were soon overwhelmed [by Germans] and dogs who were harnessed were quickly bayoneted that they might not escape with the guns.

The few Rekels who survived the horror of war were auctioned off rather than returned to their owners, and put back to work pulling carts for impoverished merchants and war widows, then faded from daily life in the ensuing years as they were replaced by trucks and cars. Belgium's Na-

Canine Emancipation

Rekels trained to lie down on the battlefield while Maxims are fired.
source: Author.

tional Federation for the Breeding of Draft Dogs, which only decades earlier had honored breeders who carefully maintained Rekel lineages spanning 150 years or more, was disbanded by war's end, its studbooks and
records apparently destroyed or lost. Little effort was made to perpetuate
the breed in the following decade, and by the fifties the last few Rekels had
passed away. So gradual was the breed's demise that its extinction went
largely unnoticed.

Ill-Made Hounds

Mechanized conveniences alone were not responsible for the end of
these working dogs. Humane organizations that once championed the cart
dog's right to a quality life turned their attention to more pressing issues
as the use of animals was made obsolete by technological innovations. Advocates celebrated the end of such exploitation, but failed to foresee that
the breeds would vanish when there was no longer any demand for their
services, in effect making the humane movement itself partly to blame for

the extinction of Turnspits and Trekhonds, if only by default rather than deliberate intent.

The institutionalized dog fancy, which could have offered the dogs refuge in the showring, was equally at fault, for imposing human concepts of status and elitism on dogs leaves little room for animals associated with the struggling underclass. And despite sweeping social reforms and the empowerment of the working class, there still was little sympathy for the plight of the poor, whose troubles were attributed to laziness, immoral behavior, and a lack of "breeding."

Ironically, dog fanciers who had fought so valiantly to end the exploitation of animals often let personal prejudice against the underclass spill over onto the working dogs, especially the Turnspits. Heartless critics picked at their appearance and alleged lack of moral character, as evidenced by their aversion to work in the wheel. Like their masters, they were degenerates, the product of mixed, illegitimate couplings. Any allusion to the dogs as breeds—as indicated in earlier works—was violently rejected.

The Reverend J.G. Wood made a point of deleting all mention of the Turnspit from the revised edition of his *New Illustrated Natural History*, all the while featuring a wealth of Spaniels, Setters, and lapdogs. The author of *Anecdotes of Animals* (1864) was none too sorry to learn that Turnspits were becoming scarce, since they were "ill-made hounds" whose very existence was proof that "the perpetuation of malformation in several breeds will produce a Turnspit." Such alleged mongrels were "miserable, degenerated animals, cast off by the better classes," according to naturalist and author Alfred Brehm, and if anything, detracted from efforts to elevate the canine race through the institution of pedigrees and studbooks.

Some authors were not content to let the dogs simply vanish from the face of the earth, but called for an eradication campaign to purge canine society of all adverse influences. Speaking on dogs kept by the rural peasantry in 1847, R.L. Allen asserted "that the farmer needs only such as may be found in the Shepherd, the Drovers' dogs, and the [rat] Terrier." The rest of lower-class dogdom were like roving gangs of delinquents, which worried livestock and harbored rabies, and justified the "extermination by law [of all] curs of low degree."

Turnspits and Trekhonds were emblematic of an earlier, more primitive time, and no longer fit into popular notions of progress. A mechanized clockwork roasting jack invented around 1870 was eagerly accepted by cooks, who in turn quickly abandoned the use, and hence, the breeding of Turnspits. Even the most comprehensive published works on dogs scarcely mentioned the breeds, although the National Geographic Society's 1927 edition of *The Book of Dogs* did include a photo of a Trekhond on the last page—in a chapter titled "The Outcasts of Dogkind."

Dogs of various kinds continued to turn butter churns in remote parts of Wales into the early decades of the twentieth century, but today the Turnspit has completely vanished, the last survivors reabsorbed into a vast canine melting pot of other breeds that constituted the mongrel class of the time.

Prior to her inclusion in an exhibit of household utensils at the Abergavenny Museum, Whiskey the Turnspit went largely unnoticed in the window of "The Old Shop" in the Welsh hamlet of Cross Ash near Ross-on-Wye, where she had been displayed for decades. Now she enjoys the dubious distinction of being the only known specimen of her breed in existence. But unlike the distinguished dogs of Tring, most visual hints of her personality were lost to the hands of an amateur Victorian taxidermist. The tragedy is compounded by the disappearance of documents which reportedly detailed her life and death around 1850—the museum's file was loaned out and never returned.

Although no taxidermied examples of the Rekel are known to exist, cart dogs have fared a little better in the historical record than Turnspits. An abundance of tourist postcards have survived from the turn of the century, depicting milkmaids and Matîns sauntering along quaint country roads, in addition to snapshots taken by visiting American soldiers who borrowed or adopted abandoned Rekels. A troupe of Rekels accompanied the King of Belgium to the United States in 1919 to participate in a parade celebrating the liberation of his country. And a Rekel, harnessed and ready for combat, is among the beasts cast in bronze in 1934 and erected in Brussels in the Place Poelaert as a tribute to the Belgian Infantry.

Masquerading as a children's story, Louise de la Ramée's *A Dog of Flanders* is a scathing indictment of society's indifference to the poor and indigent as represented by Nello, an orphaned boy, and Patrasche, an unemployed, geriatric Trekhond. Turned out by a heartless landlord and snubbed by neighbors, the dog and child expire in each other's arms inside Antwerp's cathedral while gazing at Rubens's *Descent of the Cross*. "The

Welsh butter churn dogs at the turn of the century.
source: Author.

Erected in 1934, this monument to the carabineers at the Place Poelaert in Brussels includes a Rekel-drawn machine gun.
source: Count Geoffroy de Beauffort.

Canine Emancipation

Whiskey the Turnspit.
source: Abergavenny Museum.

people of the village, contrite and ashamed, implored a special grace for them, and making them one grave, laid them to rest there side by side—forever." Twentieth Century Fox's 1959 movie of the same title presented a sanitized, commercial version of the story, despite the author's graphic descriptions of Patrasche and his fellow Matîns as the "slaves of slaves . . . beasts of the shafts that lived straining their sinews in the gall of the cart and died breaking their hearts on the flints of the streets." Instead, the movie starred a pleasingly plump, floppy-eared Golden Labrador Retriever who, along with Nello, lived happily ever after.

And the reinterpretation of Trekhond history continues. Modern fanciers choose instead to honor the positive aspects of man and dog working side by side. For as these living history buffs point out, smart merchants and farmers have always known that animals work willingly when they are well fed and treated kindly. Using Greater Swiss Mountain Dogs, Newfoundlands, and other breeds with a penchant for pulling, they turn out for parades in traditional costumes, their dogs harnessed to restored antique carts decorated with ribbons and flowers. Tentative efforts are even under way to recreate the Belgische Rekel by combining other, similar-looking and -behaving breeds.

Today, as questions and debate rise anew over notions of class or pedigree, dogs unlucky enough to lack impeccable family credentials are still the "have-nots" of canine society. Victimized by their sheer abundance, they are worthless, slated for "humane disposal" at animal shelters. They are the flotsam of society's continuing obsession with pedigreed dogs, who continue to be widely regarded as superior animals, aristocrats by birth. Still, in this modern era of disposable goods, many pure breeds also are left at shelters, the victims of impulsive buyers. Meanwhile, arguments for and against the rights of dogs continue to echo those expressed over the Turnspits and Trekhonds, with Kennel Clubs rallying against their critics, calling them animal rights "terrorists," and hosting seminars on "media management" for member breeders desiring to counter criticisms at the local level. Also like their predecessors, they continue to accuse any who question their policies as having hidden agendas seeking the abolition of the dogs altogether.

Perhaps the lesson to be found in the story of the Turnspits and Trekhonds is that the way society treats animals often is a reflection of how it treats people as well. Some of the more passionate Victorian proponents of humane education have since been proven surprisingly accurate in their speculations that animal abuse and human abuse were irrevocably intertwined. Two hundred years after Richard Martin, father of the English humane movement, declared that it was time for "a revolution in morals," Western society is finally beginning to acknowledge the importance of a compassionate ethic that respects both animals and people, regardless of pedigree or affiliation. Lord Bacon's "excellent affection of mercy" may be hobbled by the stilted, sentimental prose of another era, but the notion that the ability to empathize is integral to a healthy mind and society has proven to be anything but old-fashioned.

The Turnspit Taught

The dinner must be dished at one;
Where's this vexatious Turnspit gone?
Unless the skulking cur is caught,
The sirloin's spoilt, and I'm at fault
Thus said (for sure you'll think it fit
That I the cook-maid's oath omit),
With all the fury of a cook,
Her cooler kitchen Nan forsook;
The broom-stick o'er her head she waves,
She sweats, she stamps, she puffs, she raves—
The sneaking cur before her flies;
She whistles, calls, fair speech she tries;
These nought avail, her choler burns,
The fist and cudgel threat by turns.
With hasty stride she presses near;
He slinks aloof, and howls with fear.
'Was ever cur so cursed (he cried)!
What star did at my birth preside!
Am I for life by compact bound
To tread the wheel's eternal round?

John Gay (1685–1732)

Seven

The Other Native Americans

Somewhere at a place where the prairie and the Badlands meet, there is a hidden cave. In it lives an old woman who has been sitting there for a thousand years or more, working on a blanket strip for her buffalo robe. Resting beside her, licking his paws and watching her all the time, is Sunka Sapa, a huge black dog. His eyes never wander from the old woman. Every now and then she gets up to stir the soup in a huge earthen pot. The moment her back is turned the dog starts pulling the porcupine quills out of her blanket strip. This way her quillwork remains forever unfinished. The Sioux people used to say if the old woman ever finishes her blanket, then at the very moment she threads the last porcupine quill to complete the design, the world will come to an end.

—Jenny Leading Cloud (White River Sioux), 1967

PRIOR TO THE late nineteenth century, when a tidal wave of Anglo settlers swept across the North American continent seeking new, unfettered destinies, Native American dogs were as plentiful as their masters, varying in both form and function from region to region and culture to culture. Some performed no obvious work except as camp scavengers, while others were valued hunting assistants, pack animals, and spiritual guides.

As in so many cultures around the world, canines figure heavily in Native American mythology as dual icons, representing both death and birth (or rebirth). Like Anubis and Hermanubis, they were sentries of the afterlife, standing guard at a bridge over the "river of death," and determin-

Wood with gesso statuette of the
Egyptian god Anubis as embalmer,
ca. 304 B.C.
source: The Metropolitan Museum
of Art, gift of Mrs. Myron C. Taylor,
1938 (38.5).

Painted icon of St. Christopher, ca. 1685.
source: Courtesy of the Byzantine
Museum, Athens.

Renaissance dog collar of red silk velvet with gilded wire decoration. Incorporated in the embroidery are the arms of Bartolomeo Visconti and Philomena Nicoli, who were married in September 1488. No other decorative collar from this era is known to exist. source: Geoffrey Jenkinson.

Oil painting on paper (laid down on canvas) of a lion-clipped Lowchen, reputed to have belonged to Madame de Pompadour, mistress of Louis XV. Signed De Lamarre. source: Private collection.

Portrait of Madame de Porcin and her spaniel, late eighteenth century.
source: Cliché Musée des Beaux Arts, Angers.

Nineteenth-century parody of the woman-dog relationship, titled
"When Other Lips."
source: Teenie Hefner.

The proud owner with his flock of sheep and obedient Sheepdog.
Unknown artist, ca. 1840.
source: Mr. and Mrs. David A. George.

Dog exhibit at Tring. Ah Cum can be seen in the lower right corner.
source: Author (with kind permission of the Zoological Museum at Tring).

An adult standard Xolo named Toni, owned by Carol Clarke.
source: Carol Clarke.

Modern miniaturized
version of the Xolo,
named Hubie, owned
by Carol Clarke.
source: Carol Clarke.

World War I morale-boosting poster titled *The Soldier's Friends,* showing a
Red Cross rescue dog and a nurse.
source: Author.

Vietnam Dog Handlers Association wreath-laying ceremony at the
Vietnam War Memorial.
source: Vietnam Dog Handlers Association.

Hartsdale war dog
memorial, erected after
World War I to honor
Red Cross dogs, and later
expanded to recognize
dogs who served in
World War II.
source: Mike Lemish.

Eighteenth-century Austrian brass collar lined in leather, the lead attachment emerging from a lion's mask in high relief.
source: With the kind permission of the Trustees of the Leeds Castle Foundation.

Turn-of-the-century white metal collar with brass studs and colored felt lining, inscribed "Count Kuzki," ca. 1900.
source: With the kind permission of the Trustees of the Leeds Castle Foundation.

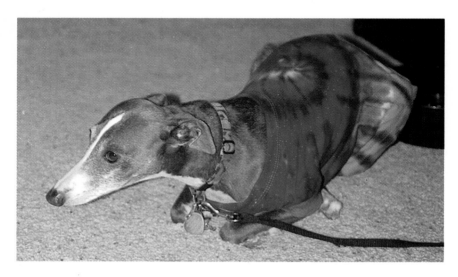

Italian Greyhound wearing tie-dyed shirt and neon collar, 1993.
source: Author.

A creatively groomed Standard
Poodle, dyed pink and decorated
with rhinestones and feathers.
source: Welge Photography.

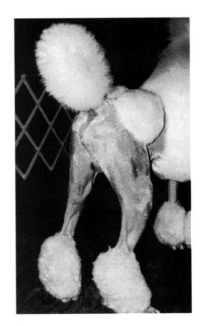

Shaved hindquarters of a
modern Standard Poodle.
source: Author.

"Biker"-style canine fashions, 1994.
source: Sam and Sally Creature Comforts.

American-made leather and
turquoise collar, made in the
early twentieth century.
source: With the kind permission
of the Trustees of the Leeds
Castle Foundation.

Austrian leather and red velvet collar bearing a copper-gilt repoussé cartouche with the arms of the Prince-Archbishop of Salzburg, Sigmund III Christoph, Graf von Schrattenbach (1698).
source: With the kind permission of the Trustees of the Leeds Castle Foundation.

Turn-of-the-century celluloid collar with red bow and brass bell, imitating Edwardian gentlemen's dress collars.
source: With the kind permission of the Trustees of the Leeds Castle Foundation.

Interior of Teca Tu pet boutique in Santa Fe, New Mexico.
source: Diane Burchard.

Nigerian dog modeling a traditional hunting collar. This fringed and feathered accessory has been made for centuries by tribal elders, but may become a lost art as it is replaced by mass-produced, disposable nylon collars.
source: Mercedes De La Garza.

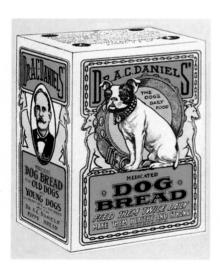

A.C. Daniels's Medicated Dog Bread, ca. 1910.
source: Author.

"Pup-E-Crumbles," ca. 1920.
source: Author.

Ad for a hamburger-patty–shaped semimoist dog food, ca. 1960-65.
source: Author.

Hyde Park Dog Cemetery headstones.
source: Author (with kind permission of the Royal Parks Service).

The Hartsdale Canine Pet Cemetery as it appears today.
source: Hartsdale Canine Pet Cemetery, Hartsdale, New York.

Headstone in Hyde Park Dog Cemetery, "To My Dear Moussoo."
source: Author.

Modern headstone with inset
photo of a deceased poodle
in the cemetery at Asnières,
reading "To My Bibi."
source: Author.

Modern pet mummification,
"Egyptian style," of a dog named
Butch, who is encased in a polished
bronze sarcophagus.
source: Summum Mummification,
Salt Lake City, Utah.

Chelsea and Sydney, two disabled dogs who help one another.
source: Donna Sadjak.

ing whether the deceased led an honorable life before granting his soul passage to eternity. In deference to just such a myth, some Inuit (Eskimo) tribes interred the skull of a dog in the graves of children to assist and lead the young soul on its journey to paradise.

Indians in the Aleutian Archipelago considered dogs the sole forebears of humanity, believing that the "First Father" descended from heaven in canine form. Likewise, the Chippewas of Alaska credited a dog as their forebear and for a short time were so beholden to canines that they ceased using them as draft animals, replacing them with women. And it was said that the world's first woman had ten children fathered by a dog, five of whom remained in the New World and became Indians while the others set to sea on a raft and ultimately gave rise to the Europeans.

Considering the difficulty of taming large wolves native to North America (as previously discussed), it is possible that the first Native American domestic dogs actually harked back to the small Asiatic wolf. Such canids (whether in a wild, semitame, or tame state is not known) could have followed prehistoric caribou hunters across a temporary northern land bridge from the steppes of the Eurasian continent into the Western Hemisphere. Tracking the migratory herds, successive generations of Stone Age humans unwittingly immigrated to the New World, beginning as early as thirty-five thousand years ago, until the land bridge resubmerged at the end of the Ice Age, perhaps as late as nine thousand years ago. Subsequently as these canids became truly domesticated, they could have interbred with resident populations of wolves (or coyotes in the south), and given rise to new, more specialized canine varieties. Some of them, such as the sled dogs of the Far North, maintained a strong resemblance to the wolf, while others evolved to mimic Old World breeds such as Fox Terriers, Welsh Corgies, and Collies.

Early European explorers often remarked on the wild natures and insatiable appetites of Indian dogs, particularly those kept by the Inuit tribes of the far north. Life was hard in the Arctic, and these dogs were forced to think creatively when it came to procuring food. If hunting was bountiful they were likely to receive extra portions of fish or seal meat, expressly smoked or frozen for that purpose. More often, though, they subsisted on virtually inedible leavings, including bones, scraps of hide, and even human feces.

In his 1856 diary, Arctic explorer Elisha Kane described the team of na-

Victorian depiction of Eskimo dogs.
source: Author.

tive sled dogs he had taken onto his ship as an "unruly, thieving, wild-beast pack . . . Not a bear's paw, a basket of mosses or any specimen whatever can leave your hands for a moment without their making a rush at it, and after a yelping scramble, swallowing it at a gulp. I have seen them attempt to eat a whole feather bed, and here, this very morning, one of the brutes has eaten up two birds' nests which I had just gathered from the rocks—feathers, filth, pebbles and moss." Upon reaching a remote glacial harbor, the dogs, with "neither voice nor lash restraining them, scamper[ed] off like a drove of hogs in an Illinois oak-opening. . . . We had to send off a boat party today for their rescue. It cost a pull through ice and water of eight miles before they found the miscreants, fat and saucy, beside the carcass of a dead narwhal. After more than an hour spent in attempts to catch

Elisha Kane's Inuit dogs battle a polar bear.
source: Author.

them, one was tied and brought on board, but the other suicidal scamp had to be left to his fate." Later on, however, these same canines alerted Kane to the presence of a polar bear in camp one night, fought the beast with all their might, and in the process redeemed themselves in his eyes.

Captain Hall, who frequented Greenland throughout the late 1800s, watched a pack of Inuit dogs devour a thirty-foot-long rawhide whip. In another instance "a single dog ate in seven seconds a piece of walrus hide and blubber six feet long and an inch and a half square." Indeed, ravenous appetites often motivated them to devour their harness trappings or even the sled itself if they were left unattended for extended periods of time, behavioral problems that sometimes were remedied by knocking out the animals' teeth. Two Inuit dogs who found their way to England around 1860 were famous for standing "hour after hour before a candle maker's workshop, smelling the fumes of the melted tallow with great enjoyment."

Sled dogs often became entangled in their traces, creating a veritable Gordian knot of struggling animals and harness trappings that brought overland convoys to a screeching halt while handlers labored to separate and subdue quarreling individuals. "They are apt to snarl and snap at one another as they gallop along," remarked J.G. Wood in 1870. "Then a general fight takes place, the whole of the dogs tumbling over one another and entangling the traces in a manner that none but an Esquimaux [Inuit] could hope to disentangle."

Canoe Dogs

In addition to the more familiar sled dogs used by the Inuit and other nomadic tribes, there were substantial populations of Indian dogs who bore no resemblance to wolves. Robust, long-backed dogs with short legs were just one of a variety of canines common to widely divergent parts of the New World, as hinted at by a number of nineteenth-century observers who, sadly, only mentioned the dogs briefly as they documented their travels. An 1877 account by S.T. Livermore listed a colony of such short-legged dogs native to Rhode Island, "with a fierce disposition that makes little distinction between friend and foe." (Zoologist John Richardson told a similar story in 1829, adding that he had seen them living with tribes farther south as well.) And an 1860s railroad surveyor in California noticed a "peculiar looking dog on the Eel River among very wild Indians, with short legs and a long body, like a Turnspit," who was the beloved playmate of women and children.

Little other information exists about these dogs, although canines matching their description are known to have been prized hunting companions of Canadian and New England forest-dwellers who canoed

Modern "Canoe Dog" living among the Chibugamau Cree Indians of Canada.
source: Royce McWharter.

through hundreds of miles of inland waterways hunting beaver to appease Europe's growing appetite for furs in the seventeenth century, and distinctive, stout-bodied, short-legged dogs still live and boat with some Cree Indians along the forested inland waterways of southeastern Canada to this day.

"When [the] dogs encounter a beaver outside its house, they pursue and take it easily," wrote a Jesuit priest in 1633 while living in Quebec. Even in periods of famine, the Indians could not be persuaded to sacrifice their dogs, threatening that "if the dog was killed to be eaten, a man would be killed by blows from an axe." An account in an 1897 issue of *Forest and Stream* brings to mind Old World breeds such as Dachshunds and Rat Terriers trained to fetch formidable game such as badgers from underground burrows; apparently, the Cheyenne employed short-legged dogs who were "small enough to enter the [beaver lodge hole] and worry the beaver till it followed the dog out, when an Indian waiting outside clubbed [it] to death."

Alcos and Wool Dogs

Another Indian dog known to New World explorers as the Techichi (Technichi or Alco) was small and sprightly, with erect ears and a curling tail. It lived predominantly in farming communities throughout the Southwest and parts of northern Mexico, although similar dogs also were reported in Canada and even along the North Atlantic seaboard. But whether the regional populations were genetically related is not known. Environmental or social pressures could have resulted in the creation of similar yet unrelated canine varieties.

In his 1578 diary, Francisco Hernández dismissed the Techichi with a few words, saying only that it was one of three types of Mexican dogs and "similar to our spaniels"—then admitted that he had never actually seen one. While living with Pueblo Indians around 1590, the Jesuit priest Juan de Acosta saw many Techichi and reported that the natives "love so these little dogges that they will spare their meat to feed them, [and] keep them only for company." In later centuries, attempts to locate living examples of Techichi were unsuccessful, leaving modern historians to speculate that the introduction of Old World diseases or outcrossings with Spanish dogs contributed to their extinction—theories bolstered by the absence of eye-

The Lost History of the Canine Race

CANIS.

A spotted Techichi (right), cowers in the presence of an Old World Mastiff, in this engraving made around 1800.
source: Allen Sims and Lynn Carson.

witness accounts of the dogs after 1800. In *The Naturalists' Library* (1840), author Hamilton Smith reported no luck in finding anyone who had seen the Techichi, leaving him to describe the dogs from one poorly taxidermied specimen on display along with other "Mexican curiosities" at the British Museum. "We at first considered it to be a Newfoundland puppy. It was small with a rather large head and in color it was not entirely white excepting a large black spot covering each ear and another spot on the rump. How much of its appearance is due to the taxidermist's efforts, however, is to be considered."

Pre-Columbian petroglyphs found as far south as Peru depict small spotted dogs accompanying their masters as they hunt birds, small mammals, and deer. Excavations at ancient cliff pueblos have uncovered fragments of nets that might have been used to snare rabbits or small birds, and an account of Paiute hunting techniques by western explorer J.W. Powell suggests a scenario of how such dogs might have been employed in prehistoric times. A hand-knotted net, "a hundred yards in length, is placed in a half-circular position with wings of sage brush. They then have a circle hunt [with dogs] and drive great numbers of rabbits in the snare, where they are shot with arrows."

Archeologists photographed this two-thousand-year-old burial cyst in White Dog Cave upon its discovery in 1907. One of two mummified dogs found in the cyst can be seen lying on top of a carrying basket on the right.
source: Peabody Museum of Archaeology and Ethnology, Cambridge, Massachusetts.

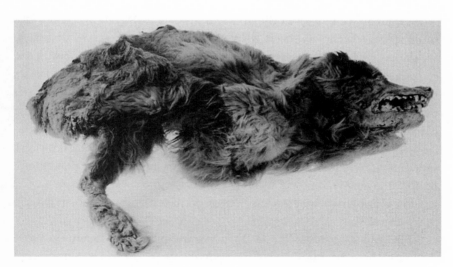

A naturally mummified spitz-type dog, recovered from White Dog Cave (shown above).
source: Peabody Museum of Archaeology and Ethnology, Cambridge, Massachusetts.

A naturally mummified Techichi, also recovered from the burial cyst in White Dog Cave. source: Peabody Museum of Archaeology and Ethnology, Cambridge, Massachusetts.

Tantalizing clues about the Techichi may yet await discovery in a museum storage facility at Harvard University, in the form of two singularly well-preserved dogs recovered in 1907 from an ancient settlement in the cliffs of northeastern Arizona. Estimated to be at least two thousand years old, the small spotted puppy and larger, buff-colored, Spitz-like dog were buried with two humans, along with carrying baskets, a finely woven fur blanket, a tumpline (strap slung across the forehead to support a load carried on the back), and a pad made of dog hair. Seventy years ago these specimens could not be studied without destroying them, but new nonintrusive imaging techniques such as X-ray tomography (CAT scans) could yield new information about the lives of prehistoric people and animals in the Southwest.

The "Spitz" found in White Dog Cave was probably the same as those described by a Spaniard named Mendoza, the traveling companion of Francisco Coronado, in his 1540 report to the King of Spain. At the Cibola Pueblo (present-day Zuni), Mendoza observed "hairy animals, like the

Wool dog sashes retrieved from a pre-Columbian site in southeastern Arizona. source: Arizona State Museum, the University of Arizona, Tucson.

large Spanish hounds, which they shear and make long colored wigs from the hair, like this one which I send your Lordship." In modern times, several examples of textiles made from dog hair have been recovered from pre-Columbian sites in the Southwest, most notably a cache of six intricately woven decorative sashes and a small pot of unspun dog wool from Obelisk Cave in Arizona.

Woolly dogs similar to those in the Southwest also lived with coastal Indians in the Northwest, where British navigator George Vancouver said they had been numerous prior to the introduction of sheep. Valued for its remarkable softness and warmth, dog fur was woven into blankets and clothing after being mixed with the sheddings of wild mountain goats, eiderdown, or pounded and spun cedar bark. In 1798, Vancouver was received by forty of these dogs at Puget Sound, "all shorn as close to the skin as sheep are in England. So compact were their fleeces that large portions could be lifted up by a corner without causing any separation." Thirty years earlier, British explorer J.K. Lord saw the same white, long-haired

Painting by Paul Kane titled *Clal-lum Woman Weaving a Blanket,* with wool dog in the foreground.
source: Royal Ontario Museum, Toronto.

dogs in Vancouver confined by the tribes "on small islands to prevent their escaping." (Such quarantines could have been prevented outcrossings with other canines.) Since it is questionable that Indians employed shears or scissors to remove the dogs' fur—unless they obtained the instruments through trade with Europeans—prehistoric Indians probably combed their dogs at the end of each winter to collect loosening clumps of wool. Tragically, the wool dogs vanished soon after the introduction of inexpensive, mass-produced Hudson's Bay Company trade blankets at the turn of the century.

Sacred Dogs

Perhaps the most unusual of native canine varieties, the Xoloitzcuintli (pronounced show-low-EATS-queent-lee), a sleek hairless dog, was a popular companion animal with Indians throughout much of Latin America. Evidence of these dogs, in the form of ceramic sculptures and wall paintings, dates back to 3500 B.C., but the exact circumstances under which hairless canines came into existence and were cultivated by ancient New Worlders remains a mystery. Several unlikely theories have been put forward over the years to account for their distinctive lack of fur, some crediting their origins to virtually anyone save the Indians who lived with them. But there is no evidence to support the notion that Xolos originated in ancient Egypt or elsewhere in Africa, or that they crossed the Bering Strait with the first New World inhabitants at the end of the Ice Age. Modern genetic research has already revealed that hairlessness is a mutation common to many mammals, even humans, cats, and horses (and in time may yield new information about the origin of these dogs). It is not unreasonable, then, to assume that the Xolo first appeared in Latin America as an unexpected mutation and was cultivated into a "breed" over successive generations.

The sight of a dog with smooth, naked skin who perspired and tanned like humans inspired deification. Ancient Toltecs and Mayans, whose vast agricultural/trade empires dominated the southern half of the Western Hemisphere already believed that the love of a dog for its master was the most perfect manifestation of selflessness. This philosophy, combined with dogs who seemed partly human, inevitably it seems, resulted in the belief that Xolos were earthly observers for the deities of truth and goodness.

Xolos exhibited a variety of colors, ranging from light ash to purplish black and brilliant bronze, hues imbued with spiritual symbolism, as evi-

Xoloitzcuintli pups of differing colors.
source: Countess Lascelles de Premio Real.

denced by the Toltec tradition of sacrificing chocolate-colored dogs to honor the god of cacao. Royally pampered with lavish meals of freshly baked, sweetened corn cakes or potato and Guinea pig stew (the only other mammal cultivated by prehistoric Indians), they often slept on soft blankets or in people's beds. The price for such indulgence was heavy, however, since most dogs were killed on the death of their owners to serve as their guides in the afterlife—here again we encounter the belief that the animal's spirit accompanied the human soul to the brink of heaven, testifying to the past conduct of the deceased and helping to determine whether entry into eternity would be granted.

Around A.D. 1200, when the warring Aztecs overthrew the Toltecs to establish an empire of their own, the sweet life of Xolos came to an end. Although the conquering tribe absorbed some aspects of Toltec culture, the Aztecs used religion as an excuse for canine slaughter, and these once-revered living representatives of spirits in the netherworld now were coveted as culinary delicacies. Natural calamities and holy holidays triggered mass sacrifices, particularly if the rains failed and crops withered as a consequence. Transported on flower-decorated litters to sacrificial altars, dozens of Xolos would be ritually slain, their hearts cut out (as were human sacrifices) and their flesh consumed by the masses.

Travois Dogs and Canine "Degenerates"

The acquisition of horses in the mid-1700s revolutionized western Native American Plains cultures, transforming struggling, subsistence-level societies into the most prosperous and powerful hunter-gatherers in the world. But through much of the nineteenth century, even after horses became an integral part of Plains tribes from Canada to Mexico, dogs continued to be relied on as beasts of burden. Often more coyote or dingo-like in appearance than their wolfish Inuit peers in the north, Plains Indian dogs were used primarily for backpacking camp goods or dragging luggage-laden *travois*. One of the earliest mentions of travois dogs comes from Coronado's account of his 1540 journey through the Texas Plains, where he encountered a migrating band of Haxa Indians north of the Pecos River. "They travel like the Arabs, with their tents and troops of dogs loaded with poles and Moorish pack saddles and girths. When the load gets disarranged, the dogs howl, calling someone to fix them right." One of the explorer's men, in mentioning the same encounter, added that some dogs were burdened with both satchels and travois, which made "their backs sore on the withers like pack animals." Such work could be perilous as well, because hungry wolves often followed the tribal migrations, stalking, killing, and eating straggling, overburdened dogs.

"Five or six hundred wigwams, with all their furniture, may be seen drawn out for miles, creeping over the grass-covered plains of this country," wrote nineteenth-century Indian portraitist George Catlin after witnessing a tribe of several thousand Plains Indians on the move:

> Three times that number of men [on horses] stroll along in front or on the flank . . . [and] at least five times that number of dogs fall into the rank, following in the company of the women. Every cur is encumbered with a sled on which he patiently drags his load—a part of the household goods and furniture of the lodge to which he belongs. Two poles, about fifteen feet long, were placed upon the dog's shoulder in the same manner [as the horses], leaving the larger ends to drag upon the ground behind him. With it he trots off amid the throng of dogs and squaws, faithfully and cheerfully dragging his load till night and occasionally loitering by the way.

After accompanying a Comanche tribal migration in 1834, Catlin remarked that, "many dogs and squaws are traveling in such a confused mass, with so many conflicting interests and so many local and individual rights to be pertinaciously protected. Each dog, that is, each dog that *will* do it (and there are many that will *not*), dragging his pallet on a couple of poles, and each squaw with her load, often bring them into general conflict, commencing usually among the dogs and sure to result in fisticuffs of the women—whilst the men, riding leisurely, take infinite pleasure in overlooking these desperate conflicts, at which they are sure to have a laugh and as sure to never lend a hand."

Such firsthand accounts of Native American dogs are quite rare, as are drawings and photographs, contributing to the mystery surrounding Indian dogs and their roles in native cultures. Unlike Catlin, most nineteenth-century essayists who did write about Indians usually had never met an

Indian, much less an Indian dog, and simply echoed the popular bias of the time against "heathens." Writers were eager to condemn the appearance, intelligence, and belief systems of aboriginal peoples—even the foremost university scholars could not resist the temptation to throw scientific objectivity to the wind. Calipers in hand, anthropologists busied themselves comparing the minute details of the physiques of aboriginal peoples to Christian, "civilized" Caucasians, gleefully pointing out any differences as evidence of racial inferiority. "A singular intellectual defect has been noticed in [Amerindians], and it is doubtless connected with a peculiarity in the configuration of the head," wrote the author of an English mid-nineteenth-century tome titled *The Natural History of Man*. "The intellectual and moral character of the Europeans is deteriorated by the mixture of red blood, while an infusion of white blood tends to improve and ennoble the qualities of the dark varieties."

Just as Native American people were portrayed as biological degenerates, so were their dogs, who were dismissed as coyotes and wolves, the popular enemies of civilization's divine plan to design a new order in the natural world. Native canines were subject to derisive comparisons with Old World "pure" breeds, leading naturally to the conclusion that they were inferior creatures (just like their masters), even a "notch below" the mongrels of Europe. The more "domesticated"-looking Indian dogs weren't above the criticisms, either, as evidenced by Carl Linnaeus's description of the Techichi, which despite its similarity to "the small dogs of Europe, [is] wild and [has] a melancholy air."

The notion of a genetic affiliation between pedigreed European dogs and wolves had to be challenged, lest anyone attack such Indian dog judgments as askew or hypocritical. Dr. B.S. Barton absolved himself of such heresy by asserting in an 1803 essay that Indian dog lineages were "much more that of the wolf than of common domesticated dogs. Our dogs, once attacked by these Indian dogs, always shun them. It is very curious that the Indian dog will never attack or pursue the wolf, which common dogs readily do. . . . They have less fidelity and will steal from their masters. In short, everything shows that the Indian dog is a much more imperfect animal than the common dog." Mrs. R. Lee, author of *Anecdotes of Animals* (1864), wrote that domesticated dogs would hunt down and kill aboriginal canines, but "show signs of great disgust afterwards, always, if they can, plunging themselves into water to rid themselves of the contamination caused by such contact." Negative sentiments toward Native American dogs penned in earlier times were repeated as gospel by experts in this century as well, including the National Geographic Society's *Book of Dogs* (1927), which derided the Xolos of Mexico as "degenerate . . . for the purposes of a dog, they are useless."

Further evidence of the depravity of the Indian mind was sought in accounts of their alleged cruelty to dogs. "Owing to the scanty allowance of food, the Indian dogs are often so weak that they are obliged to lean against a tree or some other prop whilst they bark," one writer claimed in the late 1700s. Passages describing Native American conduct in a 1788 work titled *The History of America* added to the wave of condemnation. "Instead of that fond attachment which the hunter naturally feels toward those useful companions of his toils, the [Indians] requite their services with neglect, seldom feed and never caress them." At least Barton conceded that the precarious nature of aboriginal life sometimes left little room for emotional attachments to animals who "must share in the hardships of his state. The miserable condition of the Indian dogs is a necessary result of the miserable condition of the Indians themselves."

Western military explorer Lieutenant John Frémont was invited to a Plains Indian tribal feast in his honor in 1845, where chunks of dog flesh simmered "in a large pot over the fire in the middle of the lodge, and immediately on our arrival was dished up in large wooden bowls, one of which was handed to each. [It had] something of the flavor and appearance of mutton. Feeling something move behind me, I looked around and found that I had taken my seat among a litter of fat young puppies."

While living with the eastern Sioux, Catlin, too, was one of several Anglo guests at an honorary dog feast. Eight kettles, each filled with "a huge quantity of dogs' flesh floating in a profusion of rich gravy," was served with great formality after the chief announced, "We give you our hearts in this feast. We have killed our faithful dogs to feed you—and the Great Spirit will seal our friendship. I have no more to say." If his accounts of Plains Indian life in its golden era are taken at face value, the killing and eating of dogs was not so much evidence of cruelty to animals as an intimate gesture of lasting friendship. Catlin was one of the few observers of the time to recognize the deeper significance of dog sacrifice:

Among all Indian tribes the dog is more valued than among any part of the civilized world. They hunt together and are equal sharers in the chase. Their bed is one. On rocks and on their coats of arms they carve his image as the symbol of fidelity. Yet the Indian will sacrifice this faithful follower to seal a sacred pledge of friendship he has made. I have seen the master take from the bowl the head of his victim and talk of its former affection and fidelity with tears in his eyes. And I have seen civilized men by my side jesting and sneering at Indian folly and stupidity. I have said in my heart they never deserved a name as honorable as that of the animal whose bones they were picking.

Untransacted Destinies

The forced unification of the New World with the Old, a process begun by the Spanish in the fifteenth century, was catastrophic for Indians in both North and Latin America as their cultures and societies were altered by incoming Europeans, livestock, industrial and agricultural development, and foreign belief systems. Decimated by epidemics, famine, and war, the native human population had plunged 90 percent by 1880, and as devastating as these factors were for people, they were even more apocalyptic for canines.

Like their masters, Spanish dogs and pigs carried a dangerous medley of diseases for which there was no natural resistance in the native animal population. Something as simple as a mild case of kennel cough could spread and kill swiftly, leaving villages that once reverberated with barking silent and void of canine life. Enterprising conquistadors and missionaries arrived ill-equipped to feed their own troops or followers, and quickly took advantage of native hospitality, deleting stores of beans, maize, potatoes, or other staples. And from the beginning, Spanish culinary attentions focused on the temptingly plump, hairless canines found in abundance in native villages. The few Xolos who survived the attacks of vicious, combat-trained Alaunts were at risk of slaughter to supply meat for both Spanish dogs and people. As one Portuguese observer dryly remarked, "he who could catch a dog in any village thought himself a happy man, but the soldier that sent not a quarter to his captain suffered for it, paying dear for his incivilities." Apparently the Spanish were not above killing native dogs sim-

Excavations on St. Simons Island off the coast of Georgia uncovered this Native American dog burial. The animal, whose hind leg was shattered by a Spanish musket ball, was likely shot in 1526 by Pedro de Quejo or one of his men during their failed attempt to establish a colony on the southeastern coast of North America.
source: Jerald T. Milanich.

ply for spite either, for in 1575 Francisco de Toledo, the viceroy of Peru, ordered that all the Indians' dogs be slain in retaliation for an assault on a Christian messenger.

Genetic contamination of native dog lineages by Old World stock probably began with the first contacts. By 1820, travois dogs of the northern Plains had been largely replaced by Newfoundland hybrids, the progeny of British canines originally introduced into the Hudson Bay area. Such intermixing proved the undoing of Inuit dogs, as the last of their kind vanished into a canine "melting pot" of Newfoundlands, German Shepherds, Collies, and St. Bernards brought along by miners to pull sleds and small mining cars during the Klondike gold rush.

"The untransacted destiny of the American people is to subdue the continent, to rush over this fast field to the Pacific Ocean," said Manifest Destiny political orator William Gilpin in 1846, as the United States embraced war with Mexico over vast stretches of western territories in North America—the first of many events to clear the way for the largest peacetime migration in human history. Over the next five decades, millions of European immigrants would settle the West, encouraged by passage of the Homestead Act, the discovery of gold in California, South Dakota, Wyoming, and Alaska, and completion of the first transcontinental railroad in 1869.

Hunter-gatherer societies and their claims to ancestral territories were viewed by many people as obstacles to an almost holy mission to "civilize" territories west of the Mississippi. The Indians, with their pagan customs, not only obstructed this "progress" but actually were an evil presence to be eradicated along with other indomitable pests, particularly wolves and coy-otes, who were accused of livestock predation. Acting in the interests of its growing citizenry, the U.S. government refused to enact legislation to protect the buffalo, effectively paving the way for their wholesale slaughter, and not incidentally, the destruction of Indians who depended on them for sustenance. In less than a decade, hide collectors had decimated the herds, and by 1900 only a thousand animals still survived. As intended, this was devastating to the Plains tribes.

Any resistance by the Indians was harshly dealt with by U.S. military forces. "It was the grandest demonstration by the army ever seen in the west," wrote an eastern reporter assigned to cover the massacre of Black Kettle's band of Cheyenne at Sand Creek, Colorado, in 1864. More than three hundred Indian men, women and children perished, caught in a hailstorm of bullets, their bodies bayoneted, stripped, mutilated, and scalped, their camps set afire and belongings plundered. Government soldiers were not always satisfied with killing the Indians, but rounded up the dogs and ponies for torture or execution as well. (The genocidal campaign would finally climax with the battle at Wounded Knee in 1890, after which surviving Plains Indians were banished to inhospitable reservations.)

"The red man is fast disappearing from the continent over which his fathers once held undisputed sovereignty," commented an insightful reporter for the *Illustrated London News* in 1860. "He will, in all probability, become as wholly a thing of history as the aboriginal Briton that opposed the landing of Julius Caesar." The few canines who did manage to survive the Indian Wars faced further peril due to their physical resemblance to wolves and coyotes. Who knows how many of these dogs, torn from their human families and hopelessly lost, wandered onto farms or ranches, attracted by kitchen smells or the sounds of laughter, only to be shot as predators? Some Plains Indian dogs probably abandoned all affiliation with people to join roaming bands of coyotes or wolves, eventually fading into a vast, wild gene pool. Life as an adopted member of the wolf community was not without difficulty, either, since they were adversely affected by the decimation of native game populations. Cattle and sheep often were the only alternative to starvation for feral dogs and wolves, so ranchers retaliated with strychnine-laced bacon bait or engaged in a form of "ranch sport"—lassoing, dragging, beating, and shooting wolves they encountered

Oil painting on canvas by Charles M. Russell titled *Cowboy Sport—Roping a Wolf*, 1890.
source: Courtesy Sid Richardson Collection of Western Art, Fort Worth, Texas.

on the range. By 1900, the packs of travois dogs that once numbered in the thousands were but a childhood memory for most tribal elders.

Last of the Tahl Tans

Similar in appearance to the small, spotted Techichi of the Southwest, Tahl Tan Bear Dogs were treasured as hunting assistants by inland northern tribes such as the Tlingit, Casca, and Tahl Tan Indians, who used the animals to corner dangerous game, including caribou, lynx, and most notably, black bears. Nineteenth-century northern explorers described them as "a smaller size than the Esquimaux breed but with broad feet, which prevent [them] from sinking into the snow. One, only seven months old, ran beside his gentlemen's sledge for nine hundred miles, frequently carrying one of his masters mittens in his mouth."

Efforts to save the Tahl Tan Bear Dog from extinction have proven unsuccessful, despite seven decades of decline noted by zoologists, ethnographers, and dog fanciers. The Canadian Kennel Club recognized the breed but by 1948 had registered only fifteen dogs, all owned by one woman. In the early fifties, she packed up her kennel and moved to California. Subsequent efforts to track the woman and her Tahl Tans have failed.

Nancy Dill, the last Tahl Tan Bear Dog.
source: Leslie Kopas.

John Carilick, a Tahl Tan Indian elder, recalled that "they were very smart dogs. They could find a bear's den through deep snow [and] chase up grouse and ptarmigan. They could find rabbits, anything—if you had a bear dog you could find game; if you didn't, you starved." The dogs' decline began around 1900, as bows and arrows (and antique muzzle loaders) were replaced by high-powered, long-range rifles, rendering the small canines obsolete so far as many Indians were concerned. Outsiders, particularly one big-game outfitter named J. Frank Callbreath, exported dozens of the dogs to wealthy clients as far away as Southern California, inadvertently accelerating the depletion of local breeding stock. Once in lower altitudes, some of them succumbed to contagious diseases, unfamiliar diets, and heat exhaustion caused by warmer, damper climates (the fate of most exported dogs was either never recorded or lost over time). Also, trading parties of Tlingit Indians reported that the Tahl Tan Bear Dogs they acquired in exchanges of goods quickly sickened upon reaching the Coast, invariably perishing from "pulmonary troubles." After decades of disorganized, halfhearted attempts to promote the breed, all hope of saving the Tahl Tan Bear Dog ended in 1979 with the death of Nancy Dill, the last known unspayed female, never having been mated with her own kind.

Leslie Kopas, a Canadian freelance writer, tracked down the last Tahl Tan Bear Dogs and photographed Nancy Dill. He believes the breed was rendered obsolete by technological innovations and cultural contamination. "When the Indians no longer needed the breed because Europeans had caused a change in their way of procuring sustenance, they stopped protecting the dog. Sled dogs often killed them. If the snowmobile had been invented before the rifle, the sled dogs would have disappeared first, and the Tahl Tan Bear Dog might have survived." Delicate physiologies tailored by centuries of isolation in the rural far north made the dogs intolerant of other climates or an artificial, urbanized lifestyle, and in Kopas's opinion, "the Canadian Kennel Club was acting in ignorance when it registered them—it had expectations that could not be met."

In light of such tragic history, it is remarkable that any Native American dogs have survived to modern times in their original state, but some efforts to save the dogs from oblivion have indeed been successful. Acknowledging the importance of preserving their native heritage in the late forties, the Mexican government sponsored a project to collect remaining examples of hairless dogs. Countess Lascelles de Premio Real was among a team of dog enthusiasts who spent months canvassing isolated mountain villages rumored to still keep hairless dogs, but most Indians were suspicious of outsiders and reluctant to help. "The villagers would say, 'Oh, yes, I had a Xolo but gave it to my brother/uncle/cousin' They just were not anxious to sell us any animals," the countess recalled in 1991. "I should mention that although Mexico has a liberal quota of stray and abandoned dogs, one never sees a homeless Xolo wandering about."

Jealously guarded by owners who still honor ancient beliefs in the dogs' mythical curative powers, Xolos often are secreted away by their Indian caretakers. Even so, project participants eventually obtained several dogs and in 1956 the Mexican dog show world formally recognized the Xolo as a true breed, even going so far as to classify them as "working dogs" in deference to their heritage as healers and spiritual guides. The Mexican government then declared the Xolo a living national treasure and put its likeness on postage stamps. Today they often are seen at specialty dog shows in Mexico, the United States, and Europe, and are becoming increasingly popular as elegant household companions, often touted as ideal animal companions for people allergic to dog hair and dander.

More recently a small group of feral Indian dogs believed to be virtually unchanged since prehistoric times was discovered in the remote forests of South Carolina. Possibly descended from dogs left behind by the Cherokees when they were forced off ancestral farms in the early 1800s, these canines retreated into the wild and were forgotten by the outside world. Named for their home state, Carolina Dogs are Dingo-like in appearance and weigh around forty pounds, with short, dense, reddish brown or beige fur and wolf-like heads. University of Georgia zoologist I. Lehr Brisbin collected quite a few of the animals (including some who were mistaken as strays by animal control authorities and impounded) and created the first official Carolina Dog kennel, the goal being to establish a breeding standard by which the animals can be preserved and perpetuated in captivity, and in the process, shed new light on prehistoric canine physiology and behavior.

Bart the Carolina Dog.
source: Hazel Campbell.

Like the New Guinea Singing Dogs, many of the Carolina Dogs have now been reintroduced to human society, and have adjusted to life as household pets. Until his death in 1994, Bart the Carolina Dog was a cherished member of the family of Tom and Hazel Campbell. In many ways, the Campbells report, he was a gentle, devoted pet, no different from any other happy companion animal, although he retained much of his wild instinct, playfully attacking food, even pouncing on something as tame as a doggie biscuit.

In the wild, Carolina Dogs live in extended family units much like wolves and work cooperatively to hunt feral hogs, rabbits, and birds. Floridian Ralph Wright owns a female named Ogeechee and believes the Carolina Dog is superior to traditional Old World hunting breeds. "When a Beagle spots a rabbit and begins the chase, the pack follows the quarry," he says. "Not so with the Carolina Dogs. The one who sees the rabbit first begins the chase while the others go out at angles, heading off not straight after the animal but to the right and left of it. This might not make sense to someone watching the pursuit, until they realize that a rabbit always runs in circles. When the rabbit veers to the left or right, a dog on the periphery will catch it." Carolina Dogs also habitually bury their feces, a hitherto undocumented behavioral trait in any canine population. Most frequently seen among nursing mothers, Carolina Dogs use their nose and paws to cover their feces with sand, a behavior that may have resulted from the need to conceal their offsprings' presence from sharp-nosed predators in the wild. "When I leave Ogeechee's droppings in her pen, she reaches through the chain-link fence with a paw to pull in dirt to cover the waste," Wright says. "Also, she has the strangest habit of urinating while standing upright, with her front paws on the fence, but I think this is just one of her quirks."

Farther west, some attempts have been made to seek out surviving, unadulterated Plains Indian travois dogs, but with questionable results. The remote corners of western Indian reservations have been combed for surviving native dogs, but it has proven difficult to determine and document the true heritage of the animals found, even though some look very much like Plains-type dogs. Considering the Plains Indians' cultural upheaval over the last hundred years, and the lack of documentation of dog lineage histories, it is difficult if not impossible to state conclusively

Crow Indians (a Plains tribe) some time after the turn of the century, in the company of a hybrid or non-native dog.
source: Author.

whether collected animals are "purebred" travois dogs, mixed Old World breeds, or wolf hybrids.

The problems inherent in trying to determine whether a canine is truly "native" raise the question of whether any aboriginal dogs can be accurately preserved on the advent of the twenty-first century when the fluctuating natural and cultural environments that molded their development no longer exist. Indian dogs cannot conform to modern society's inflexible definition of a breed without undergoing radical changes brought about by the application of Old World pedigree systems. Miniaturized Xolos have appeared in recent decades, for example, and in 1994 the Xoloitzcuintli Club of America debated the policy of recognizing the minority of "powderpuffs" (haired Xolos) born in most litters, who resemble Techichis as adults. The argument to reclassify powderpuffs as flawed animals was inspired by the Mexican Kennel Club's long-standing tradition of regarding the haired variety as degenerate, even though evidence that the Toltecs or Aztecs ever culled haired dogs is lacking. Moreover, the role of these dogs in maintaining a healthy gene pool remains to be fully determined.

There is no easy answer to the dilemma of how to preserve native dogs as they were in earlier times. The modern definition of the word "breed" stresses conformity to minute physical details. By its very nature, the institutionalized fancy demands the elimination of variations in appearance that are historically characteristic of so many aboriginal dogs. This is true particularly of those living in migratory societies, who were the products of genetic mixtures occasioned by contacts with other groups as well as their wild cousins—representing centuries of interactions between regions and cultures. As zooarchaeologist Stanley Olsen points out, Indian dog varieties are difficult to compartmentalize because they "grade into one another in size [and] form if a large enough collection is examined." In this sense, Olsen observes, "prehistoric Indian dogs were not registered American Kennel Club breeds, but were instead free-breeding, socializing mongrels."

As great as the loss of aboriginal dog varieties may be, the loss of personal and cultural lore inspired by Indian dogs is equally significant. The impact of the dog on the Native American psyche may never be fully comprehended, although surviving bits of history hint at the deeper importance of dogs beyond that of simple beasts of burden, and that they played a pivotal role in planting seeds of compassion in the hearts of their owners, just as dogs do in other societies today. For the modern world, Native American dogs are reminders that humans living in divergent circumstances and time periods are also inspired to both laughter and tears by dogs, who like their descendants, offered unconditional comfort and companionship. As such, surviving Indian dogs embody the experiences and aspirations of people who lived centuries ago; they are emotional links to a distant but nonetheless shared past, where dogs were the only creature companions humans could depend on in an otherwise inhospitable world.

The true significance of Indian dogs—those "other" Native Americans—remains to be fully realized, not simply as dusty, forgotten museum specimens or snatches of exaggerated trivia in out-of-print volumes, but as reminders of the importance of steadfast animal companionship. Whether in our day-to-day lives or in metaphor and myth, dogs remain a part of who we are, not only in ancient tales but in the present, as demonstrated in this contemporary Native American commentary:

An impoverished Tlingit woman and pack dogs in Valdez Creek, Alaska, ca. 1920.
source: Author.

We don't think much of the white man's elections. Whoever wins, we Indians always lose. Well, we have a little story about elections. Once a long time ago, the dogs were trying to elect a president. One of them said, "I nominate the bulldog for president. He's strong and can fight."

"But he can't run," said another dog. "What good is a fighter who can't run? He won't catch anybody." Then another dog said, "I nominate the greyhound because he sure can run." The other dogs cried, "But he can't fight. When he catches up with somebody, he gets the hell beaten out of him!"

Then an ugly little mutt jumped up and said, "I nominate that dog for president who smells good underneath his tail." And immediately an equally ugly mutt jumped up and yelled, "I second the motion." At once all the dogs started sniffing underneath each other's tails. A big chorus went up:

"Phew, he doesn't smell good under his tail."

"No, neither does this one."

"He's no presidential timber!"

"No, he's no good, either."

"This one sure isn't the people's choice."

"Wow, this ain't my candidate!"

When you go out for a walk, just watch the dogs. They're still sniffing underneath each other's tails. They're looking for a good leader, and they still haven't found him.

—Lame Deer (South Dakota Brule Sioux), 1969

Eight

The Dogs of War

S INCE THEIR TASK was to literally tear the enemy troops to bits, war dogs were valued for their strength and savage personalities, as demonstrated by the zeal with which Spanish conquistadors unleashed bloodthirsty Alaunts such as Becerrillo on scantily clothed and poorly armed Indians in the sixteenth century. It was an idea that would continue to be popular well into the eighteenth century, even in colonial America. Benjamin Franklin suggested that dogs be incorporated into the militia because the animals' keen hearing and sense of smell could help protect citizens from Indian (and British) ambush. Writing to a colleague, he was of the opinion that such dogs should be:

> . . . large, strong and fierce. . . . Only when the party come near thick woods and suspicious places should they turn out a dog or two to search them. In case of meeting a party of the enemy, the dogs are all then to be turned loose and set on. They will be fresher and finer for having been previously confined. . . . This was the Spanish method of guarding their marches.

The employment of war dogs was urged by John Penn, the Lieutenant Governor of Pennsylvania between 1763 and 1771. In a letter to James Young, Paymaster and Commissioner of Musters, he proposed that "every Soldier be allowed three shillings per month who brings with him a strong Dog that shall be judged proper to be employed in discovering and pursuing the Savages."

But no action was taken to implement dogs, not even after the Revolution of 1776. In 1779 yet another plea for war dogs was made, this time by William McClay of Pennsylvania's Supreme Executive Council. "I have sustained some Ridicule for a Scheme which I have long recommended, that of hunting the Scalping Parties with Horsemen and Dogs," he wrote in 1779, recalling that "it was in this Manner That the Indians were extirpated out of whole Countrys in South America."

Even Napoleon overcame a personal distaste for dogs (Josephine's lapdog frequently bit him), and understood the advantages of canine sentries during his Egyptian Campaign. Lured by campsite garbage, pariah dogs prowled the perimeter of his fortifications and alerted to any strange noise or movement. The Emperor took more deliberate steps to incorporate dogs into his militia in 1798 by chaining a number of large, aggressive hounds to the walls surrounding Alexandria.

Considering that Napoleon was not really a dog lover at heart, what he later wrote about seeing a dead soldier during a battlefield inspection at the end of his Italian Campaign is all the more remarkable. Sitting by the body was a small dog, crying and licking the man's hand. "No occurrence of any of my other battlefields impressed me so keenly," he said, explaining that:

> This soldier, I realized, must have had friends at home and in his regiment, yet he lay there deserted by all except his dog. . . . I had looked on, unmoved, at battles which decided the future of nations. Tearless, I had given orders which brought death to thousands. Yet here I was stirred—profoundly stirred—stirred to tears. And by what? By the grief of one dog. I am certain that at that instant I felt more ready than any other time to show mercy toward a supplicant foeman. I could understand just then the tinge of mercy which led Achilles to yield the corpse of his enemy, Hector, to the weeping Priam.

During the American Civil War (1861–64), dogs who were inclined toward viciousness found employment in the military as prison guards. Spot, a 150-pound "Cuban Bloodhound," was one of a pack of thirteen ill-tempered dogs owned by Captain Henry Wirz at the infamous Andersonville Prison in Georgia. According to eyewitnesses, his pack was kept "for the purpose of recapturing Union soldiers who had escaped," and fugitives "frequently were killed or mutilated by these dogs." Many attempts were made on Spot's life, but he survived to live out his remaining days in civilian life with the captain.

Confederate and Union soldiers alike adopted dogs they found wandering the war-torn countryside and made them regimental pets or mascots. The mere presence of a friendly dog could work wonders for the morale of troops who were hundreds of miles from home. Fan, the pet of Captain J.W. Byron of the 88th New York, repeatedly demonstrated her bravery under fire, according to an eyewitness who wrote:

> Fan went into every battle, and while the firing was brisk lay down behind a big log or in some other secure place. And when a lull would follow she'd sally out and run along the regiment to see if any of her friends were killed or hurt. She was very much attached to [one] man of the company, who during the firing fell mortally wounded. When Fan came up to him, she threw herself on him and cried. She wept and licked him, while the poor fellow would throw out his hand to pat her as he feebly exclaimed, "Poor Fan! Poor Fan!"

Volunteer firemen in Pennsylvania's 102nd Infantry brought along a spotted Bull Terrier named Jack, who stayed with the regiment through the entire war, taking part in battles in Maryland and Virginia. Like Fan, he searched for wounded soldiers after each skirmish. Jack shared everything with his human comrades, even being captured by the Confederates at Salem Church, Virginia, in 1863. After a six-month incarceration he was

Jack the Union mascot.
source: Soldiers and Sailors Memorial Hall, Pittsburgh.

exchanged for a human Confederate prisoner at Belle Isle. Later, at Malvern Hill, the somber terrier was shot through the back and shoulder and for several days hovered near death. Thanks to the tender ministerings of his friends, he recovered, only to be wounded twice more. While on furlough in Pittsburgh in August 1864, the 102nd Regiment held a ball and collected seventy-five dollars—an incredible sum at that time—to purchase a silver collar and honorary medal for Jack. Then on December 24 in Frederick, Maryland, Jack vanished and was never seen again—the men sadly concluded their champion had been ambushed and killed for his valuable neckwear.

England also had its share of unofficial war dogs, such as Bobbie, mascot of the 66th British Regiment. He went into action during the Afghan War of 1879 and was wounded in the Battle of Maiwand. Queen Victoria personally decorated the hound for his valor in 1881—just before he was run over and killed by a carriage.

Dogs of the Great War

At the onset of the First World War, Germany had fifty thousand dogs trained and ready for combat, leaving Allied forces with the dilemma of how to acquire dogs of their own in time to assist troops at the front. Britain took the lead by enlisting the help of the country's foremost authorities on canine obedience, and launched a nationwide recruiting drive. Two thousand dogs were volunteered by their owners within the first week of the campaign, including Airedale Terriers, "Scotch Collies," Old English Sheepdogs, and a plethora of mongrels.

Selected animals were relocated to doggie boot camps, where their nerve under fire was tested. Handlers attempted to desensitize them to the sights, sounds, and smells of war by throwing firecrackers in their faces, exploding grenades near the kennels as they slept or ate, and firing machine guns or rifles overhead as the dogs traversed obstacle courses of barbed wire interspersed with mud quagmires. Any dog unable to pass this rigorous test was granted an honorable discharge and released to a sometimes embarrassed owner. Those who passed were officially classified as military personnel, and went on to specialized training for locating wounded men on the battlefield, sentry duty, the laying of telephone and

Red Cross dog trained to canvass the battlefield for wounded soldiers, then return to the
trench with a helmet or bit of garment to alert stretcher bearers.
source: Author.

telegraph wire, pulling cargo sleds and wagons, or even functioning as decoys to draw enemy fire (thereby revealing the enemy's location).

War dog schools in France, Italy, Belgium, and England attempted when possible to assign canine recruits to tasks best suited to the particular talents of their breed. In the best Molossus tradition, the British trained Irish Wolfhounds to chase down and knock enemy messengers off their bicycles, while Greyhounds (whose exceptional eyesight can detect the flicker of a rabbit's whisker at over a hundred yards) were taught to bark an alarm at the first sign of movement on the front. England's fleet of Scotch Collie sentries was credited with saving troop water supplies from contamination by enemy spies, and at one point in the war Germany attempted (but failed) to bomb the Collie kennels at West Hartlepool.

The desolate landscapes of battlefields were nightmarish in their vastness—bleak oceans of barbed wire, twisted metal, and knee-deep mud studded with huge, water-filled craters. Soldiers were impressed with how

"Dolly," a French messenger dog, in the trenches awaiting her next mission.
source: Author.

seriously the messenger and rescue dogs took their duties. They were repeatedly featured on morale-boosting posters—often in the company of
lovely young nurses. On seeing a messenger dog "running, hopping, jumping, skipping over the terrible shell hole," one English officer was struck by
the "earnest expression on the dog's face as he passed." Many of these canines carried on despite being wounded, and in one case it was discovered
only after a postmortem examination that a dog had been carrying messages for weeks with a bullet lodged in his lungs and shrapnel in his spine.

The United States alone failed to establish a canine unit of its own in
time for World War I, a decision military strategists soon came to regret.
Once they arrived in France, American troops had to beg or barter for the
use of French, Belgian, and English war dogs, particularly those trained as
sentries and couriers, and also made use of canines inadvertently left behind at the front by their regiments. Many a Belgian cart dog, found
wounded or abandoned, and sometimes still wearing tattered bits of harness, was put back into action pulling a small ambulance or passenger
wagon.

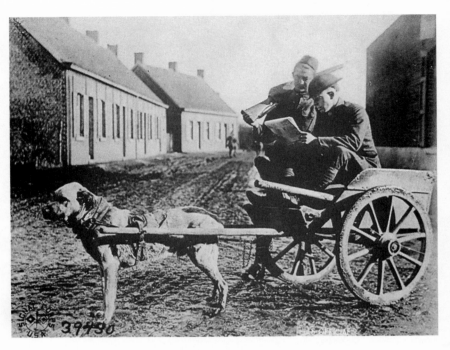

Belgische Rekel with American soldiers.
source: Author.

America's First Canine War Hero

Although the United States had no organized canine corps, one of the most remarkable of wartime stories involves the only American dog known to serve overseas. Stubby, a homeless Bull Terrier-Boxer cross (so named for his nublike tail), wandered into the training camp of the Army's 102nd Infantry at Yale University in the summer of 1917. Quickly endearing himself to the troops, particularly Private J. Robert Conroy, he was adopted as an unofficial member of the division. Despite a no-pets-allowed rule, Stubby shared meals and sleeping quarters with the men—even, it was said, mimicking their drills and marching exercises. When it came time to go to the war, Conroy and his colleagues smuggled the dog aboard the steamer headed for Europe.

Stubby reached the trenches of the front line in February 1918, in the midst of a horrific battle. Although the dog never formally trained to cope with such nightmarish conditions, he calmly endured an unceasing barrage of shelling for the first thirty days. Stubby's caretakers, in fact, were amazed by his cool under fire, and absolutely stunned when he voluntarily ventured out into the battle zone to seek out and comfort wounded soldiers still caught in the crossfire. News of the little dog's heroism and fidelity reached the French village of Domremy, and after the fighting subsided, the women of the town presented him with a hand-sewn chamois coat decorated with Allied flags and his name stitched in gold thread.

By war's end Stubby had been credited numerous times with saving his regiment from certain disaster. He would warn the men of incoming mortar shells by barking or hurling himself to the ground, and once prevented the escape of a German spy by sinking his teeth into the seat of the man's pants and refusing to let go. Whiffs of mustard gas, too faint to be detected by the human nose, sent Stubby into a barking tirade that warned the soldiers to don protective gear. One time he roused a sleeping soldier just in time to get both his and the soldier's masks on—the regiment had provided Stubby with his own makeshift gas mask, custom-fitted to accommodate his round head and flattened snout.

Stubby also was an experienced "therapy dog" long before animal visitations were proven to shorten the recovery time of sick or seriously injured people. He ministered to the troops in his own canine fashion, often cuddling up to wounded or shell-shocked soldiers, keeping them warm through a long winter night. Sometimes he simply sat staring intently into the men's faces, his piercing, hypnotic gaze calming and distracting them from pain or grief. During a lull in the fighting at Toul, Stubby ventured out onto the battlefield and was wounded in the chest by a burst of enemy shrapnel. Yet during his own convalescence, Stubby took it upon himself to get out of bed and wander through the field hospital, visiting soldiers who, like him, were recovering from injuries received in the line of fire.

At one point, when Conroy was wounded and evacuated to Paris, the administrators of Hospital 57—having heard of Stubby's legendary healing effect on homesick, demoralized patients—granted an exception to their no-pets rule and allowed the dog to keep his master company. Medics found his conduct impeccable, and the cathartic effect of his visits to the ward was noted by the physicians. On extended convalescent leave with

Conroy in France, Stubby's fame continued to grow. He became the toast of Paris when he saved a little girl from being run over in the middle of a busy thoroughfare, and was frequently seen strolling about town wearing his chamois blanket, which now sported a rapidly growing array of honorary medals donated by friends and admirers.

Eighteen months after Stubby debarked on foreign soil, the Armistice was signed, ending the "war to end all wars." During that time he saw more action than most human soldiers, participating in at least eighteen major battles, including Champagne-Marne, Aisne-Marne, St. Mihiel, and Meuse-Argonne. Back home he became a nationally acclaimed hero, and eventually was received by presidents Wilson, Harding, and Coolidge. Even General Pershing presented him with a gold medal and declared him a "hero of the highest caliber." After the war, Stubby led more regimental parades than any dog in American history, and was promoted to honorary sergeant, becoming the highest ranking dog to ever serve in the Army. He was an honorary member of the Red Cross, the American Legion, and the YMCA, which issued him a membership card good for "three bones a day and a place to sleep."

Stubby, the only American dog known to serve in World War I.
source: Author.

Stubby leads a regimental parade in Washington, D.C., after the war.
source: National Museum of American History (Smithsonian Institution #75024).

Despite his nationwide fame, Stubby at times encountered prejudice against his kind. In the 1920s, thousands of spectators hoping to see the little hero packed a national dog show in Boston. Breeders attempted to block his guest appearance, complaining that he was a mongrel and therefore had no business at an exhibition of pedigreed dogs. But a judge ruled against them, saying, "he may be a mutt, but he's done more than all of your dogs put together—Stubby stays." When Conroy and Stubby sought lodging at the famous Hotel Majestic in New York City, they were informed by the desk clerk that "the Majestic does not permit guests to bring in dogs." An incensed Conroy shouted, "This is no dog—this is a war hero!"

The K-9 Corps

In the mid-thirties the Nazis eagerly capitalized on Allied dog handler expertise, patterning their training regimens after those perfected by Lieutenant Colonel E.H. Richardson, founder and commander of Britain's first military dog schools. "After World War I, when I was living in Germany, I saw vast numbers of Dobermans and German Shepherds being trained to attack, jump hurdles, trail and carry packs," Frederick Simpick, a writer for *National Geographic* reported. "Ostensibly, these were for police work, though everybody knew they would eventually wind up in the Army." Intelligence reports suggested the Germans were amassing a force of war dogs numbering in the thousands. Furthermore, there was growing concern that Japan might mount an invasion against the United States, or at least covertly sabotage key military installations.

It was for these reasons that the U.S. War Department decided to follow its Allies in implementing its first official military dog program—and turned to the public for help. Enter Dogs for Defense, Inc. (DFD), a New York–based civilian organization established in 1942 to coordinate and promote a national recruiting drive for canine soldiers. Spurred on by the public's lingering adulation for Stubby, and under the leadership of Harry I. Caesar (who also was a director of the American Kennel Club), a network of DFD regional chapters popped up around the country to host fundraisers and process dogs donated by patriotic civilians. Specialists responsible for overseeing some of the foremost European canine corps of World War I were called in to assist in the formation of the new war dog regiment, unofficially titled the K-9 Corps.

The years between the two World Wars saw the development of new planes, bombs, land mines, flamethrowers, rockets, and cannons capable of deadly precision. But despite the technological innovation, military strategists realized that dogs formed an important adjunct to the new arsenal of mechanical and electronic equipment. For the first time, detailed manuals and a steady stream of memos specified every aspect of the animals' care and training, inadvertently fueling the bureaucratic perception of war dogs as weaponry rather than soldiers. Eventually, the War Department even demonstrated a preference for pure breeds, on the basis that it was more efficient to house and train dogs of uniform size and temperament.

The enlistment of pedigreed purebred animals, some reportedly worth hundreds of dollars in the show world, was pointed to as proof of the supremacy of America's K-9 Corps, which in turn proved a tremendous marketing tool for soliciting public donations and new recruits. (Not incidentally, it also stimulated consumer demand for pure breeds after the war.) Thirty-two breeds initially were recommended for military service, among them the Airedale Terrier, Alaskan Malamute, Belgian and German Shepherd Dog, Bouvier des Flandres, Boxer, Briard, Bull Mastiff, Collie, Dalmatian, and even Basset Hound. The list was progressively pared down, causing not a few hurt feelings among fanciers whose breeds had been culled. By war's end the German Shepherd was designated the official dog of choice by the Army (until the end of the Vietnam War). Only after the number of purebred volunteers dwindled were certain types of mongrels grudgingly accepted. Female dogs made the cut for wartime service, but difficulties in their care and housing arose when they were unspayed—or worse, in heat. Some were already pregnant when they enlisted, or after an indiscreet dalliance in the kennels, were shipped overseas and gave birth at the front. Finally, orders were issued to the dog training centers to spay all bitches on hand—a "military necessity," according to orders from on high (castration of the male dogs apparently was never even discussed).

Public support for the K-9 Corps was bolstered by celebrity endorsements. Norman Sadler, a famous champion Smooth-Coated Fox Terrier, made guest appearances at fund-raisers, as did Boots, an Oscar-winning canine trick artist. Albert Payson Terhune, the much-loved dog writer and

Performing dogs rallied support for the American war effort.
source: Author.

philosopher, donated one of his Collies amid a flurry of press and radio coverage. But life in the Army did not appeal to the canine "son" of the famous Collie Lad, and he ran away from canine boot camp, effectively flunking out. Once the press coverage died down the dog was unceremoniously returned to his famous owner. A troupe of vaudeville "trick dogs" made the final cut, as did a canine thespian reportedly valued at ten thou-

**ENROLLMENT APPLICATION
U. S. COAST GUARD DOG PATROL**

PHILADELPHIA DISTRICT

Date September 15, 1942

To the Commandant of the Coast Guard:

    I hereby apply for enrollment for active service in the Coast Guard Reserve.

Period of Enlistment Duration   Duties Dog Patrol

    I hereby agree to perform active service, without pay or allowance, other than subsistence.

I am (Breed) GERMAN SHEPHERD Shoulder Height 25" Age 2 Years
Call Name "RONNIE" Sex Male
Are you registered at the American Kennel Club? NO If so, what is
your number? -- Have you lived in a kennel or a house? HOUSE
How long have you lived in your present place? 2 YEARS Are you
nervous? NO Do you run away? NO Have you been
living in the city or the country? CITY Are you afraid of gun
fire or loud noises? NO What is your attitude toward strangers?
SUSPICIOUS Have you been a good watch
dog? YES Have you had any obedience training? NO
With this application you must furnish us a picture.
General Remarks (Give the general outline of your disposition, training, background, or any special habits): I am loyal to my master, alert, and love to jump. I have never had distemper, and I have not been innoculated.

Sign "RONNIE"
    Dog's Name
Sign *Josephine Druwiega*
    Owner's Name
1712 West Cayuga St., Philadelphia, Pa.
    Owner's Address

(Prepare in triplicate)

U.S. Coast Guard Dog Patrol enrollment application for a German Shepherd named Ronnie in 1942.
source: National Archives.

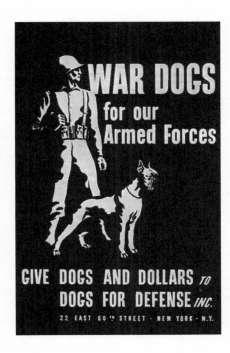

Dogs for Defense promotional poster.
source: Author.

The first batch of American canine inductees in 1942 were stationed for a month's training with the Quartermaster Corps in Front Royal, Virginia.
source: National Archives.

sand dollars. But according to one recruiting officer, even this distinguished dog was "just another buck private who used to be a movie star."

While Hitler's army numbered at least thirty thousand German Shepherds, Russia had the most respected canine force on the Continent, totaling well over a million animals. Renowned as a tireless seeker of land mines, one mongrel named Zucha unearthed two thousand buried explosives in less than two weeks. Other canines were trained to sneak into the enemy camps to steal maps and documents. And "suicide" dogs, loaded with thirty pounds of explosives, sought food under rolling tanks, whereupon wooden levers attached to their backpacks depressed, triggering an explosion capable of cutting through the steel underbelly of the machine.

The United States also trained suicide dogs, but the experimental project was fraught with problems. One was that if the press should get wind of the program it would seriously undermine DFD fund-raising and recruiting drives. In the end the idea was shelved, not because watching a dog blown to pieces was traumatic for soldiers, but because the animals couldn't distinguish between our own and enemy tanks. (Yet as late as 1993, the Russians still had a suicide tank dog program.) Likewise, according to a 1945 government memo, operation "Demolition Wolf" was terminated when it was determined that explosives-laden dogs trained to infiltrate enemy strongholds constituted "a danger to friendly troops [because they are] unable to distinguish between enemy-occupied bunkers and captured enemy bunkers occupied by friendly troops." (In the 1950s the United States seriously considered a proposal to reinstate the program, this time strapping small tactical nuclear weapons to dogs.)

Also unknown to the public at the time, the American military considered implementing a "killer dog" program in the Pacific, the idea being that packs of savage, assault-trained canines could be unleased to annihilate the Japanese, just as Alaunts had been deployed by Spanish conquistadors in the New World. Under great secrecy, the dogs were tortured with electric shocks and bullwhips, dragged behind galloping horses, starved, and forced to fight for food—all in the name of "training." A formal demonstration of the program in 1943 was conducted before an audience of officers, who watched as Japanese-American soldiers bedecked in padded, protective garb allowed the dogs to wrestle them to the ground.

It was pronounced a dismal failure and the program was disbanded, because, according to eyewitness Lieutenant-Colonel A.R. Nichols, "The performance of the animals appeared artificial and forced."

The United States never had more than ten thousand dogs in service at any one time during WWII. Trained in a similar manner to WWI messenger dogs, many canines dispatched telephone wire from large spindles mounted on their backs to link two strategic points. Large, hardy pack dogs were essential to operations in rough, mountainous terrain, untiringly carrying heavy loads of ammunition and food supplies essential to the soldiers' survival. Some sled dogs were trained for aerial drops into remote mountain areas to search for downed airmen, and during the Battle of the Bulge, these dogs were hastily flown across the Atlantic to help carry wounded soldiers to medical centers.

Canine paratroopers—dogs who participated in parachute jumps behind enemy lines—were hailed as another strategic innovation. England was rather proud of its "Parapup Battalion," while the United States never officially adopted an active airborne dog program. On occasion four-footed commandos were dropped behind enemy lines to assist troops on stealthy nighttime excursions into enemy territory. One such dog, a quiet-natured crossbred Collie named Bob, led more forays into German territory than any other canine or human in the Allied Army. Parachuting scout dog Ricky, a Welsh Shepherd, sniffed out booby traps, and continued to clear a path for troops through an enemy minefield even after being wounded in an explosion of a charge he found.

Sometimes canine parachute drops went awry, as in the case of Bing, an Alsatian dropped into Normandy on D-Day with the 13th Battalion of England's Parachute Regiment. Bing landed in a tree and endured enemy shelling through the night until soldiers cut him down the next day. Though he suffered wounds to the neck and eyes, after medical treatment he resumed his place at his handler's side.

When veteran American paratrooper Bill Krummerer and fourteen other men from the 463rd Parachute Field Artillery jumped into southern France shortly before D-Day, a cantankerous Doberman Pinscher was unceremoniously kicked out the plane's door as well. Within hours of landing and concealing their gear, the dog began to growl and look toward a small rise. "Sure as hell, over the rise came four Krauts in a wagon," says

Krummerer. "We opened up with a 50-mm machine gun, and don't you know it, they never made it back to the Rhineland." As it turned out, the dog not only disliked Germans but exhibited a healthy contempt for his partners-in-arms as well. "I tried to pat the dog and thank him," said Krummerer, but "all I saw were teeth and he just about took my hand off."

A number of dogs were decorated for valor after the war, including the first troop of Doberman Pinschers enlisted by the U.S. Marines for duty in the Pacific theater. Affectionately known as "Devil Dogs," they assisted their handlers in taking beachheads and enemy troops in densely forested islands. One Doberman known as Duke flushed fifty Japanese out of hiding, was responsible for the capture of twenty-two others, and several times alerted to enemy patrols before they could ambush the Americans.

Chips, a short-tempered German Shepherd-Collie-Husky cross, was the most highly decorated and celebrated American dog of the Second World War. Working as a tank guard dog, he accompanied Patton's Seventh Army through eight campaigns in Africa, the Mediterranean, and Europe, and was a sentry at the Roosevelt-Churchill conference in 1943. His true mettle under fire was finally tested on the beaches of Sicily. Against the orders of his handler, Chips bolted off and leapt into what was thought to be an abandoned pillbox. In fact it held six Germans, poised to open fire with a machine gun on the Americans. Chips subdued the gunner and convinced the rest of the soldiers to surrender, though he was wounded in the process. He received a Purple Heart and a Silver Star, for his actions reflected "the highest credit on himself and on the military service," according to Allied Force Headquarters. General Eisenhower went out of his way to congratulate the dog in person—Chips repaid the gesture by very nearly taking a chunk out of Ike's hand.

As the war drew to a close, eight thousand American service dogs were demobilized and it was leaked to the press that the Army planned to auction the animals off rather than return them to their civilian owners, as had been promised. The public was incensed. "It is not the intention of the War Department, the Treasury or Dogs for Defense, to permit the dogs which have faithfully served their country to become the object of barter," the DFD president Harry I. Caesar reassured a reporter for the *New York Times* (November 24, 1944). DFD subsequently assumed respon-

sibility for resocializing and then returning the dogs to their rightful owners or placing them in new adoptive homes. Each animal underwent a "de-
militarization" program to unlearn its wartime lessons. (Those who
remained aggressive were humanely put to sleep, but three thousand canines went home to live long, happy lives in peacetime.)

Chips returned to civilian life in 1945 by train and debarked in Front
Royal, Virginia, amid a mob of reporters. His family reported that he did-
n't seem much changed by his wartime experiences, although he acted a
little more tired and less interested in chasing the garbagemen when they
rattled the cans.

Canines Reclassified

Objecting to the national acclaim Chips received for his heroic actions,
William Thomas, a high school principal and the 1943 Commander of the
Military Order of the Purple Heart, penned an angry letter to President
Roosevelt and the War Department. "It decries the high and lofty purpose
for which [this] medal was created," he wrote. Thomas went on to say that
military accolades for animals not only demeaned anyone (human) who
had ever received a Purple Heart, but made a mockery of the entire nation. Embarrassed by the criticism, the Army quickly rescinded the honors
bestowed both on Chips and other dogs who served in World War II. Fearful of further public reprisals, Dogs for Defense opted not to fight the rev-
ocation of Chip's medals—even though the organization had eagerly
capitalized on Chip's exploits to promote their recruiting program. He was
the last dog officially decorated for wartime valor by the United States government.

Beyond the debate over awarding animals formal honors, Thomas's
letter lent fateful impetus to the government's desire to reclassify military
dogs as "equipment," thereby making them increasingly exploitable—and
disposable. Not only did canine soldiers lose their right to recognition for
wartime services, they also lost their status as living creatures.

England's war dogs also returned to their homes, but as heroes receiving the Dickin Medal, the animal equivalent of the Victoria Cross. Donated by the People's Dispensary for Sick Animals, each honorary medal
was engraved with the words, "For gallantry, we also serve." Some pro-

posed that the United States offer an equivalent medal, but nothing ever came of it. And the idea of asking civilians to "loan" their dogs to the military for limited tours of duty was abandoned after the war, as were tentative efforts by the DFD to breed their own dogs for the military, effectively putting an end to the organization's function as a "middleman" between the military and the civilian populace. From then on the government purchased dogs outright from independent breeders, or bred the dogs themselves, making the animals federal property, free and clear. The War Department would never again be bothered with having to explain to nosy civilians how their dogs were used or disposed of.

In the Korean War, canines continued to be deployed much as they were in WWII, working as sentries and scouts. Staff Sargent Melvin Powell recalls that in the course of thirteen months of steady fighting, the dogs "were really remarkable, particularly on patrols during those bitter-cold, black nights when we couldn't see anything. Whenever they pricked up their ears and whined a little, we knew the enemy was within 150 yards of us and moving in, so we made ourselves ready. [The dogs] were never wrong, to the extent that we got so we staked our lives on their ability." It was later determined that when dogs were used in times of imminent contact with the enemy in Korea, they reduced casualties by more than 65 percent. Unlike the canines of the first two World Wars, these animals received only passing interest from the press, and almost fifty years later, the dogs— like their human comrades—are becoming lost to history, anonymous faces in a war that some veterans accuse Americans of forgetting.

The K-9 Corps was officially decommissioned in 1958, ending the Army's supervision of war dog training and transferring responsibility for all surviving animals to the Air Force's Military Working Dogs Agency at Lackland Air Force Base in San Antonio, Texas.

Dogs in Vietnam

Despite the creation of electronic devices that could detect motion and allow men to see in the dark, dogs continued to be the most reliable means of tracking the enemy. Between 1965 and 1972, two Marine sentry dog platoons, ten Air Force security police dog squadrons, and three Army Sentry Dog companies were assigned to American military compounds in Vietnam (at least four thousand dogs served in the course of the war, state-

First free fall of a military dog took place in 1969, as part of an experimental program to determine the feasibility of air-dropping handlers and dogs into Viet Cong territory. Despite the success of the experiment, the program was never implemented by military strategists. Shown jumping are SFC Jesse Mendez and scout dog Pal.
source: Jesse Mendez.

side and overseas), where they patrolled base perimeters or accompanied platoons on expeditions into enemy-controlled territory.

In the thick, steaming jungles of southeast Asia, footpaths could harbor a multitude of booby traps, some of them spring-loaded with lethal, feces-covered spikes (the intent being that if the stabbing didn't kill, infection surely would). An array of homemade mines dotted woodland trails, and often when one was tripped it activated a daisy chain of explosions, killing every soldier in line. Many draftees were ill-prepared to deal with the Viet Cong or VC, a stealthy foe unlike any they had been trained to fight. In the words of veteran handler Harold Bell, "we were a mixture of surfers from L.A., brothers off the block and college kids from suburbia."

Strategists failed to anticipate the full scope of guerrilla combat in this terrain, leaving troops both physically and emotionally vulnerable to an untraditional kind of enemy. Once again dogs proved instrumental in saving American lives—by some estimates, upward of ten thousand men. For instance, one German Shepherd named Tiger led two hundred American troops through the jungle on a search-and-destroy mission. Several hours into the mission, the dog stopped and stared at a tall stand of grass about seventy-five yards down the trail. As it turned out, the grass concealed three hundred Viet Cong.

Joseph White, who served with the 47th Scout Dog Platoon, fondly remembers his own canine charge, a black German Shepherd named Ebony:

> She was truly a great scout dog, a hero in every sense of the word. She would find booby traps before any soldier could get maimed. She could even hear a mortar being loaded on a distant hill. More guys than can be counted are alive today because of this dog. Some guys remember the day we put headphones over Ebony's ears, and she bobbed her head to the beat of a Jimi Hendrix record. Others forever remember her as the dog who didn't like the Army. You'd say, 'Ebony, would you rather be in the Army or be a dead dog?' And she'd drop over dead every time. It really cracked us up. But all of us remember her as the dog who found the booby-trap, or heard the impending ambush, and saved our lives.

With the sanity of even the most hardened of soldiers strained to the limit, the dogs served in still another way, as an emotional anchor to reality back home; a connection to the families and lives the men had left behind in the States. These were memories that could be triggered by a war dog, a creature who brought to mind happy recollections of childhood or family pets.

As much as the VC hated American soldiers, they hated American dogs even more. By war's end U.S. scout dogs had uncovered over a million pounds of stockpiled corn, depriving the enemy of a much-needed staple as well as thousands of pounds of ammunition, firearms, enemy documents, and over three thousand booby traps. At first the enemy tried to distract scout dogs with bait or perfume, but the animals were undeterred. Then, as the war progressed, the VC promised to handsomely reward anyone who killed dogs. Canines in Vietnam faced other dangers as well, as many a scout dog saved his handlers from fatal snake bites, often sacrificing themselves in the process. And the first American canine casualty in Vietnam was a dog named Mac, who upon arrival on July 17, 1965, collapsed and died of heatstroke, just one of many to eventually succumb to the stifling heat and humidity.

In March 1973, the United States formally announced its withdrawal from Vietnam. In the frantic scramble to evacuate troops, orders came down to leave most of the scout and sentry dogs behind. Classified as "surplus equipment," they were to be handed over, along with other supplies and weaponry, to our South Vietnamese allies. Dog handlers were stunned and heartbroken. After all these dogs had done for them, many considered it the height of betrayal to not bring the animals home, too.

Despite the years spent familiarizing Vietnamese allies with U.S.-made weaponry, cultural and linguistic barriers made the task difficult if not impossible when it came to handling the dogs. Sergeant Jesse Mendez performed three tours in Vietnam as an adviser and handler instructor, and recalls that none of the training manuals had even been translated into Vietnamese. That meant all instruction had to be carried out using interpreters. But the biggest problem, Mendez says, was "trying to get the handlers to praise their dogs if they performed well, or did what was expected of them."

Military strategists failed to take into account that most Vietnamese had little experience interacting with any companion animals, but particularly dogs, which are still regarded as livestock throughout much of Asia. To make matters worse, the Vietnamese were intimidated by the imposing size of the German Shepherds. "After all, many handlers only outweighed their dogs by a few pounds," Mendez points out.

Veteran handler Tony Montoya witnessed the final processing of some war dogs at the Dog Training Detachment facility in Ben Hoa, "along with a whole truckload of horse meat. When we got there to hand the dogs over, none of the [Vietnamese handlers] wanted to come close to the dogs. We had to get the dogs off the trucks ourselves and take them to their stake-down area."

Almost all of the dogs not transferred to the Vietnamese were euthanized, for reasons ranging from old age to minor ailments. Official memos expressed concern that some of the dogs might carry a mysterious tick-borne blood disease—soon after the war it proved curable with antibiotics. Animals who passed their physicals had their names posted on a bulletin board. Montoya's dog Patches was one of the lucky few to obtain passage back to the States. "I cannot express in words how I felt when I saw his name on the list of dogs to be sent home," Montoya says. Other stories circulated through the ranks regarding the fate of the dogs, feeding the anxiety felt by many handlers. Henry (Fred) Dorr, who was stationed near Freedom Hill, recalled that he and his comrades "were told that the last man out would open the kennels and let the dogs run free." It also was rumored that before the Marines shipped out, an order was issued to not transfer their dogs to the Vietnamese, but to euthanize them. Fifty canines were allegedly killed and buried in a mass grave, along with all their records. To this day, some handlers feel certain their dogs met horrible fates after the American withdrawal, either perishing from neglect in the hands of uninterested and incompetent Vietnamese handlers, or killed outright and eaten. Twenty years later, memories of evacuating via jeep or helicopter, all the while straining for one last glimpse of a canine comrade still chained to its makeshift kennel, continue to haunt many veterans. The experience has forever affected their lives and their relationships with others.

Dr. Howard Hayes, a veterinary researcher at the National Cancer Institute, has endeavored to collect any and all surviving documentation pertaining to the fate of sentry and scout dogs who served in Vietnam, and he willingly shares his findings with veteran handlers seeking to put to rest decades of wondering about what became of their canine comrades. In 1990 Hayes published an unprecedented mortality survey of Vietnam war dogs, which concluded that canines who worked in combat zones where the herbicide Agent Orange was sprayed suffered double the normal incidence of testicular cancer. Yet funding for further study to determine if there is a correlation with the men who served alongside them has been slow in coming, despite Hayes's conclusions that "the magnitude of the observed excess risk of testicular seminoma and dysfunction in Military Working Dogs serving in Vietnam strongly suggests that military service in Vietnam be considered a risk factor for testicular cancer."

More recently Hayes discovered a higher incidence of malignant lymphomas among pet dogs who live in households where American-made lawn herbicides are used, notably those containing 2,4-dicholorophenoxyacetic acid—better known as 2,4-D, a chemical component also found in Agent Orange. The implications of this are suggestive, to say the least, since one study done in Sweden found a higher than normal incidence of soft tissue carcinomas in civilian men exposed to 2,4-D herbicides.

So in still another way, it appears, the war dogs of Vietnam are continuing to serve their country.

"I was raised up with animals in the John Wayne era," reminisced veteran Michael Cagle, "so it seemed natural to enlist as a dog handler in 1966." In Vietnam he was paired with Heidi, a sixty-pound scout dog. "I always think about her. We lived together, slept together, ate together." Today Cagle suffers from Post Traumatic Stress Disorder (PTSD). "For most of the guys, problems start when they think about friends. My problems start when I think about [Heidi]."

Dog handlers apparently are at exceptionally high risk for PTSD because they held the most stressful of combat jobs—always on the front line, traveling alone for extended periods with only their dogs for companionship and comfort. For Cagle and others, the stress that pushed them too far is the memory of being forced to abandon these intimate companions to uncertain fates, while they returned home to the land of suburbia and consumer excess. Today Cagle lives with several dogs and cats, whom he loves and regards as members of the family, but no animal or person can alleviate the anguish he feels whenever Heidi comes to mind. "You just can't get close to people who haven't been through what I've been through. That dog saved my life."

After decades of wondering what happened to their canine friends and fellow handlers, a handful of veterans like Cagle and Mendez have united in a quest to remember and share this difficult past. Established in 1994, the nonprofit Vietnam Dog Handlers Association (VDHA) is dedicated to helping veteran handlers by serving as a clearinghouse for those hoping to find old friends. Together they seek closure by sharing personal recollections of their experiences during the war.

On Veterans Day, 1994—for the first time—an official wreath-laying ceremony was held at the Vietnam Memorial in Washington, D.C., to commemorate Vietnam dog units. Escorted by U.S. Army handler Paul Morgan and his dog Cody Bear (the first dog ever allowed to visit "the Wall"), dog handler representatives presented a wreath of flowers with the letters "K-9" prominently displayed in the center. VDHA member and newsletter editor Tom Mitchell described his experience at the event in this way:

> There were over a thousand veterans, [and] grouped together in front we met a couple of Vets who were handlers who knew nothing about the VDHA. A number of [them] yelled "Hey, a dog? Great! They were great!" The Vet next to me said, "Hey, that's cool, I didn't even know they had dogs over there.". . . They marched proudly down the walk and placed the wreath next to The Wall. With tears swelling in my eyes, I could hardly see. I was very proud to be a part of the VDHA. Other vets nodded to me knowingly.

Censorship by Omission

Much of the history regarding America's war dogs and handlers has been lost or destroyed. This tragedy is compounded by the public's general lack of awareness about war dogs, and by scholars and curators who fail to even mention either their existence or their service, whether in writings or in exhibits on military history. A great deal of what has survived— in the form of photos, papers, film footage, dog equipment, and personal recollections—remains to be discovered, documented, or preserved for posterity. The military routinely shredded and burned papers pertaining to the war dog program, leaving huge gaps in the history of canines who served in World War II and the Korean and Vietnam Wars. In addition, a great deal of documentation was left behind with the Vietnamese, along with scout and sentry dogs. The National Archives houses a substantial body of government memos, reports, and correspondence pertaining to war dogs, but much of it can only be obtained by filing a request under the Freedom of Information Act, a time-consuming process. Other federal documents, many a half-century old, for some unexplained reason remain classified, unavailable to researchers.

After the end of World War II, when Dogs for Defense went out of business, founder Harry Caesar packed up all DFD files, documents, photos, and memorabilia, and stashed them in his private kennels. Upon his death years later, Caesar's heirs liquidated much of his estate, and having no interest in dogs, took all the DFD materials to the city dump.

Nemo was one of the handful of Vietnam sentry dogs to return to the United States. Hailed as a hero by the press after battling with the Viet Cong and losing an eye from a bullet wound to his muzzle, he received thousands of get-well cards from children. On his demise, Nemo's hide was saved in the hope that it could be preserved and mounted by a taxi-

Vietnam sentry dog Nemo.
source: Lackland AFB Working Dogs
Agency, San Antonio, Texas.

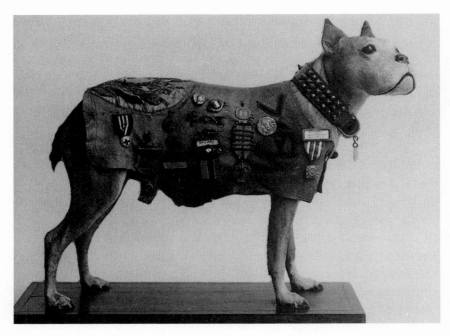

Taxidermied body of Stubby.
source: National Museum of American History (Smithsonian Institution #43998).

dermist, as a lasting tribute to his heroism. But due to an oversight, it was left in a shipping box until it had become a useless, putrid mass.

Eight decades after turning the world on its ear with his selfless feats of courage, Stubby is virtually an unknown soldier, except to a small, select following of military history buffs. Upon his death in 1926, his hide was preserved and stretched over a lifelike, plaster body cast housing a small urn filled with his ashes. Conrad then donated Stubby, along with a scrapbook of photos and newspaper clippings and the dog's halter and metal-covered chamois coat, to the Red Cross Museum in Washington, D.C. He stood on guard there, so to speak, in a glass case until the mid-fifties, when he was permanently transferred to the Armed Forces Division of the National Museum of American History at the Smithsonian. Many a civilian Bulldog was christened "Stubby" following the Great War, but curiously, Fairfax Downey's 1955 biography of Dogs for Defense, which included a detailed review of pre-WWII dog heroes, didn't even mention him once.

The Dogs of War

Researching an article about war dogs for the *Washington Post* in 1993, reporter Tom Dunkel made a pilgrimage to the Smithsonian to inspect the little dog he had heard so much about. He found America's first and most highly decorated canine war hero in a packing crate, shelved in a storage room

> reminiscent of the walk-in equipment closets where high school gym teachers stash moldy wrestling mats and volleyballs. The once-fearless [dog] stands mounted on a cheap wooden pedestal to which someone has stuck a piece of masking tape upon which is scribbled, "Stubby the dog—fragile." Here he stands, sharing storage space with the world's largest collection of salamanders. The fact that the country's most honored war dog could meet such an ignominious end says something about man's curious relationship to his best friend. Something not altogether uplifting.

At this writing the National Museum of American History has no plans to put Stubby back on display because their exhibits now are thematic in nature, and administrators currently consider the dog to be an oddity with little educational merit. Nor do any of the museum's newly renovated, state-of-the-art displays mention the fact that over thirty thousand dogs served in America's armed forces over the last half century.

By comparison, the history of England's war dogs seem to have fared much better. London's Imperial War Museum houses a collection of artifacts, documents, and photos pertaining to the role of animals in both World Wars. In 1992 a special exhibit was unveiled, highlighting the contributions made in wartime by all kinds of English creatures, ranging from pigeons and horses to rats, cats, and dogs. Displays featured the best of the museum's permanent collection as well as privately owned items (including several Dickin Medals). It drew thousands of British and foreign spectators, children as well as adults, and was heralded by curators as a runaway success.

In recent years, war dog materials have become popular with private collectors of military memorabilia. Once monetary or nostalgic value has been assigned to such items their preservation is probably insured, but so long as the bulk of these artifacts circulates in the private sector, their whereabouts remain unknown to researchers. And with time, the likelihood increases that historical contexts and provenance may become separated from the items themselves. In defense of private collectors, however, it should be mentioned that James Flurchick has one of the largest holdings of American war dog memorabilia and artifacts. Displayed in his New Jersey home, his private exhibit currently constitutes America's only War Dog Museum. Without such collectors, most of these artifacts and documents would by now have been irretrievably scattered or destroyed.

War Dogs Remembered—and Forgotten

The United States has been alone among the world's powers to *not* pay formal tribute to its war dogs. Italy, Russia, Belgium, Germany, and the Netherlands have all sanctioned the creation of memorials honoring canines. Japan boasts seven war dog memorials, including a shrine containing hair clippings from 250 service dogs. But after a recent flood of memorial site requests to honor World War II gliders, the Peace Corps, Hispanic Vietnam Veterans, African-American Vietnam Veterans and Female Vietnam Veterans, government bureaucrats are in no mood to consider yet another request—especially for something as seemingly insignificant as dogs.

Some people have opted not to wait for the government. In a proud American tradition dating back to 1922, a small group of private citizens pooled their money to erect a tribute to dogs who served in World War I. Situated in the Hartsdale Canine Cemetery, in New York, the life-size bronze statue of a Red Cross German Shepherd stands atop a ten-ton boulder of Vermont granite. After World War II, the inscription was revised to extend appreciation to the dogs who served in Europe and the Pacific. In celebration of the fiftieth anniversary of the American K-9 Corps in 1992, American Legion Post No. 8, under the guidance of veteran Bill Krummerer, conducted a full military service on Memorial Day, including the playing of the "Star-Spangled Banner," "Taps," and the firing of three volleys—a tribute traditionally paid to fallen human comrades. The ceremony was attended by over a hundred people, many of them civilian dog lovers. And many cried, according to a newspaper report.

More recently, another memorial to America's canine soldiers appeared in Lincoln, Nebraska, courtesy of the late Gordon Greene. As a ten-year-old, he volunteered his pet dog Buster for service in World War II. In 1944, Greene was informed by the Army that Buster had been killed in action, whereupon he made a lifetime vow to honor his fallen pet. Forty-nine years later, in 1993, Greene was granted permission to erect a tribute in Antelope Park as part of a larger military memorial garden. An angled, polished black marble slab commemorates the K-9 Corps: "America's unsung heroes of all wars—they never complained."

Greene says, "I chose to have it placed on this knoll in order to depict the point of view that the K-9 dogs are posted on the outer perimeter and on an elevation as if they were still on guard, watching over the other veterans."

In 1994 the U.S. government caved in a little on honoring war dogs and sanctioned the unveiling of a privately funded life-size bronze sculpture of

General Eisenhower maintains a respectful distance from Chips, after the dog attempted to bite the commander's hand when he was decorated for exceptional valor.
source: National Archives.

Killed by an artillery blast on the Iwo Jima beachhead, this war dog made the supreme sacrifice for his country.
source: National Archives.

a Doberman Pinscher at the naval base in Orote Point as part of a larger commemoration of the fiftieth anniversary of the liberation of Guam. It was installed overlooking what is thought to be the war dog cemetery, but the original headstones and grave markers were lost some years earlier in a tropical storm.

War dog memorial advocates agree that the unveiling at Guam was a step in the right direction, but still feel that an official tribute to the thousands of dogs and handlers who risked their lives for their country, beginning with Stubby, needs to be erected somewhere in the continental United States—in a prominent, accessible location. The entrance to Arlington National Cemetery in Virginia would be an ideal spot because as some veterans point out, soldiers always sleep peacefully when dogs stand guard. A more obscure but no less appropriate location for a memorial would be at the gates of Lackland Air Force Base in San Antonio, Texas, where military dogs continue to live and serve. Until the public becomes more aware and appreciative of the contributions made by dogs and dog handlers in wartime, however, the dream of one great national memorial on public land is likely to remain just that.

Fighting a Losing Battle

Dismayed by the Army's obvious apathy for returning war dogs to civilian life, DFD founder Harry Caesar complained in 1944 that "the place of the K-9 veteran is in a home and not in some kennel on an Army post. To say that a dog should be kept confined to a kennel, robbed of the pleasures of the companionship only to be found in the home [is] just like arguing that the soldier, for whom no job is in sight, should be kept in uniform indefinitely." Half a century later, the federal government persists in classifying canine soldiers as equipment rather than personnel, and euthanizes them when they can no longer work. "A constant vigil needs to be mounted to ensure that a dog has basic rights and is treated with the same respect as any soldier, male or female," says Mike Lemish, author of *War Dogs: Canines in Combat* (1996), the first definitive treatise on America's mil-

Ever vigilant, war dogs enabled exhausted soldiers to relax and sleep in the field without fear of ambush.
source: National Archives.

itary canines published in half a century. Many veterans concur, and would like to see the military extend an appreciative hand to the thousands of canines and handlers who have served since the corps' inception. As the VDHA's official historian, Lemish has launched a national campaign to petition the United States Post Office to issue a commemorative stamp honoring canine veterans, notably those who were in Vietnam. "This shouldn't be a difficult decision for the [postal] advisory committee," remarked Paul McNamara, a columnist for the *Middlesex Daily News*. "Richard Nixon cost thousands of U.S. soldiers their lives in Vietnam—the dogs *saved* lives. Nixon got a stamp."

In 1992, the Military Working Dogs Agency at Lackland declined to officially sanction a traveling exhibit on American canine soldiers. "We cannot endorse an exhibition that petitions for a major change in governmental policy," said Hildegard Brown, then chief of publicity for the agency when she was interviewed in 1993. "The giving of awards to animals for outstanding performance is demeaning to servicemen." Brown also described campaigns to reinstate the status of dogs as personnel instead of equipment "unreasonably critical of military operations."

Today's military dogs are drafted for life and are kept alive only as long as they are useful. As the dogs age, they are returned to the San Antonio base and continue to serve their country as practice dogs for beginning handlers. They never retire, according to Brown, but are euthanized when they can no longer work. The military claims that the dogs can never be reintegrated into normal civilian life, yet civilian police dogs receive virtually identical training and are routinely "retired" to live out their remaining years in nurturing home environments—and as already discussed, thousands of dogs returned home after World War II. In labeling these animals as equipment, as if they are automatons or inanimate accessories, the military appears blind to the true value of canines to human soldiers, as spiritual allies. For the attachment or feeling of love that develops between a dog and human who have fought together to stay alive goes deep and is never forgotten.

Staff Sergeant Christopher Batta and an explosives-detecting Belgian Malinois named Carlo are just the latest in a long line of human-dog bonds that defy federal policy. Stationed in the Persian Gulf during Desert Storm, Carlo and Batta uncovered booby traps set for American troops, in one instance locating a massive cache of plastic explosives hidden by Iraqi soldiers in a Kuwaiti high-rise. By the end of their sixty-day tour of duty, Carlo had alerted to 167 concealed explosives—averaging three potentially deadly situations each day. He also discovered a cache of cluster bombs hidden under a case of MREs (Meals Ready to Eat), two hundred feet of detonation cord, and several cluster bombs buried in neighborhoods where children were playing.

The U.S. Armed Forces publication *Stars and Stripes* described a formal ceremony held on October 10, 1991, in which Batta received the Bronze Star for his service in Kuwait. But the sergeant found the regulation bar-

Belgian Malinois sentry dog named Tosca with handler Sgt. Lena Norris in 1993. Only in recent years have there been women handlers in the American military. source: Author.

ring animals from receiving military honors unfair, and after the ceremony removed the medal from his uniform and pinned it on his dog's collar. "Carlo worked harder than me," he said. "He was always in front of me."

The bond between handler and dog goes deep. This dog took a bullet in the head at Guam during World War II.
source: National Archives.

Nine

Eye of the Beholder

AS PART OF THE URBAN middle class's insatiable demand for affluent material trappings in the latter half of the nineteenth century, sales of pedigreed dogs boomed. This, in turn, inspired a multitude of secondary industries, not the least of which were grooming and fashion accessories for pets. Elaborate coiffures and fanciful collars and costumes were eagerly embraced by the public as a means of further obscuring the "beastly" qualities of dogs and adding a finishing touch to the breeder's art. The dog's body was eyed as a "work in progress," an irresistible invitation to embellishment.

But as with so many other aspects of dog history, this contrived beauty culture is rooted in centuries of tradition. It may even predate human history itself, being founded in the maternal bonding instinct common to so many social mammals, most notably canids and primates. After all, grooming with the tongue (or hands) strengthens emotional ties between two individuals, especially mothers and offspring. Wolf bitches, for instance, "wash" their offspring from head to toe, an act that leaves each pup coated in the parent's scent, thereby reinforcing the maternal bond. For humans, the most basic act of grooming—strokes of the hand—would have helped to cultivate a young canid's sense of identification with its adoptive human family. In use since the Neolithic period, the simplest of all collars, a sturdy leather or woven fiber strap, served one basic purpose—to control the animal. But as the role of the dog in human society became more complex, such neckwear was repeatedly reinterpreted to accommodate more specialized needs.

Ancient Assyrians and Egyptians were probably the first to redesign this fundamental collar, fashioning primitive choke chains out of twisted hemp and leather, which when combined with simple leashes effectively restrained lunging, savage war dogs. By contrast, classical Greek sheep-dogs wore more sophisticated and dangerous gear, particularly thick leather bands set with needle-like spikes, essential to protect the animals when they confronted wolves. Roman war dogs also wore formidable spiked, leather collars, while civilian canines in middle-class homes and business establishments wore more user-friendly collars—simple leather straps with adjustable hammered metal buckles and decorative brass riv-ets, much like those manufactured today. Toy Spaniels and Terriers cra-dled in the arms of doting Roman ladies rarely had such sensible collars; their mistresses were more inclined to drape them with gold chains, glass beads, or semiprecious gems, amber and pearls, as a sign of affluence. It also was during this time that collars first became icons of subservience; by their very design, they implied a servant-master relationship with respect to power. As a result, slaves often were required to wear dog collars com-plete with identification tags bearing their master's name and address.

Collars came to be perceived as supernatural accessories—a means of harnessing unearthly and malevolent powers for personal benefit. It was rumored, for example, that the Roman general and statesman Marcus Agrippa (63–12 B.C.) depended on a dog named Monsieur, who wore a magical collar decorated with satanic symbols, which were conduits to limitless, infernal knowledge. The dog willingly shared this wisdom with his master, enabling his rise to the status of the Emperor's confidant. Years later, as the elderly Agrippa lay on his deathbed, he unbuckled the collar from the canine's neck and gasped, "Depart, unhappy beast, the cause of eternal damnation," at which Monsieur threw himself into the Saône River and drowned. It is interesting to note that Dog Toby, the canine char-acter in the Punch and Judy show (performed since 1662), wears a ruffle garnished with bells—to keep the devil *away* from his master.

Roman collars designed as offensive weaponry were difficult to im-prove on in subsequent centuries. Outfitted in coats of felt padding, jointed metal plates, or chain mail, medieval war dogs went into combat in col-lars studded with razor-sharp blades. Similarly vicious implements were later worn by Spanish Mastiffs, who facilitated the conquest of the New World in the sixteenth century. Then during the Renaissance, variations on the Roman spiked collar came into use as war dogs gave rise to canines

Sixteenth-century German iron collar consisting of four large plates linked by spiked rings. source: With the kind permission of the Trustees of the Leeds Castle Foundation.

bred for sport. And bloody sports they were—bear, wild boar, stags, and bulls were cornered by packs of nimble, aggressive hounds who tore the animals to pieces while their lordly owners looked on. A special banquet arranged for Queen Elizabeth I (1533–1603) included just such a spectacle for the entertainment of the diners, with the royal Greyhounds set loose on sixteen red deer trapped in an arena.

Packs of hounds numbering in the hundreds required constant attention, and "dog-boys" were hired by the lord's huntsman to tend to their needs. For example, in the fifteenth century, the Duke of York ordered his dog-boy to live full-time in the kennels, sleeping among the pack at night and leading them to meadows each day where they could sample medicinal herbs. Then they were to be rubbed down with a "great wisp of hay" to make them "kindly and clean . . . and goodly to all manner of folks save to wild beasts, to whom they should be fierce, eager and spiteful." Showing their station as servants (and patterned after Roman slavery customs), the dog-boys as well as the dogs often wore collars.

Renaissance canines fortunate enough to live with doting aristocrats also enjoyed the same opulent fashions as their owners, from silk ribbons and heavy brocade collars to jewel-encrusted chains. Kings and country barons expressed their affection for a particular hound by giving it a collar showing its elevated station in the family, decorated with wide bands of plush silk velvet covered in gold embroidery. For prized Mastiffs, hinged solid bands of bronze, silver, or gold, bearing griffins, lions, or other emblems of power were common.

Complicated clips for sporting dogs first became prevalent in the Renaissance, particularly for curly-coated sheepdogs and water retrievers now thought to be the progenitors of Standard Poodles. Writing of the use of such hounds in the sixteenth century, Johannes Caius said they were "shorn from shoulder to hindquarters and of tail . . . so that they may be quicker," implying that a waterlogged mane of fur on the head, shoulders and forelimbs, counterbalanced by naked flanks and rear legs, enhanced a dog's balance while swimming. But in eighteenth-century France, the ability to radically alter canine appearance by styling its fur made the Poodle particularly popular with nobility, regardless of whether the animals were used to fetch waterfowl, so their coats were styled to express the aristocratic standing of their masters, as a decadent, symbolic "king of the beasts."

Lion-clipped Pomeranian, ca. 1890.
source: Author.

Despite the Poodle's reputation as a retriever, the infamous Boye and his fast friendship with Charles I laid the foundation for an enduring image of the breed as an ornamental fixture in royal social circles. The popularity of these animal courtesans kept professional canine stylists called "demoiselles" steadily employed in the eighteenth century. Recognizable for their long white pocketed aprons jangling with scissors, hand clippers, and combs, they plied their trade to a large retinue of wealthy clients. In 1774, a typical Parisian canine "makeover" started with a therapeutic bleeding (using a knife or leeches), followed by a sudsy bath and a trim, costing the equivalent of a common laborer's entire day's wages. Canine coiffures became almost as tedious as human ones. Poodles sat patiently for hours as their loose curly coats were teased to unbelievable heights, powdered and sprinkled with colored confetti to create an otherworldly look, topped off with gem-encrusted collars and anklets.

Understandably, the demand for canine coiffures temporarily subsided after the French Revolution, since the country's inventory of aristocratic pet owners had been seriously depleted. But by 1850, the stylists were back in force and enjoying an unprecedented popularity with both upper- and middle-class consumers. On Sundays, Parisians escorted their dogs to the banks of the Seine under the Pont des Arts, a major bridge linking the left

Toy dog with lion clip and ribbon in its hair, ca. 1870. source: Author.

and right banks. There, for a fee, pets were lathered, immersed in sulfur water to kill fleas, then sent fetching a stick tossed into the river, after which they were clipped to the owner's orders.

Eventually, all kinds of Victorian dogs sported fanciful coiffures. The newly miniaturized Pomeranian was trimmed in the Continental style, like the Poodles, and tiny Yorkshire Terriers and Malteses, the darlings of seaside resorts, had their silky hair tied up in satin ribbons specially dyed to match the colors of their owners' trousseaus.

As the nineteenth century progressed, canine coiffures and adornments were increasingly patterned after women's hairstyles and fashions, furthering stereotypes of Poodles and other groomed breeds as effeminate. The *tonte en macarons,* a cascade of coiled hair worn first worn by Princess Eugénie (1826–1920), the wife of Emperor Napoleon III, became the rage in the 1890s, inspiring the *caniche cordé,* or corded poodle. They still sported Continental clips, but now the fur on the shoulders and head was encouraged to mat until it formed ropelike coils that trailed the ground. Regardless of the dog's gender, the tresses around the face were knotted or tied atop the head with a large satin or velvet bow, in the style of a debutante.

Japan, a champion corded English poodle around the turn of the century.
source: Author.

Not everyone was happy to see canines with reputations as rugged, "manly" sporting breeds shaved, perfumed, draped in ribbons, and dyed red, green, or purple. Already rattled by the growing presence of women in the ranks of professional breeders, old-school sportsmen were outraged by what they perceived as canine dandification. "Under the many bridges that cross the Seine in Paris numerous dogs lie helpless in the shade of the arch," naturalist J.G. Wood fretted in 1874. "Their legs [are] tied together and their eyes contemplate with woeful looks the struggles of their fellows, who are being shorn of their natural covering and protesting with mournful cries against the operation." Wood called the partial denuding of canines while allowing remaining portions of their coats to become tangled masses a "barbarous" custom that made "it practically impossible to keep the dog clean and sweet," and found such fads "directly in opposition to the natural state of the Dog." Dog author Ernest Baynes echoed similar sentiments, complaining that "some owners tie the hair on top of [the dog's] head with a ribbon and send him out looking like a little girl going to a party. . . . it is a pity that the fashion of making him look ridiculous should have the effect of hiding [his] truly fine character." Even Charles Dickens felt guilty when he had to have his beloved Timber Doodle, a shaggy white Terrier, shaved because of a flea infestation. "[Timber] looks like the ghost of a drowned dog come out of a pond after a week or so," the author wrote to a friend. "He knows the change upon him and is always turning around and round to look for himself."

The more intimate the bond between pet and owner, the more pressing it was to seek a material outlet reflecting the elevated status of the animal. Consumers clamored for decorative collars or pet wardrobes as complete and "human" as their own. "Dressmakers in London, Paris and New York are doing a good business making traveling cloaks, evening cloaks, jackets and rubber boots [for dogs]," wrote Charles Burkett in 1907. The Galérie d'Orléans in Paris specialized in catering to the extravagant whims of aristocratic pet "parents," offering "shirts for dogs, monograms embroidered on [dog] garments," and even "overcoat[s] with velvet lapels." The Queen of Portugal was a regular customer, as well as numerous male notables, among them the Grand Duke Michael of Russia, the Turkish Viceroy of Egypt and Prince Waldemar of Denmark.

As might be expected, canine clothing mirrored upper-class fashions.

New lines of pet apparel were reviewed by fashion critics with the same *très chic* jargon found in reviews of women's attire. The author of *Les chiens de luxe* (1907) described a line of "little shirts decorated all over with narrow bands of Balenciennes lace that extend a half a centimeter around the coat, giving a special cachet to the outfit." And French essayist Paul Mégnin noted that "our chic dogs have a special bathing outfit—in blue cambric with a sailor's collar hemmed in white with embroidered anchors in each of the corners, and on one of the sides, embroidered in gold, the name of the beach—Cambourg or Trouville." For canines traveling in style there was "a checked cloak of English cloth with a turned down collar, belted, [and] a small pocket for the train ticket."

Chien de Luxe, a well-dressed French dog at the turn of the century.
source: Author.

Just a Gigolo by Parisian artist "Zito," who sketched the people and pets of Paris in the 1920s.
source: Author.

In Trouble with the Law

As urban animal populations soared, periodic outbreaks of rabies increasingly became a source of concern with health officials. Sensational news coverage of dog bite incidents triggered wholesale panics, inciting communities to purge their streets of "ill bred" animals. Failing to discover how the disease was transmitted and completely at a loss for a cure, the medical community cast rabies as some sort of social disease, attributable to dogs of "low moral standing"—just as the human underclass was blamed for the spread of syphilis. This provided justification for a genocidal campaign against "curs of low degree" in the final decades of the Victorian era. English bobbies received orders to apprehend animal "criminals," easily identified by their lack of collars. Poison-laced bait was scattered in London alleys where homeless animals were known to live and forage, and as the "rabies wars" escalated, police were ordered to blud-

Begging poodle with belled collar, ca. 1880.
source: Author.

Overfed Bull Terrier wearing typical Victorian leather and brass collar.
source: Author.

geon any pet caught off leash, and in some places, even those on leash but without a muzzle. Collars bearing inscribed plates or mandatory registration tags with the owner's name and address were essential to the Victorian dogs' survival away from the watchful eyes of their owners. The demand for collars increased dramatically as citizens scrambled to protect their pets from the rabies "vice squad." Vendors hawked leather and brass collars on London's Portobello Road as well as on busy street corners in High Kensington, at prices ranging from sixpence to three shillings.

Concern with fashion affected the design of even the cheapest collars, with plain leather bands often giving way to adornments such as bells, buttons, and colorful stitching. Some owners patterned their dogs' attire closely after the classic styles worn by dogs belonging to nobility, and ordered stamped or engraved collars made of rolled brass, copper, or silver. Housebound lapdogs wore silk ribbons, bows, scarves, and swatches of velvet or lace with applied beadwork.

Terrier wearing beaded collar, ca. 1900.
source: Author.

French dog wearing padlocked collar, ca. 1890.
source: Author.

Extravagant accessories could compromise a dog's safety, however, since dognappers prowled fashionable districts of big cities, abducting pets from the private gardens of their doting owners and holding them for a reward. Canines who were small, weak, or overly trusting of strangers were often mugged for their fancy neckwear (as evidenced by the sad fate of Civil War mascot Jack), so many collars came fitted with keyed padlocks to deter theft.

One tale of canine splendor from 1930s India involved his Highness Nawab Sir Mahabet Khan, ruler of the state of Junagardh, who was deeply attached to Roshanara, his female white Bull Terrier. To commemorate her pending mating he sent out fancy wedding invitations and organized a feast befitting a princess. On the day of her wedding, Roshanara was bathed in perfumes and decorated with a jeweled necklace specially designed for the occasion, while the "groom," a Golden Retriever named Bobby, who belonged to a neighboring Nawab, was bathed and adorned in similar fashion, with gold anklets and chains for his neck.

The Nawab of Junagardh and his beloved Roshanara.
source: Courtesy of the Guernsey Museums and Galleries, Guernsey, Channel Islands.

Boat Rockers and Jet-Setters

Within the first two decades of the twentieth century, women's corsets and crinolines gave way to flimsy, short-hemmed cocktail dresses with riotous cascades of sparkling beads, ushering in the "Roaring Twenties." As stars of the stage and silent screen made public appearances in the company of dogs, now both women and poodles had their tresses bobbed in perky page boys, reflecting a new spirit of rebellion against rigid Victorian moral strictures. Dog fancier Oscar Schultheis remarked with some sarcasm that "milady has seen to it that the dog has been selected with a care to showing her off, just as she shows off the dog. Those sedate old dogs of drab color went well with a hoop skirt but in these days something high-stepping and flashily colored is wanted." Many newly "liberated" European women—single, independently wealthy, and in no hurry to settle down—abandoned their dainty lapdogs for more manly breeds such as Great Danes, Newfoundlands, St. Bernards, and German Shep-

German actress Fern Andra with her poodle-clipped German Shepherd in the mid-twenties.
source: Author.

herds, and impertinently had the animals sheared and adorned in the same feminine fashion as the Poodles.

The Depression era of the 1930s put a damper on such excess, and as women's dresses became simple, understated, and functional, so did dog fashions. Pet catalogs of the time featured "sensible" plain leather collars, and garments were limited to plaid woolen sweaters or overcoats in subdued plaid patterns. With the advent of World War II, however, thousands of American women left their their kitchens to fill factory jobs and run businesses, and for the first time, fashion designers offered women garments to fit their new roles—in the form of blazers, comfortable slacks, and low-heeled shoes, all patterned after men's fashions. Accordingly, groomers responded to clients' demand for a less-contrived image for their Poodles, trimming dogs' coats to an even, comfortable length over the entire body, with the fur "hemmed" like pants at the ankles.

The postwar 1950s brought a new era of prosperity and a resurgence of interest in material goods. Consumer demand for mass-produced purebred dogs reached a peak unseen since the pet boom of the 1860s, and owning the "right" sort of dog again became a statement of personal status. The son of financier Otto Kahn, Count Alexis Pulaski, quickly ingratiated himself in New York City's high society by opening a combination grooming salon/pet haberdashery called "Poodles Incorporated." Catering to the likes of Gary Cooper and Arthur Godfrey, the shop provided sixteen coiffure styles for pets, jeweled accessories, and mink coats. It also offered Poodle puppies and championship-quality stud services from Masterpiece, the first internationally acclaimed gray Toy Poodle, valued at over twenty thousand dollars. Frequently seen dining with celebrities at the 21 Club, Masterpiece was in high demand as a professional model and media personality. Then, in 1953, at the height of his career, he vanished from the shop in one of the most celebrated cases of dognapping in history. Despite an ample reward and a media blitz calling for his safe return, Masterpiece was never seen again. Three years later Pulaski's shop folded, but by that time Poodles were the rage with Hollywood's leading ladies, who draped the dogs in rhinestone (and real diamond) chokers and collars, or dyed their fur to match pink Cadillacs and living room upholstery.

During the fifties and sixties, transatlantic luxury liners boasted canine beauty parlors and kennels furnished with hammocks and blankets, and one kennel master on the ocean liner *America* recalled a female passenger requesting that he dab her poodle with French perfume every day (the woman supplied two different scents—one for "each end" of the dog, she explained).

Berkeley Rice, author of *The Other End of the Leash* (1968), recounted an American dog wedding that would have made any Nawab envious:

> Along with its dinner parties and lawn parties the Palm Beach pet set recently attended a fashionable wedding of its own when two well-connected toy poodles were joined in matrimony at the Poodle Boutique. Miss Petite Brabbam, the bride, wore a dual-length ivory satin gown trimmed with Alençon lace, and a long veil of French Illusion hanging from a crown of seed pearls. The groom was Muggins Carvey, son of Signature's Silver Pride and Suzette Al'Kahira. He was conservatively attired in a white top hat and a black bow tie. Among the notable guests—all poodles—were the Smith brothers. Beau Smith wore a sunlight-yellow double-faced wool coat with collar and martingale in jonquil velvet, while his brother Michael appeared in a pink velvet coat with fuchsia-colored yarn fringe. Gigi and Mouton Kimberley were also there, Gigi in a pink sequined evening coat with white mink collar, and Mouton in a royal-blue sequined day jacket bowed at the back. After the wedding party posed for pictures, everyone retired to the patio for a short reception.

Alternative canine fashion statements first seen among rebellious Parisian pet owners of the 1860s resurfaced in the 1960s as symbols of revolt against the social and cultural conservatism of the 1950s—as well as in protest of the war in Vietnam. By the late sixties, hair and clothing styles popularized by student protesters filtered into mainstream fashions, influencing canine styles as well. Now poodles seen strolling in New York's Central Park were adorned with real or plastic flowers, or in a few cases, dyed in psychedelic swirls of green, pink, and yellow. As racial barriers and sexual inhibitions crumbled in the 1970s, for the first time it became politically correct to own a mongrel—the more mixed the animal's "racial" makeup the better. These animal companions reflected their owner's identity with the "counterculture" by wearing tie-dyed scarves and red bandanas. Their coats, of course, were left long. Twenty years later, upwardly mobile, corporate-driven, fashion-conscious baby boomers are wearing high-dollar L.L. Bean sportswear, driving new Lexuses and BMWs, and dreaming of owning condos in Colorado or Wyoming. Out of a faddish nostalgia, they have co-opted the "hippy" canine accessories of the sixties, and pet stores offer complete lines of tie-dyed T-shirts and bandanas, in California surfer-style neon and Hawaiian floral prints. And instead of adorning only the necks of well-mixed mutts, they are seen on papered, pedigreed Poodles, Cocker Spaniels and Golden Retrievers.

As the twentieth century draws to a close, technological innovations also are influencing collar designs. Christmas catalogs offer satin and velvet bow ties for dogs and cats fitted with miniature batteries to make the rhinestones twinkle. The Beverly Hills–based Protect-a-Pet Company has devised an "ultra-modern" nighttime safety collar made of flashing lights encased in clear tubing, designed by aerospace engineers at NASA, and other companies promote high-tech electronic collars they claim repel fleas and control barking. Today, many a jeweler in Beverly Hills sells strings of cultured pearls with diamond and gold clasps—for dogs. And in London, Harrods Department Store recently offered "a wealth of items [that] whilst not absolutely vital, nevertheless contribute imaginatively to a pet's lifestyle," including an eighteen-carat gold collar fitted with diamonds priced at £7,500 ($12,000).

Still, the leather collar with brass and nickel-plated knobs—mere vestiges of lethal spikes—endures as a classic, particularly for male dogs and

Futuristic collar made by Protect-a-Pet (PAP).
source: Protect-a-Pet.

"masculine" breeds. Though its history as a form of weaponry is not widely known today, it still connotes danger and power in canine imagery and popular satire. Even a Loony Tunes cartoon often features the stereotypically gruff Bulldog in a collar with protruding metallic knobs—and invariably, the character's name is Spike.

Fancifully coiffed Poodles also are subject to parody, as in a recent cartoon by Lynda Barry that depicts a defiant, snarling Poodle with spiked hair, reading, "He's small, he's black, he's MAD AS HELL—he's a POODLE WITH A MOHAWK. You'll never call him Fifi again!" An instant hit, the cartoon has been reprinted on posters, greeting cards, and T-shirts. In the same vein, unkempt Poodles have become metaphors for anarchy, as reflected in the popular movie *Batman Returns* (1992), in which a bizarrely matted Miniature Poodle is employed by the evil Penguin to carry bombs around Gotham City. Showring Poodles of the 1980s and 1990s, like their mistresses, sport long, voluminous tresses covering the ears, topped off with a crown of stiffly teased bangs. All the while, the dog's rear torso and hind legs are shaved naked, save for a few carefully placed pompoms.

Trendy salons double as fashion boutiques, featuring everything from miniature black leather motorcycle jackets, wedding trousseaus, party dresses, vacation apparel, hats, and sunglasses to costumes for Easter and Halloween. The Pet Set in Atlanta, Georgia, sells mink coats for dogs, with prices starting at around four hundred dollars, and does over one million dollars in business annually. Some regular customers spend an average of five thousand dollars per trip at the shop, on French chateau doghouses, marble feeding bowls, dinner jackets, brass beds, jogging suits, and high chairs. Teca Tu, a boutique of southwestern-style doggie vests, collars, and coats made of Indian trade blankets and decorated with suede fringe, recently opened near the old square in Santa Fe, New Mexico, as has Spirit Dog, the jewelry firm specializing in hand-tooled leather collars adorned with custom-designed coral-and-turquoise-inlaid conchos.

"The urbanization of America has put pets and their owners in closer confinement than ever before, and so the status of the pet has increased," observes Dr. Michael Garvey, chairman of the Department of Medicine at the Animal Medical Center in New York. "It was easier to ignore the needs of your pet when it was roaming outdoors. If you're living in a two room apartment with your two cats and dog, it's hard to ignore their needs." Canine beauty culture is overcoming its image as a snobbish excess to be reborn as a legitimate way to express concern and affection for an animal who now is regarded as a full-fledged member of the family. People living alone or with demanding careers feel particularly compelled to reward their dogs' love with luxury items and grooming services, partly out of guilt for not spending enough quality time with their animals. "There are a lot of 'latchkey' dogs out there whose owners can't make time for a regular bath or brushing session," says Jeffrey Reynold, executive director of the National Dog Groomers Association. Like their Parisian predecessors, some modern stylists call on their canine clients at home, bathing and grooming them in mobile salons—air-conditioned vans outfitted with bathtubs, dryers, and other beautifying equipment. A growing number offer not only bathing and styling, but teeth-cleaning and anal gland expression services as well, because pet owners realize that the more often a dog is handled the more likely infections, tumors, or injuries will be discovered before they become life-threatening.

Hundreds of professional groomers from Europe and America flock to annual conferences to attend seminars and workshops to learn new scissoring techniques or compete for high-dollar prizes in styling competitions that encourage creative expression—the more fantastic the better. Dog "models" are clipped, colored, and accessorized to resemble panda bears, elephants, zebras, bees, or even people. Some stylists prefer to treat the Poodle's sides and back like a blank canvas, and use fine-pointed scissors, spray paint, and stencils to create intricate landscapes, still lifes, or even depictions of horse-drawn carriages and frolicking dolphins. Others simply decorate their dog models in bold, abstract swirls of color, adding gems and feathers.

Traditionally, such lavish beautification rituals for dogs have been limited to Western industrialized cultures. But on the brink of the twenty-first century and the emergence of a global, urbanized middle class, societies lacking in intimate canine traditions are undergoing rapid change. Large portions of Asia and Africa are experiencing radical socioeconomic changes in the face of Western technologies and consumer goods, and accordingly, people increasingly are viewing dogs as fashionable adjuncts. In these situations, animal stylists—what few there are—educate pet owners about the benefits of regular grooming, and indirectly, the benefits of intimate relationships with pets. Angeli Lin-Yen Siow operates one of the first dog salons established in Singapore and says grooming pets has successfully made the transition from being perceived as an excess to "a sensible way of protecting one's investment."

"When I first opened my business, every dog I trimmed—and there weren't very many—was a tick-infested, matted mess," she recalled. "I tried to make the owners imagine the discomfort of their pets. 'How would *you* feel after four months without a bath?' I would ask, and show them the painful sores caused by those ever-tightening mats of fur." Ten years after opening, Lin-Yen Siow has more customers than she can tend to, and she believes that because of her admonishments, "life for Singapore pets has improved greatly. There are many more people today taking a personal interest in the health and happiness of their animals."

African dog culture has changed very little since the Neolithic era, and understandably, groomers are a rare breed. Tribal huntsmen in Nigeria and Kenya employ packs of golden-coated, aboriginal-looking hounds (resembling Dingos or large Basenjis) to canvass fields and wooded areas in search of game. The simple, practical relationship is based on the exploitation of dogs as tools, although some of the canines do wear distinctive collars of dyed, rolled, camel leather decorated with profusions of fringe, which have been made for centuries by tribal elders and village leatherworkers. Ostrich feathers affixed to the collar project over the dogs' heads to help hunters avoid shooting them by mistake as they run through dense grass. But today this traditional neckwear is about to become yet another piece of lost history, as dog owners opt for inexpensive, mass-produced neon plastic flea collars imported from the West.

The cheap collars are just one of many signs that traditional African dog cultures are changing or disappearing altogether. As racial and class barriers collapse and new urban job opportunities open up for the masses, the material trappings of Western affluence are being zealously embraced—everything from blue jeans, fast food, and pedigreed purebred European dogs has become an emblem of status in this new society. Still, some traditions persist, namely the animals continue to stay outdoors, chained in courtyards or corralled on apartment balconies, where they are expected to guard their masters' property against both human and animal intruders. "It is a lonely business for me because in the whole of Nigeria I have not seen or heard of any other groomer," remarked Chris Okafor, a self-taught animal stylist in Nigeria, who operates a fledgling salon out of the back of his family's pharmacy in the town of Enugu. "On rare occasions, hunters may bathe their dogs in a stream after a chase through the bush to remove thorns, dirt, and debris, but most canines receive no personal attention from their owners, let alone veterinary care." Okafor sees grooming and imported pet accessories—even those that hasten the decline of traditional forms of canine adornment—as essential to fostering a compassionate ethic. "In learning to become more responsible pet owners, my people will finally discover the true joy of living intimately with animals."

Whose Dog Are You?

Unlike other artifacts and documentation of canine history, many collars have survived to become highly coveted antiques in the 1990s. "Considered a somewhat quirky, rather esoteric pursuit which many more or less kept to themselves, dog collar collecting has now come into the mainstream," says art dealer William Secord, whose gallery of Edwardian canine portraits by famous animal artists draws customers from all over the world. Responding to growing demands for canine memorabilia, he has expanded his gallery to offer other top-dollar items, including antique collars.

Secord is not the only one to take notice of historical collars. English dealers in fine collectibles and antique jewelry offer vintage canine neckwear when they can obtain it, but admit that the market is fast dwindling as the number of collectors grows and values skyrocket. Prices for an ordinary, late-Victorian leather and brass collar (like those once sold by London street vendors for a few shillings) command from eighty to five hundred dollars (fifty to three hundred pounds), depending on their condition. But these are paltry prices compared to what might be paid for a collar of exceptional craftsmanship or provenance. The extent to which collectors will go to acquire such an item was demonstrated at a 1993 Christie's auction of items from a Scottish estate, including a small, engraved silver collar. While not remarkable itself, the collar originally was a gift to Sir and Lady Stuart Threipland in 1750 from England's Prince

Charles, then living in exile in Italy. Bidding on the collar escalated quickly to an incredible forty-one thousand pounds (sixty-eight thousand dollars).

Geoffrey Jenkinson of Guernsey (Channel Islands) was a connoisseur of antique collars long before collecting them became popular. His fascination with the artifacts began twenty-five years ago when he acquired one inscribed "The Honorable Mr. Jenkinson"—the collar of the dog of a remote ancestor. His collection now features a unique assortment of canine neckwear with documented histories, including an elaborately embroidered Renaissance collar made of doeskin and red velvet that commemorates the 1488 wedding of Bartolomeo Visconti and Philomena Nicoli. In a fashion typical of the era, its gilded wire stitching incorporates the coat of arms of both aristocratic families. Similar fashions are featured on hounds depicted in paintings and tapestries, but no other collar from this period is known to exist. Jenkinson also owns a heavy leather collar originally worn by Derby the Devil Dog, a Mastiff who belonged to a close friend of Sir Arthur Conan Doyle (Derby is thought to have been the inspiration for his *Hound of the Baskervilles*). A kid leather–lined collar worn by the beloved dog of actress Sarah Bernhardt bears an engraved plate reading, "Hamlet, 21 Rue François 1er, Paris / To be or not to be, that is the question."

As fantastic as such private collections are, the Dog Collar Museum at Leeds Castle in Maidstone (Kent) is unrivaled for its inventory of mint-condition collars spanning four centuries of canine history. Presented to the Leeds Castle Foundation by the widow of well-known medievalist John Hunt, the collection formerly was broken up and displayed intermittently in museums throughout Europe. Today, as a cohesive body of artifacts, the collection traces the social evolution of canines in Western civilization since the Middle Ages, supplemented by paintings and engravings. Many are engraved with family crests or emblems of aristocratic power, reflecting the status of the dog's master, while others bear inscriptions reflecting the owner's affection and humor, such as the one that reads, "I am Mr. Pratt's Dog—Whose dog are you?" Another admonishes, "Stop me not but let me jog for I am S. Oliver's Dog, Bicknell."

Many collars predating the industrial era are extremely large, suggesting they were worn by Mastiffs or Wolfhounds, who by their very nature connoted masculine, aristocratic power. By contrast, collars dating from the late Victorian era reflect the growing social diversification of dogs as a variety of breeds became pampered household pets. Lucky was the small dog who once wore an American-made leather collar with polished ovals of real Persian turquoise set in brass bezels, or one of the first celluloid (early plastic) collars, patterned after a man's turn-of-the-century starched collar.

Certainly such artifacts have an intrinsic value as works of art, but a greater part of their popular fascination probably lies in their nostalgic appeal. For in our modern, mechanized, mass-produced world of throwaway goods, handcrafted items from bygone eras fuel our yearning for a slower, less impersonal age. At the same time, hard evidence that past generations also had intimate relationships with their dogs provides modern pet lovers with a sense of continuity and connection to history, enhancing their appreciation for the canines who live with them today.

In the late nineties Western society is experiencing an "antifashion" movement, as wool suits and dress-and-hosiery ensembles (symbols of the corporate world for over fifty years) are being supplanted by button-fly jeans and T-shirts. Historically, such garments were popular for their comfort and economy, but now they have become emblems of creative genius, individuality, and financial independence. Oversized, mismatched articles of clothing, baggy sweatpants, Bermuda shorts, and traditional white undershirts (even "grunge" and "slacker" looks) have moved into the mainstream of fashion, destabilizing long-accepted dress codes in the business world—perhaps because the business world itself has been so drastically changed by home computers. With such unpretentiousness on the rise, will the contrived appearance of some pedigreed pets give way to a fashionably "sloppy" look? Could coiffures parodying baggy-seated pants be on the horizon for Poodles, or perhaps torn, Seattle slacker-style flannel shirts for lapdogs?

Now a groomed and adorned dog seems not so much to imply the superiority of civilization over nature as it suggests an animal's mastery of its owner's heart—a turning of the tables, so to speak. The emotional and physical isolation of individuals in modern society continues to make companion animals coveted personal accessories, not so much as fashion doppelgängers but as intimate life partners. As such, their unconditional devotion and ability to understand and reciprocate human emotions are generously rewarded with material trappings. Historically, canine beauty culture reflected domination and control. Now it celebrates the elevation of dogs to stations within the family unit previously reserved for other humans.

The Way to a Dog's Heart

BEFORE THE INDUSTRIAL Revolution, canine nutrition for working-class dogs was much like the diet of their working-class owners—basic, simple, and sometimes not very good. Although they worked all day within a whisker of glistening sides of beef or lamb, Turnspits were lucky to get anything beyond a crust of bread or a greasy knuckle of bone. Trekhonds fared a little better, although their diets also were identical to those of their peasant masters—meatless fare consisting of bread, potatoes, onions, and boiled cabbage. In general, the greater the wealth and status of the master, the more varied the diet of the dog. Canine dinners at the French court in the 1700s were lavish, for instance, including succulent bits of roast duck, consommé, cakes, and candied nuts or fruit.

The Chinese empress Tzu-tsi was said to have ordered her beloved Pekingese amply fed with "shark's fins, curlew's livers, and the breasts of quails . . . and for drink, tea that is brewed from spring buds or the milk of the antelope that pasture in the Imperial Park." Prince Albert, consort to Queen Victoria, was insistent on supplying his beloved Greyhound, Eos, with a steady diet of pâté de foie gras and fresh unsalted butter. When Eos died suddenly, Albert lambasted the scullery maid assigned to care for him for serving him salted butter, generally the fare of "commoners."

Dogs belonging to urban working-class owners in the mid-1800s fared somewhat better than their peasant predecessors. According to art historian Campbell Lennie, it was common in cities like New York and London to purchase rations of horse meat for dogs and cats, "since horses were dropping dead in the street everyday, the passersby scarcely sparing them a glance as the contractor or coster haggled over the price of a carcass with the cat's meat man." These inexpensive cuts of meat, combined with var-

The Breakfast Party by Sir Edwin Landseer, ca. 1860.
source: Author.

ied leftovers from their master's table, meant that many Victorian urban dogs enjoyed richly varied diets.

In the latter half of the nineteenth century, as pets came to be regarded as luxury items, the question of how best to maintain one's "investment" sparked new interest in canine nutrition. Fanciers were inspired to look beyond breeding and grooming for additional ways to "civilize" and elevate the canine race. In an era when medical breakthroughs cast new light on the world of microbes, the gastrointestinal tract was viewed as a brewery of disease fueled by a diet of bulky, unprocessed vegetable matter, which could result in an array of maladies loosely categorized as "blood poisoning." Harsh, antiseptic high colonics and even radical "colectomies"—elective surgeries to remove healthy colons—were employed in conjunction with disciplined diets of heavily processed foods void of dietary fiber and generous doses of laxative tonics or candies. In essence, imposing a "modern" diet on the body became a means of controlling an embarrassing inner, natural world.

Canine bodily functions were subject to the same obsessive concerns. Since the eating of meat (particularly raw meat) was natural to canines, dog experts often pointed to that as a corruptive influence that led civilized pets to lives of savage depravity. The more well bred the urban dog, the more important it was to control its behavior through diet. It might be acceptable to feed large, mongrel, country dogs a carnivorous diet, but according to Victorian British dog expert Francis Clater, meat caused mange or cankers and could "overexcite" pedigreed lapdogs adapted to life in city townhouses and apartments. Fresh meat brought out the worst in unspayed females, too. When the animals were in heat their primal passions could be inflamed by a "primitive"—and therefore "wrong"—diet, leading to disgraceful bouts of nymphomania. To head off such a crisis, ice water baths and meals of crustless bread, ground hemp seed, and milk were prescribed to calm the animal's nerves.

Writing in the 1880s, French author Jean Robert pointed out that highly processed meals for dogs were "contrary to their carnivorous nature." Other dog authorities of the time, such as Charles Burkett, agreed and argued for a more rational approach to canine nutrition, adding that "it is not bad to vary the food with rye bread, brown bread and vegetables." In a conciliatory nod to modernist thinking about dogs, however, even these experts advised the meat be cooked. American veterinarian A.C. Daniels prescribed a recipe for homemade "canine cakes" of boiled, minced beef or mutton, mixed with rice and vegetables, then baked, at the same time reluctantly admitting that canine nutrition was still "a subject of opinion."

Victorian kennel masters took pride in their own dog food recipes, some handed down from generation to generation. Most prepared huge pots of fresh vegetables and slaughterhouse leavings such as calves' heads, feet, and entrails, with a few "secret ingredients" that might be anything from a splash of sherry to a pinch of gunpowder. The kennel master to Queen Victoria took offense when Lootie the Pekingese came with special feeding instructions: "[the dog] is very dainty about its food, and won't generally take bread and milk, but it will take boiled rice and a little chopped chicken and gravy mixed up in it," wrote Captain Dunne, Lootie's savior. Not only unimpressed but unsympathetic, the man retorted that this "Imperial" Pekingese would get the same "nice cooked meat with breadcrumbs and powdered biscuit" as the other dogs, and "after a little fasting and coaxing, will probably come to like the food that is good for [it]."

Commercial Dog Foods for Urban Dogs

Despite recommendations for wholesome canine suppers of vegetables, whole grains, and fresh meats, consumer interest in controlling the "inner nature" of dogs persisted. The notion of a mass-produced, machine-processed pet food—inexpensive, easy to serve, and touted as superior to home cooking—was increasingly appealing to busy urban consumers, and commercial pet food became part of the new status associated with being "modern."

In the mid-1800s, a young entrepreneur named James Spratt journeyed from Cincinnati, Ohio, to London to sell lightning conductors. On his arrival, he was surprised to see vast hordes of homeless dogs lurking quayside, gobbling moldy, discarded hardtack (biscuits) thrown onto the piers by the sailors. Shortly afterward, he turned his attention to creating the first commercially produced biscuit expressly for dogs, unveiled in 1860 as Spratt's Patent Meat Fibrine Dog Cakes. A baked mixture of wheat, beetroot, and vegetables bound together with beef blood, Spratt's cakes were touted as a superior way to feed pets.

Within a few years other prepackaged dog foods appeared, often employing marketing techniques first used for patent medicines. Their biscuits, breads, and cakes not only gave a sheen to the dog's coat, but could prevent everything from tapeworms to distemper—claims bolstered by the paid endorsements of veterinarians such as Dr. A.C. Daniels, who willingly affixed his good name to a "Medicated Dog Bread," which unlike the competition was "free from cheapening ingredients such as talc powder and mill sweepings." Pioneering pet-food makers tried to discourage consumers from supplementing their products with other foodstuffs. Fresh beef, Spratt claimed, could "overheat the dog's blood," and even the most wholesome "table scraps will break down his digestive powers, [making] him prematurely old and fat." Meat was a necessary part of the dog's daily meal, the company agreed, but "should be in a form best suited to the requirements of his present existence," namely Spratt's biscuits. Playing on

To LOVERS OF DOGS.

Fac-simile of a Scarab in the possession
of the Philocynic Society,
date about 2000 B.C.
Translation of the Hieroglyphs:
Child·feed·thy·dog·wisely·and·thou·shalt·
prevail·at·the·Bench show."

Send for gratis pamphlet on dog feeding etc. to:

SPRATT'S PATENT, L?

239 East 56ᵗʰ Street, New York City.

Advertisement for Spratt's Patent
Dog Biscuits, playing on widespread interest in ancient Egypt
after the discovery of King Tut's
tomb in 1922.
source: Author.

doting pet owners' worries that commercially made biscuits contained inferior ingredients, Medicated Dog Bread spokesman Daniels claimed that
other biscuits might result in "constipation, indigestion and skin ills," but
his product was made with only "the best winter wheat, rice meal and
fresh meat."

Still, there was continued concern that an overly processed diet might
not be good for a dog's mental or physical health. "To live on dog biscuits
alone would be a very dull diet," said British author E.M. Aitkens. "A finely
grated carrot or a little chopped raw cabbage and other greens will be hun-
grily eaten if mixed well with meat and broth in which plenty of vegetables have been cooked." And veterinarian Dr. Raymond Garbutt, one of
the first to use X-ray technology to diagnose canine maladies, reported
that he was seeing a growing number of dogs suffering from the "piles"
(hemorrhoids), which he attributed to the feeding of "too many consti-
pating foods," particularly dry kibble.

Between 1890 and 1945, the manufacture and sale of pet foods continued to increase despite such criticisms, as consumers became more pos-

sessive of their leisure time, opting to spend it on anything but "slaving over a hot stove" for their dogs. Seen by many as an ideal entrepreneurial business opportunity—utilizing raw materials nobody else wanted (mostly inedible meats and grains) to produce a product eagerly sought by a growing population of dog owners with increasing disposable incomes—several new dog food companies were founded, many of them still in existence today. Others began as outgrowths of financially strapped companies looking for ways to turn a profit from the large quantities of waste materials produced by their granaries and slaughterhouses.

After World War II, the burgeoning success of commercial dog food was part of a sweeping societal trend toward modern conveniences that would both improve the overall standard of living and maximize the consumer's leisure time. Women embraced anything that would free them from the kitchen or ease their household chores. Like drive-through restaurants and frozen entrees, prepackaged dog food was just one more culinary advantage.

Frozen-food recipe booklet cover, 1942.
source: Author.

Beginning in the 1950s, companies switched their promotional strategies to emphasize the convenience of canned and bagged dog foods. "Feeding a dog is simple today," declared a Kasco dog food company advertisement. "It is unnecessary to cook special foods, measure this and that—why bother when it takes less than a minute to prepare a Kasco meal for your dog?" Calo dog food played on a similar theme, promising to do "away with all the fuss and bother in preparing food for your dog." Ken-L-Ration bragged about the lightning speed with which their dog food could be served and cleaned up, since it did not "stick to the feeding bowl [and is] easier than ever to mix. Ken-L-Meal absorbs water almost instantly." By 1961, Gaines was advertising "dog food that makes its own gravy," in just sixty seconds.

As the pet food market became increasingly lucrative through the 1960s, it caught the eye of American industrial giants looking to diversify. Quaker Oats, Ralston-Purina, and other breakfast food conglomerates began producing grain-based kibbles and biscuits, and meat-packers such

Ad for "sixty-second" Gravy Train dog
food, 1961.
source: Author.

Ad for Friskies, 1955.
source: Author.

as Armour and Swift marketed the first canned dog foods with a meat base. (During this time, too, questions about the safety of cigarettes first prompted tobacco companies to diversify their holdings, and pet food was one of the more popular investments.) Competition among these industrial "big boys" brought new, stylishly packaged products and eye-popping promotional campaigns created by Madison Avenue hotshots, which torpedoed smaller, independent companies like Spratt's, as well as most regional "mom and pop" pet foods.

But too many dog owners persisted in supplementing commercial dog food with table scraps, so companies retooled their marketing strategies. Advertisements ceased to even acknowledge the idea of home cooking for dogs, and put an increasingly derogatory twist on "scraps," while commercial foods were powerhouses of proteins, minerals, and vitamins. At a 1964 meeting of the Pet Food Institute (PFI), a Washington-based lobbying association representing American companies, George Pugh, an executive of Swift and Company (makers of Pard dog food) described ongoing efforts to discourage the feeding of anything but commercial dog food. Thanks to PFI press releases, he reported to industry colleagues, "we got stuff in one thousand daily and weekly papers." PFI staff also "assisted" *Good Housekeeping, Redbook,* and fourteen other popular magazines in the preparation of feature articles about dog care, which not incidentally advocated commercial pet food to the exclusion of everything else. And a script prepared and distributed by PFI, warning of the dangers of table scraps, got airtime on ninety-one radio stations throughout the country.

Beef Wars

For the next decade the industry's primary goal was to convince consumers that dogs were carnivores, pure and simple, and so required a diet of meat such as only they could provide. In 1967, television advertising for the industry totaled fifty million dollars, most of it spent on a "beef war" in which each company claimed that their product contained the most. "Feed more than just HALF A DOG!" one company urged, implying that the more beef a dog gets, the happier and peppier it is. Alpo hired television's *Bonanza* star Lorne Greene to hold up a perfectly marbled sirloin steak before the camera and exhort the virtues of pure beef dinners for

"More beef" advertisement for
Ideal Dog Food, 1956.
source: Author.

1948 Dash brand dog food advertisement. Its very
name suggests a harvest of high-energy nutrition
for pets.
source: Author.

dogs. To spur sales of new products, companies supplemented television
campaigns with special promotions costing hundreds of thousands of dollars. To introduce a semimoist food packaged in the shape of hamburger
patties, kept perpetually soft with a generous dose of ordinary corn syrup,
one company gave away almost half a million dollars' worth of free samples—approximately one million pounds of the product. Another special
promotion backfired on Ralston Purina, which in the mid-sixties tested
consumer interest in a new Bonanza Dog Meal in Wichita and Kansas City.
Ads claimed the product was "preferred in taste tests six-to-one over the
largest selling dog meal"; only after the promotion was under way did
company executives learn that the biggest selling dog meal in the test area
was Purina Dog Chow, their own product.

Sales continued to rocket and by 1975 there were more than 1,500 makers of dog food, as compared to only 200 forty years earlier. Consumers

Canned dog food became more profitable than ever after World War II, when tin rationing was lifted, freeing the way for manufacturers to prepackage a wider selection of processed foods for consumers. source: Author.

A 1943 advertisement for Pard, suggesting a link between the food and canine vitality. source: Author.

embraced prepackaged dog food, spending seven hundred million dollars a year on canned and dry products. As America's pet population climbed through the seventies, signaling a growing emotional attachment to dogs, industry analysts correctly predicted a trend in "humanized" pet foods, molded and packaged like those for humans. Company budgets for color television commercials quadrupled, while promotions shifted from sermons on sound nutrition to visual appeal. Novelty was the industry buzz word, and the race was on to concoct ever more entertaining types of pet food. Sitting in their living rooms, consumers were treated to an enticing, colorful banquet of "hamburger" patties with grill marks and a mock-cheese garnish, or stews, meatballs, and gravy-covered filets tender enough to cut with a fork—but for pets.

Stampeding Lilliputian chuck wagons careened across the floors of TV kitchens, leading frantic, wild-eyed dogs to steaming bowls of moist,

This canned food was marketed in 1947 as "complete nourishment" for both dogs and cats, a strategic marketing factor well into the 1960s, when nutritionists concluded that felines and canines had different nutritional needs.
source: Author.

A 1943 advertisement for "dehydrated" dog food, packaged to resemble canned dog food. According to the ad, the addition of warm water would restore food to its "pre-war form," by softening and making a gravy.
source: Author.

meaty chunks swimming in rich brown broth. Even dry dog food took on a festive air, with kibble in every color of the rainbow, just like kids' cereals. Free brochures on housebreaking or training the family dog to perform simple tricks were used to hawk new lines of pet treats in the shape of little fish, eggs, and milk bottles in "six gay colors," with a slogan that flew in the face of earlier industry advice against between-meal snacks: "Whatever else your dog eats during the day, he needs treats too!" The industry also dabbled in some far-out advertising ploys during this time, such as the high-frequency whistle known as the Bowser Rouser. On hearing the whistle, the family dog would supposedly run to the television set, barking and jumping, to convince his owner that he wanted that particular brand of food.

Healthy Food Redefined

By 1980, growing consumer worries about artificial additives in their own diet convinced many companies to tone down outlandish marketing ploys and return to advertisements that stressed the nutritional value of their products. To counter accusations that pet foods contained harmful additives, the industry cast itself as a "scientist" rather than a recycler, dedicated to the never-ending search for the perfectly formulated dog food. The PFI acknowledged that "pet health officials increasingly voiced a need for more information and verification . . . concerning nutritional claims for pet foods," so the organization announced a "self-enforcement program" to provide pet health professionals and pet owners with added assurance of quality nutrition in their pet foods. By 1991, sales of pet food had topped out at over eight billion dollars. Canned and kibbled fare occupied more supermarket shelf space than breakfast cereal or baby food. A whole generation of consumers now could not recall a time when pets ate anything but commercial dog food, and the campaign to discourage alternative food sources had been so successful that some consumers were fearful of feeding their dogs even a piece of soda cracker.

Lorne Greene notwithstanding, veterinarians and pet food spokesmen proclaimed, thanks to industry-sponsored research, that they had discovered dogs actually were omnivores, thereby requiring a diet of whole grains and vegetables instead of pure meat. One company recently ran a magazine advertisement featuring a raw, well-marbled T-bone steak under the caption, "It's about as natural as feeding a dog cheese puffs," before launching into a diatribe on the all-natural ingredients in their product. Cornucopias of fresh fish, lamb, chicken, turkey, brown rice, golden ears of corn, carrots, brown eggs, garlic, and freshly picked parsley still covered with dew are featured in other ads—again attempting to appeal to the changed palates of pet owners, who now clamor for organic produce and free-range poultry.

In fact, the industry walks a fine line when it makes such announcements about dog nutrition. Fearing that all the talk of farm-fresh ingredients might spur consumers to take their skillets in hand and resume cooking for their pets, dog food companies make a point of emphasizing that canine nutrition is a science best left to qualified experts—namely them (or research projects sponsored by them). Ads for "super premium" and "prescription" dog foods incorporate actors or models wearing goggles and white lab coats, shown holding clipboards as they measure out healthy-looking ingredients amid a clinical forest of test tubes, computers, and diagnostic equipment. Echoing Victorian bowel obsessions, companies eagerly point to the superiority of their products as indicated by the small, dark, firm feces they yield. Hypnotized by the prospect of dog foods so scientifically advanced they could sustain astronauts on prolonged space missions, consumers are torn between intimidation and awe. Terms such as "chelated minerals," "metabolizable energy," and "amino acid profile" combine to both intrigue and confuse even the most savvy consumers, who are left to puzzle over ingredient lists and nutritional charts on dog food packages.

But when pets are treated like children or spouses, convenience ceases to be the driving force for buying commercial dog food. In fact, many consumers now would be offended at the suggestion that they buy prepackaged pet food simply because it is quick and easy. And because they pride themselves in buying only the best for their dogs, they sometimes are attracted to products that actually are inconvenient to purchase. Cable TV "infomercials" touting new brands of pet food sell like wildfire, even though the product is available only by phone, and great quantities must be ordered each time. Other new products are available only from select distributors. Hill's originally made its Science Diet available exclusively through veterinarians, an ingenious marketing strategy that grabbed the attention of millions of yuppie consumers seeking reassurance that they were providing their pets the best nutrition money could buy, and moving Hill's to the forefront of superpremium foods in the early nineties. Such foods may cost triple the amount of grocery store brands, but high sticker price is just another incentive to buy when a dog owner reasons that the more it costs, the better a food must be.

Play It Again, Sam

Now consumer activists are again accusing the dog food industry of using substandard and harmful ingredients to cut costs and increase profits. Leading the quest for more truthful labeling on dog foods is the United Animal Owners Alliance (UAOA), a nonprofit organization that publishes research findings on the safety of ingredients and preservatives used in commercial pet foods. One controversy involves the long-term use of ethoxyquin (brand name Santoquin), an antioxidant/preservative found in both pet and human foods. Over the last few decades it has become an integral part of the modern food chain, commonly sprayed on livestock feed, and for a time, even stirred into the drinking water of chickens to make their egg yolks bright yellow. Pet food companies use it to stabilize canned and bagged products, especially those made from spoiled or rancid grains, chicken feathers, hooves, beaks, animal feces, and even blood-soaked sawdust squeegeed off slaughterhouse floors, all of which fall under Food and Drug Administration (FDA) definitions for pet food ingredients called "meal" and "by-product."

A growing number of pet owners, professional breeders, and veterinarians have questioned the safety of ethoxyquin as an ingestible preservative. Investigating its history through government documents, the UAOA found the preservative listed in the *Consumers' Dictionary of Food Additives* as an "herbicide," while OSHA had identified ethoxyquin as a "hazardous chemical." As of this writing, the FDA limits this chemical in human foods to five parts per million—dog food, however, may include up to 115 parts per million. Articles in veterinary journals and popular pet magazines suggest that ethoxyquin may be partly responsible for a wide array of health problems now plaguing the canine race, especially animals whose immune systems have been compromised by generations of intensive inbreeding. According to Dr. W. Jean Dodds, DVM and Director of the Comparative Hematology Laboratory at the New York State Department of Health, a nearly tenfold increase in immune-mediated canine diseases "has coincided with the introduction of ethoxyquin into premium brands of pet foods" (DVM *Newsmagazine*, 1991). Others suspect that ethoxyquin may be linked to canine infertility, inexplicable bouts of aggression, stillborn puppies, puppies with severe deformities such as cleft palates and hydrocephalism, recurrent tumors, kidney or liver failure, and even hypothyroidism.

Monsanto Chemical Company, the patent holder and maker of ethoxyquin, conducted a five-year study on ethoxyquin-laced dog food thirty years ago, but steadfastly refused to relinquish the findings to the public for fear of "misinterpretation." Finally in 1989, in response to pressure from consumer groups such as the UAOA, the FDA demanded a copy of Monsanto's study and found it "deficient." But the federal watchdog on health still feels there is not sufficient reason to call for a review of the use of ethoxyquin as an additive in human or animal foods. Critics have cried foul, saying the pet food industry used its political clout to quash any effort to review the substance by an unbiased, independent party. Pressure from the public did eventually result in ethoxyquin being entered into the National Toxicology Program for testing; however, it could be years before such a test is even scheduled. Then in 1991 it was announced that a new, three-year research project to study the effect of ethoxyquin on dogs would be conducted by an independent testing laboratory—sponsored by Monsanto Chemical Company. Findings were due in 1994, but in March of 1995 Monsanto announced that the study would be extended because some of the test dogs had become pregnant. At this writing, there is no word about when the study will be concluded, or if it will be released to the public.

Even so, the bad publicity has inspired many pet food companies to opt for new, safer preservatives, notably vitamins A, C, and E. Meat renderers may still add ethoxyquin to products before their sale to pet food companies, however, and under current FDA guidelines, pet food companies are not obligated to list ethoxyquin in their ingredient labels unless they have added an additional dose themselves. Critics still worry that as industrial "self-regulation" becomes more commonplace and federal regulatory agencies like the FDA are scaled back, chemical companies that manufacture pet food additives will continue to oversee the clinical trials of substances that they have a financial stake in, and determine whether the public is entitled to know the results of studies or trials.

White Bread and Gravy

Until recently, people who opted to cook for their dogs instead of purchasing commercial foods were looked on as "counterculture" pet owners, well intentioned but ill-informed. But now that natural foods have become a part of the baby-boomer culture, that attitude is changing. Many consumers now believe that responsibility for one's health begins at home, with the foods one chooses to eat. These people try to purchase groceries in chemically unadulterated and minimally processed forms whenever possible—and they're starting to believe the same dietary principles should be applied to their pets. Since its debut in the mid-eighties, *Dr. Pitcairne's Complete Guide to Natural Health for Dogs and Cats* (1982) by Richard Pitcairn, DVM, has been widely regarded as a pioneering work by consumers desiring a less-processed diet for their pets, patterned after the ones they follow themselves. "Much of the supposed protein in commercial food actually cannot be digested by dogs," Pitcairn says, "and the heating involved in the canning process destroys much of the original food value. The truth is that most pet foods on the market do little more than just sustain life." Addressing the pet food industry's age-old commandment against feeding table scraps, Pitcairn admits this could be harmful "if a person just scraped leftover cookies, white bread, gravy and canned spinach into a pet's bowl," foods from which most of the nutritional value has been destroyed by overprocessing. But he also is quick to point out that "generation after generation of healthy animals thrived on the scraps and extras of the whole natural foods of our ancestors."

Pitcairn recommends canine dinners of raw or lightly steamed vegetables, legumes, nuts, raw meats, eggs, and cottage cheese, along with breakfasts of hot oatmeal, whole milk, and a touch of honey. Cost-wise, the recipes are competitive with many grocery store brands of pet food, and batches sufficient for one or two weeks can be made in advance, then refrigerated or frozen in single servings.

Since the publication of Pitcairn's book, federal agencies and book publishers have responded to consumers desiring to educate themselves in the field of pet food. *Nutrition Requirements for Dogs,* published by the National Research Council, reports the latest in scientific studies on canine nutritional requirements. And Adele Publications (not affiliated with any dog food manufacturer) offers *Canine Nutrition and Choosing the Best Food for Your Breed of Dog,* which asserts that different breeds have different nutritional needs.

As with canine beauty culture, feeding strategies may reflect a dog's social rank within its adoptive human family. The more "human" position the animal occupies, fulfilling the role of a child or spouse, the more inclined pet parents are to supply the animal with a completely human diet. "My pet shares all aspects of my life, and food is no exception," explained the owner of Skeeter, a former shelter dog. She and her canine "child" share dinners of poached fish, home-baked breads, French cheeses, and organic produce, including tomatoes, asparagus, and oranges. "Skeeter has eaten nothing but human food—no junk food— for seven years now. His teeth are white and his breath smells better than mine."

For the dog owner in no hurry to get out of the kitchen, Richard Graham's *The Good Dog's Cookbook* may be just the ticket. This author believes humans and dogs possess the capacity to appreciate many of the same foods. Graham offers some rather complicated "human" recipes, including multiple-course dinners beginning with appetizers and soups, followed by entrees such as a "traditional Irish layered pie" of pheasant, steak, and sliced hard-boiled eggs in a light wine sauce, or "Chinese-style rabbit," braised in port wine with fresh herbs.

For many people, the more involved and time-consuming the dog feeding ritual becomes, the more emotionally gratifying it is. Retired movie star Doris Day hired six housekeepers to care for her extended family of dogs and spends hundreds of dollars weekly on their food. Her Carmel, California, home includes a kitchen set aside exclusively for cooking pet food. "I do all the shopping myself," Day says. For breakfast, she and her staff bake "[gourmet] turkey loaves with garlic, onion and eggs each day," periodically alternating with deboned chicken and plenty of fresh vegetables, whipped potatoes, brown rice, and pasta. At night, the animals often enjoy a light supper of cornflakes in milk or low-fat cottage cheese. "Although it can be expensive, my pets give me so much love that it's the least I can do," she explained.

Of ten thousand American pet-owning households surveyed in 1993 by Barry Sinrod, author of *Do You Do It When Your Pet's in the Room?*, almost 50 percent gave their dogs a steady diet of "human food," suggesting the instinct to share food still runs deep in the human psyche, despite fifty years of industry-sponsored "education." Convinced that t eir pets also detest monotonous meals, many are choosing to compro ise on disciplined diets of scientifically formulated kibble with a vast ray of interesting culinary indulgences. Owners report that their dogs njoy corn on the cob, peaches, apples, and tomatoes, not to mentio fresh-roasted turkey or a bit of steak. Some sympathetic dog owners also admitted to the occasional, sinful canine indulgences, such as home-delivery pepperoni pizza or a spin through the drive-through at McDonald's for a box of fries and a soft ice cream sundae, sometimes in celebration of the animal's birthday.

Pitcairn agrees that variety in an animal's diet is good emotionally as well as physically. He puts it in human terms: "Think about eating [the same thing] for the rest of your life. Certainly you'd refuse such a diet, even if there were a 'health food' variety. Before long most of us would be climbing the walls looking for a salad or some fresh fruit—anything relatively whole and fresh! Or just different!" In fact, regimented diets of processed food almost from birth have left some dogs at a loss as to what to do when handed a bit of bread, a vegetable, or even a bone. To deprive canines—among the most intelligent and inquisitive of creatures—the experience of eating unprocessed foods is not only a denial of their animal nature but of their need for new learning experiences.

Though largely ignored by social historians, what we humans feed our dogs, from cabbage to Kibble, constitutes a kind of diary of the increasingly important roles canines have played in our lives, not to mention the dogs' ability to adapt and thrive in changing environments. Historically, the things we feed our companion animals have reflected the psychological needs of humans, particularly the desire to conquer the "inner nature" of both man and beast. Then processed foods for humans and pets caught on as a result of Western society's post-World War II drive for convenience and more leisure time, both of which quickly became identified with being "modern," and more importantly, affluent.

Now nostalgia for a simpler time, when humans and dogs shared the same beds and breakfasts, has prompted a return to home cooking and natural foods. And the hallmark of a prosperous, leisurely life is how much time one can afford to spend tending to the needs of pets—not how little. Today, food continues to serve as both a literal and symbolic "tie that binds" our companion animals, making them dependent on us for survival. But it also is the foundation of a more complex and loving relationship between people and their pets. As we near the beginning of the twenty-first century, human and canine feeding strategies appear to have come full circle, perhaps symbolizing our yearning for a more intimate relationship with the natural world.

Eleven

Saying Good-Bye

If there is no God for thee,
Then there is no God for me.

—Anna Hempstead Branch

O N THE DEATH OF HIS BELOVED DOG Boatswain in 1808, Lord Byron was moved to compose an epitaph memorializing his pet as "Strength without Insolence, Courage without Ferocity, And all the Virtues of Man without the Vices." In subsequent decades such words have been echoed by a growing legion of pet owners who wish to memorialize their dogs in death, not for their ability to function as fashionable adjuncts to the material trappings of wealth, but as constant, loving companions.

Before the late 1800s, when the lifespan of the underclass was cut short by disease, poor nutrition, work-related injuries, and childbirth, their cemeteries were often neglected tracts of land far from church, village, or homestead. Families struggled to raise the few pennies needed to pay the grave digger, who sometimes unceremoniously tossed the deceased into a large communal pit, or interred them in graves already occupied, stacking casket upon casket until the last body was only inches below ground. Such places were rarely visited by survivors, whose lives already were filled with daily reminders of the same ignominious end. Little room was left for sentimentality when it came to the death of an animal, although there were exceptions.

Upon the death of a performing dog who was the heart's delight of his master, a parish priest, the man intended to conduct a formal Christian funeral, but news of the plan leaked to his supervising bishop, who summoned him to appear before a tribunal and face charges of sacrilege. Pleading his innocence before the court, the priest not only succeeded in getting all charges dropped, but shamed his accuser as well. "You will understand, my Lord, that I was able to put this dog, who was worth much more than a good number of Christians, in a discreet position," he is reported to have said. "The dog gave me many instances of wisdom in life, and above all in its death! It even wished to leave me its will, at the head of which is the name of the bishop of this diocese, to whom it bequeaths 150 crowns, which I have here for you now."

Even before the modern era, pet dogs were interred in small cemeteries scattered throughout England, Europe, and eastern America. But these were invariably on private land and for dogs belonging to the aristocracy, who conducted their own gravesite services often with great ceremony. "His attachment was without selfishness, his playfulness without malice, his fidelity without deceit," read the epitaph of Dash the Spaniel, the first and perhaps best-loved dog of Queen Victoria. Over the course of her long life, the vast grounds surrounding Windsor Castle became the final resting place for countless animals, ranging from full-grown horses to a tiny finch, and of course many dogs, their likenesses immortalized in life-size statues erected over each grave. Other aristocratic families followed the royal example. An obelisk was erected by Sir Henry and Lady Meux of Hertfordshire in memory of their dog Chloe, for example, and over the years this family added the names of other dogs who passed through their doors.

In the latter half of the nineteenth century, thousands of landless pet owners who lived in densely populated cities were confronted with choosing between two nightmarish options when a dog died: throwing it out with the trash or placing the body in a weighted sack and flinging it into a nearby river (2,021 dead dogs and 977 cats were pulled from the Seine in 1900 by Paris sanitation crews). Complaining of the lack of dignified options for saying farewell to an animal, Charles Burkett pointed out that ancient societies honored deceased animals, "while *our* advanced civilization, that knows so much better, casts them into the manure pit." Georges Harmois, publisher of the French newsletter *L'Ami des Chiens* and an early advocate for pet cemeteries, agreed: "No one who has petted and become attached to a good dog wishes to see his poor little lifeless body thrown into a scavenger's cart. . . . Yet, strange to say, some refined Christian people will do this, and shut their eyes and hearts to the pitiful and revolting sight."

The dilemma was exacerbated by the fact that people now living in such proximity to their pets were developing unusually strong emotional bonds with them. So untold numbers rejected both options, choosing instead to risk arrest by sneaking into public parks after dark to inter their dogs and cats. The notion of pet cemeteries for the public was a blending of two popular Victorian ideologies—one glorifying the fidelity of pets, the other romanticizing death. As medical and scientific developments gave humanity a greater sense of control over its destiny, death was transformed in popular imagery from the black-robed, skeletal "Grim Reaper" to an angelic messenger. Freed from the shackles of earthly existence, the spirit would be reunited with loved ones in an eternal, heavenly afterlife. Accordingly, the forlorn, overcrowded graveyards of previous centuries were supplanted by romantic gardens where stone paths wound through blooming hedgerows, with ivy-covered alcoves graced by the artful placement of an Italian statue or two. On any Sunday, dozens of families might be seen sitting among the tombstones enjoying a picnic.

In this climate, the exploits of pets in the service of their human masters inspired a steady stream of sentimental poetry, essays, paintings, and engravings. The outpourings were a celebration of fidelity, for in the minds of popular Victorian writers and artists, dogs embodied the highest virtue of all—unconditional love. "Is not the dog an animal we can exalt without any reservation?" pointed out Harmois. "Is he not worth as much as many men and more than some others? . . . Has he not that great superiority over the human race of possessing such remarkable constancy and sincerity of faith?" Popular social commentators struggled to make sense of the emotional pain experienced at the death of a pet. "The misery of keeping a dog is his dying so soon," reflected Sir Walter Scott, whose own Scottish Deerhound, Maida, was laid to rest under a marble likeness at Abbotsford. "But to be sure, if he lived for fifty years and then died, what becomes of me?"

By habit a woman of few words, Queen Victoria spoke surprisingly often and at length about the unwavering devotion of her favorite dogs, just as, according to Washington Irving, Scott was inclined to "pause in conversation, to notice his dogs and speak to them as if rational companions. . . . His domestic animals were his friends." Such relationships became increasingly commonplace in the modern urban world, as traditional neighborhoods of extended families were bulldozed to make way for factories and multistoried apartment buildings. Material wealth often seemed to take precedence over spiritual fulfillment, and many people felt disoriented or left behind by a rapidly changing society. Isolated from friends and families, city dwellers increasingly turned to their dogs for emotional support. In many cases, particularly for the single or elderly, animals were the only family, the only "people" they could depend on to love them regardless of their standing (or lack or it) in the community.

Little wonder then that the establishment of the first public pet cemeteries in the final decades of the nineteenth century was welcome news to

German pet funerary procession of children, probably staged for a photographer around 1900.

source: Author.

Dog cemetery at Asnières, France.
source: Author.

Victorian pet crypt with a life-size bronze statue of "Bob," the deceased dog, mounted on the lid, ca. 1890.
source: Author.

animal lovers. Founded in 1899 by feminist Marguerite Durand, the dog cemetery at Asnières lies on a forested river islet near Paris that was already a playground of the middle and professional working class, thereby smoothing its conversion into a charming garden resting place for animals. Caretakers offered a sliding-scale burial fee to accommodate wealthy and impoverished alike. For a few francs one could inter a dog in a common, communal grave, or for fifty francs reserve a private plot for ten years. One hundred francs assured thirty years of undisturbed rest, and rich pet owners gladly shelled out five hundred and more francs to guarantee an eternal resting place for their dogs.

Crushed under the wheels of a carriage barreling down busy Bayswater Road, the accidental death in 1888 of Prince, a Dachshund belonging to the Duke of Cambridge, inadvertently led to the creation of a small but extremely popular pet cemetery in the heart of London. The trembling, grief-stricken duke carried his dog into a fenced rear garden of a cottage at Victoria Gate (entering Hyde Park), and with the help of the groundskeeper, interred his companion near a large hedge. Stories of the little dog's demise touched the public, and soon other pet owners were peti-

Hyde Park Dog Cemetery, London, as it appeared around the turn of the century.
source: Author.

tioning for permission to bury their dogs in Hyde Park. Within twelve years the garden contained more than three hundred graves and had to be closed to further burials.

A larger, more lavish pet cemetery then was established at Molesworth in Huntingdonshire. By 1926, it contained over six hundred graves, many marked with marble pedestals and ornate statuary. One dog belonging to a wealthy socialite was embalmed upon its death in Italy and shipped back to England for interment in its own marble mausoleum complete with stained-glass windows.

The Humanitarian Spirit

Paradoxically, the same Victorian society that produced sentimental writings and art about dogs and death expected people to maintain a high degree of emotional detachment from their animals, at least in public. Pet owners who went to great lengths to arrange a burial befitting the elevated status of a cherished dog often were subjected to ridicule by non-pet own-ers. This was particularly true in the final decade of the nineteenth cen-tury, as the cold, clinical eye of science began to supplant earlier, more romantic views of nature. Now zoological treatises portrayed all kinds of animals as biological automatons, bereft of conscious thought, function-ing on instinct alone. Asserting that the capacity to feel and express emo-tion were exclusively human traits, public health experts expressed concerns that the burial of pets posed a health hazard and also wasted till-able soil. (In actuality it was the human burials that threatened the safety of the public, as lead casket linings eroded and leached into rivers supply-ing water to densely populated areas.)

Pet lovers rarely found comfort in the Church, which for centuries had maintained the stance that sentimental attachments to dogs were beneath divine consideration, and in fact bordered on sacrilegious. "I have not for many years identified myself with any church, chiefly because I do not know of any church which looks upon the animal world—outside of man—as included in its mission of 'good will on earth,'" reflected Mary Elster in 1899. An outspoken American animal welfare advocate, she penned strong parting words, with instructions that they be read aloud by her husband at her funeral:

> My idea of the holy Catholic church is one which shall reach out its protecting hand to every animal into which God has breathed the breath of life, which shall shelter them, defend them from torture at the hand of their most relentless enemy—man—[and] which shall esteem their rights as equal to our own; yea greater, as they are weaker and incapable of speech.

Most Victorian clergymen echoed the same old objections to the burial of dogs, calling it heresy to apply Christian funerary rites to animals. The only thing certain to incite even louder objections was the notion of burying humans and animals together, as we've already seen by the remarkable posthumous wanderings of Frederick the Great, whose dying request that he simply be buried among his little hounds in the garden at Sanssouci was ignored for two centuries. Likewise, Lord Byron's wish to be buried next to his beloved Boatswain also was ignored. The German composer Richard Wagner (1813–83) fared better—when his dog Russ was murdered by poison, the animal was immediately placed inside the composer's own tomb. Wagner then commissioned a discreet stonemason to carve the animal's likeness by the mausoleum entrance, with the words, "Here Russ rests, and waits."

Burying dogs with humans continues to be a controversial subject, as evidenced by the reaction of the public in the late sixties to news that Monsieur Blois, a leading French industrialist, planned to inter the children's dog in the family burial plot. Backed by clergymen, government minister Pierre Cot argued that Blois "had not the right to impose such a presence in the tomb on those who have gone before him." Attempts to block the funeral were thwarted when an obscure law dating back to the Revolution was discovered still on the books, entitling the owner of a cemetery plot to place whatever he or she likes in it.

The act of loving and being loved by a dog was a profound emotional experience for thousands of people, one that forever changed the way they perceived animals. The ritualized interment of pets celebrated this revolution of the human spirit, and memorialized the presence of an emerging humane ethic in the modern psyche. "Who can say that this does not betoken the growth and spread of the humanitarian spirit, [especially] in times that try men's souls," remarked a spokesperson for the Massachusetts SPCA around 1900, upon noting the public's growing interest in funerals for pets.

Saying Good-Bye

Last Rites

With or without the support of the clergy, many urban pet owners were determined to allot the animal members of their families the same respect accorded to humans in death, and eagerly embraced the novel idea of public pet graveyards. Such facilities allowed for creative self-expression about an experience shared by thousands of people. The burial of a dog became a public declaration of one's most deeply held views on life, death, and spirituality.

Victorian pet mortuary rites could be as formal as any concocted for humans. Supported by sympathetic friends dressed head-to-toe in black, pet owners conducted their own gravesite services, reading Bible excerpts or eulogizing the lives of their dogs. In 1900 a funeral was conducted at the Hartsdale Canine Cemetery for Major, a highly trained Spaniel said to "sing in three languages," according to his owner. After a period of lying in state, wearing a gold collar, Major's satin-lined casket, complete with a crystal window in the lid, was draped in flowers and taken to the ceme-

A Victorian pet mausoleum in the cemetery at Asnières, fashioned to resemble a doghouse.
source: Author.

tery. As a small crowd of friends sang a doxology, he was lowered into the grave. In typical Victorian fashion, some deceased dogs were photographed as they reclined on lace-covered pillows, posed as though they were in blissful slumber (it was customary to photograph deceased children in the same manner). Some owners kept locks of their pet's hair, and one English woman, who interred her Pomeranian in a double-locked casket, retained and wore the keys on a chain for the duration of her own life.

The beginning of the twentieth century marked the golden era of animal cemeteries. Life-size marble sculptures of dogs marked the graves of many bourgeois pets in Asnières, for example, as did stone or mortar renderings of sentimental Victorian subjects—miniature weeping willows, doves, and angels—not to mention marble mausoleums fashioned to resemble doghouses. Other pet owners, rich and poor alike, erected small, simple headstones inscribed with the animal's name and a short epitaph.

Despite some florid prose, epitaphs from this era convey emotions common to both past and present grieving pet owners. Bible verses, excerpts from Shakespearean plays, poetry by Lord Byron, or a simple statement of the owner's own creation were common. "Not one of them is forgotten before God," many stones in Hyde Park solemnly declare. "Drowned in Old Windsor Loch," "poisoned," "run over," and "pined for his mistress" were heart-wrenching commentaries on tragic ends. "To say goodbye is to die a little," and "Could I think we'd meet again it would lighten half my pain," also reflect the anguish of parting with one's dog. And an elaborate pedestal erected over the grave of a French dog in the 1890s, complete with a marble canopy shading a canine figure asleep on a pillow, is dedicated "to the memory of my dear Emma—faithful and sole companion of my otherwise rootless and desolate life."

Other epitaphs played on the fickle nature of human affection. "In a false world thy heart was brave and true," and "One would have thought he was human, but he was faithful," were typical commentaries on the constancy of dogs as compared with people. As one Edwardian animal lover pointed out at the grave of his pet, he was "deceived by the world, but never by my dog."

Summing up the philosophy behind a second wave of sweeping change in Western funerary fashions, a turn-of-the-century landscape architect observed that "Nature, under all circumstances, was meant to be improved by human care. It is unnatural to leave it to itself." By the 1920s, the untamed natural flavor of garden cemeteries had been replaced by manicured "memorial parks," frequently characterized by rows of generic-style headstones planted in vast expanses of lawn and highlighted by machine-made replicas of classic Grecian statuary or artificial flowers.

"The landscape effects are pleasing," a promotional brochure printed in the 1930s for Hillside Acres pet cemetery near Boston, Massachusetts, proclaimed. Here a sea of close-cropped grass was dotted with hundreds of "modest, marble headstones in orderly rows" within a shiny galvanized chain-link fence. Funeral homes endeavored to make burials as convenient and painless as possible for the survivors and, as with human memorial parks, to assume a more active role in funeral services and perpetual grave maintenance. By the end of World War II, consumer response to these new pet cemeteries was so overwhelming that many were negotiating for the acquisition of neighboring tracts of land. "You ought to see this place on Memorial Day," remarked Joe Haswell, the director of Hillside Acres in the mid-sixties. "There are more people over here than over at the

Houston pet memorial park and inset of a typical plastic, fabric-lined dog casket.
source: Houston Pet Cemetery.

human cemetery. There's been a lot of friends made at gravesites. People meet, then come back next year on Memorial Day and have a picnic."

In the 1960s and 1970s, some full-service mortuary centers for pets appeared, patterned after human funeral homes. They offered a full range of services, from embalming and grooming to open casket services in air-conditioned parlors with "canned" music piped through ceiling speakers. Long Island's Animal Funeral Home, the first of its kind in America, boasted a series of "slumber rooms" in various themes. The "Ming Room" with oriental decor was touted as ideal for Pugs or Pekingeses, while the "Powder Puff Room," a gilt, rococo chamber, was better suited for Poodles.

In recent decades, surviving Victorian pet cemeteries have incorporated the memorial-park landscape philosophy, adding great expanses of velvet lawn dotted with islands of dense forest. Declared a historical site in 1987, Asnières has buried forty thousand animals to date. Machine-polished headstones featuring anodized or laminated photographs of the deceased mark new gravesites, in stark contrast to the moss-covered mar-

Pet owners planting fresh flowers in the dog cemetery at Asnières.
source: Author.

ble doghouses installed ninety years earlier. It also has lost some of its quaint, isolated character due to the recent installation of a mainland tourist park and connecting bridge over the Seine. Still, Asnières remains a peaceful setting for pet owners to meditate at their animal's graves, and in true French fashion the park still is filled with fresh flowers for the graves brought by picnicking families.

Hartsdale has expanded far beyond its original 1896 location in a small apple orchard to become nine rolling acres of lush meadow interspersed with towering stands of willow and spruce trees. The largest and oldest public animal cemetery in America, it boasts sixty thousand burials to date, representing a century of diverse animal funerary fashions. It still retains a hint of Victorian garden flavor, planting over three thousand fresh chrysanthemums each spring, twenty thousand begonias each summer, and hanging hundreds of decorated balsam and spruce wreaths in the winter.

On Memorial Day, Hartsdale is filled with hundreds of human visitors, some dressed in three-piece suits or Sunday dresses and carrying bouquets of flowers, who sit at their animal's grave and reminisce about the past. "I used to make fun of all this," recalled Alvin Miller, whose dog was recently interred. "I laughed at people who put a coat on an animal or buried their pet in a cemetery. But once I got [my dog] Farfel, I became so attached to him that there wasn't anything I wouldn't do for him." In accord with Jewish tradition, another visitor to the cemetery waited a full year before installing a permanent headstone on the grave of Apollo, her Doberman Pinscher. "He was a major part of our lives, and we miss him terribly," she said through her tears. She commissioned a headstone large enough to eventually include the names of all nine of her pets.

Lost in Time

Few animal cemeteries harking back to the first decades of the modern pet era have not been altered by the addition of modern graves or later landscaping styles, but some do exist. Victorian graveyards and memorials on private lands, like those at the old Meux estate or Windsor Castle, appear to be safe, at least for the time being. Other private pet cemeteries have not been so fortunate. As ancestral family land tracts have been subdivided for modern development, surviving headstones often lie neglected and forgotten under layers of brush in vacant lots, or in one instance, in a small island of grass in the middle of a busy English motorway.

Such a fate has befallen the once-posh Molesworth Cemetery. Hailed in 1900 as one of the finest and most ornately decorated pet cemeteries in England, it now stands on the brink of total destruction. Beautifully crafted marble sculptures that once graced the final resting places of Victorian pets have been vandalized or stolen, and what grave markers remain lie forgotten among weeds and bushes at the edge of an open field, many of them lying face-down.

Unprotected antique headstones are frequently wrenched from the ground and sold to private collectors or landscape artists desiring a touch of quaintness for new gardens. Charles Dickens's memorial to his dog Bouncer, which read, "This is the grave of Bouncer—the best, most faithful, most loving of little dogs," turned up in Germany several years ago, where it was offered for sale by an antique dealer for the astounding sum of $2,200 (£1,300). The looting of pet cemeteries is not new, as evidenced by eyewitness accounts of a lavish graveyard at the Forbidden City in Peking (Beijing), where at least one thousand Pekes were laid to rest in coffins of polished orris (a hard, fragrant root), their graves marked with ivory, lapis lazuli, silver, and gold-inlaid headstones. When French and British troops sacked the Imperial City in 1860, these markers were uprooted and destroyed for their precious inlays.

The Hyde Park Dog Cemetery in London, perhaps the oldest public pet cemetery in the Western world, may well be the last intact Victorian garden pet cemetery in existence, having undergone virtually no change since its closure almost a century ago. Hidden from view by low-hanging branches and protected from theft and vandalism by a high, spiked iron fence, the site generally is known only to cabdrivers and frequenters of the park. A groundskeeper still lives in the adjacent cottage and performs basic maintenance. Even this cemetery is in danger of being lost, however, as acid rain etches delicate stone surfaces and overgrowths of mold, moss, and vines pry loose the lead lettering on headstones.

A comprehensive photographic survey of the site was conducted for the first time in 1994, recording the location of all grave markers and inscriptions. Some headstones pose tantalizing questions that will probably never be answered—how a dog named Gerino, born in 1889 on the west

Headstone of Gerino, the Texas dog at Hyde Park Dog Cemetery.
source: Author (with kind permission of the Royal Parks Service).

Texas frontier, came to travel all the way to London and then to share the privilege of interment in the company of dogs belonging to barristers, counts, and dukes, remains a mystery.

With interest growing among scholars and history buffs in the preservation of historical human cemeteries, we can hope that the notion of protecting pet graveyards will become popular as well—before it is too late.

Transcending the Ultimate Class Barrier

Today, as the physical and emotional benefits of living with companion animals gain recognition in the scientific community, Western society is becoming more sensitive to the feelings of grieving pet owners. In an effort to educate new veterinarians about the emotional needs of their clients, many universities now offer seminars and classes on the psychology of mourning and pet death. Twenty-four-hour "hot lines" for distraught animal lovers are offered in some places, and several of the larger veterinary hospitals have full-time counselors to help pet owners deal with the pending death of their animals. Many animal shelters also conduct support groups for citizens who have difficulty coping with the loss of a much-loved pet.

The pet cemetery business is booming as the number of people who regard animals as members of their families continues to grow. Today there are at least five hundred graveyards in the United States alone. The traditional method of interment—a plain casket and simple stone or metal grave marker—is still popular, although one Utah-based company offers "Egyptian-style" embalming for both animals and people. The pet is mummified, wrapped in fabric strips, and encased in a polished bronze sarcophagus molded to represent the animal. Some owners have their pet cremated and seal the ashes inside a box or vase bearing the animal's name or photo, and display it on the fireplace mantel with other family mementos. In the desire to keep their animals nearby, others have resorted to taking their dogs, cats, Guinea pigs, and canaries to taxidermists, who freeze-dry the bodies and add glass eyes for a lifelike final touch. And many pet lovers still opt to bury their animals on private property, marking the grave with a simple headstone or by planting a tree.

The death of Erin, an elderly dog belonging to a Houston, Texas, woman, inspired her to create an elaborate, backyard memorial. A large plastic garbage can with an airtight lid used as a casket contains not only the body but a written account of the dog's life, several toys, and a jar of her favorite food (peanut butter). A cross bearing the dog's name was erected at the head of the grave, along with a vase for flowers, a small statue of a sleeping dog, and a crystal pyramid. "I want people in the future to get a glimpse of animal rights activists and their dogs," she explains. "It reminds one of ancient Egyptian burials, but it's a little more new age in style."

The desire to bury a pet with the same honors accorded human beings marks dogdom's transcendence of the greatest class barrier of all— the one that philosophically has separated humans from the animal world. As one writer remarked in 1925, "the best place to bury a good dog is in the heart of its master." That pet owners still choose to outwardly honor the memory of their animals in so many different ways should not obscure the revolution taking place in our concept of ourselves: that we are part of the larger world of animals, not above or separate from it—one dog and human at a time.

The Power of the Dog

There is sorrow enough in the natural way
From men and women to fill our day;
But when we are certain of sorrow in store,
Why do we always arrange for more?
Brothers and sisters, I bid you beware
Of giving your heart to a dog to tear.

Buy a puppy and your money will buy
Love unflinching that cannot lie—
Perfect passion and worship fed
By a kick in the ribs or a pat on the head.
Nevertheless it is hardly fair
To risk your heart for a dog to tear.

When in the fourteen years which Nature permits
Are closing in asthma, or tumor, or fits,
And the vet's unspoken prescription runs
To lethal chambers or loaded guns,
Then you will find—it's your own affair,
But . . . you've given your heart to a dog to tear.

When the body that lived at your single will,
When the whimper of welcome is stilled (how still),
When the spirit that answered your every mood
Is gone—wherever it goes—for good,
You will discover how much you care,
And will give your heart to a dog to tear!

We've sorrow enough in the natural way,
When it comes to burying Christian clay.
Our loves are not given, but only lent,
At compound interest of cent per cent.
Though it is not always the case, I believe,
That the longer we've kept 'em, the more do we grieve:
For when debts are payable, right or wrong,
A short-term loan is as bad as a long.
So why in Heaven (before we are there!)
Should we give our hearts to a dog to tear?

Rudyard Kipling (1865–1936)

Twelve

History in the Making

The greatness of a nation and its moral progress can be judged
by the way its animals are treated.

—Mahatma Gandhi

OUR PERCEIVED HUMAN UNIVERSE is composed of dichotomies—
rich and poor, developed and undeveloped—even, it could be said,
ignorant and enlightened. This duality weaves through the history of canine culture as well, with dogs viewed as exploitable tools and, often at the
same time, as intimate friends. Such dual value systems were critical to the
concepts of class, rank, and privilege. Prior to the Industrial Revolution,
for instance, the perception and treatment of dogs as tools or servants-
dominated canine culture, while compassion was cast either as perversity
or a luxury few could afford. Like their aristocratic masters, "pure" bred
dogs were symbols of power and exclusivity, isolated both physically and
ideologically from the general dog population. With the industrialization
and urbanization of human societies, however, the working masses acquired the means to breach this class barrier, and dogs with artificially inflated value became mainstream commodities.

When large numbers of canines began living in confined quarters with
people, it was inevitable that a new kind of relationship between the two
species would be forged. As humans one by one experienced close, everyday interactions with these animals, they discovered that, no matter the
pedigree or lineage, dogs are inherently of value—as thinking, feeling beings capable of a remarkable, unconditional love. As a result, empathy it-

self is becoming mainstream, metamorphosing from a luxury to a scientifically documented necessity for the perpetuation of a healthy society.

In this sense, the evolution of the human-canine relationship has been like a great clock set into motion by a single spark of love between one person and one dog. It is a clock that marks an emerging global humane ethic, a clock of compassion ticking off stages of human emotional development.

Farthest along on this clock may be Britain, as evidenced by the resounding success that is the Dogs' Home Battersea in London, one of the oldest and best-known shelters in the world. It was founded by Victorian socialite Mary Tealby, who on a rainy night in 1860 found herself staring into the eyes of an abandoned, dying puppy discovered lying in an alley puddle. One hundred and thirty-six years later, the refuge that puppy inspired has saved the lives of more than three million homeless pets, and the Dogs' Home Battersea is undergoing a £4.5 million ($7.4 million) renovation to become a state-of-the-art animal complex. Even so, the simple loving feeling that first inspired the shelter continues on, as evidenced by a laundry room full of hand-knit sweaters that are pulled out each winter to warm and comfort the many puppies and kittens who call the facility "home" until permanent, adoptive families can be found. "The Home," as indeed it is fondly called by Londoners, also respects its own history, for its new center was designed to wrap around a turn-of-the-century stucco and Spanish tile cattery, the oldest building on site. Archival photographs will guide restoration of the structure, which will house a Battersea Museum, featuring exhibits on the shelter's history and the English humane movement, as well as offering an array of imaginative humane education programs for children and adults.

Towering over the Battersea cattery is the only tree on the lot. According to Duncan Green, the home's director, this, too, will be preserved with reverence—as a tribute to the "half million Battersea dogs who have given their all to sustain it."

Now a second wave of industrialization is spilling beyond the confines of Western society into the world at large, and the pattern of canine transformation from tool to soul mate is taking place in developing countries as well—only the hands on the clock of humane evolution are set to where they were some one to two hundred years ago in places like London. To

Architect's model of the new Dogs' Home Battersea, construction to be completed in 1996. The cattering and "dog's tree" can be seen in the lower center of the photo. source: Dogs' Home Battersea.

the extent that this evolutionary process (first the material / technological aspects of industrialization, followed by the moral aspects) has historically been associated with the West, a societal humane ethic for animals can rightly be labeled a "Western" value in this context.

After half a century of intensive industrialization, Japan has emerged to rival England and the United States as a society of dog enthusiasts, with its own institutionalized fancy patterned after those established in the West a century earlier. Here dog ownership is widely regarded as an indicator of affluence, since much of the population lives in tiny, cramped apartments, which often ban pets. (They can take comfort from a "virtual reality pet," with computer games for feeding, bathing, and playing fetch.) Young male suitors eagerly pay high fees to "rent" dogs from pet shops, in hopes that the animals will soften women's hearts and ease the tension of a first date.

Yet Japan has become the world's largest consumer of American-made pet foods, with exports totaling over three billion dollars in 1992. Toys, accessories, veterinary and grooming services also are big sellers, as are calendars, T-shirts, and illustrated books on dogs, not to mention television programs profiling people and their pets from around the world. Even in the chaos of the Kōbe earthquake, Western observers were fascinated by the sight of Japanese survivors canvassing ruined neighborhoods in search of lost or injured dogs and cats. Temporary animal shelters consisting of tents and stacked airline kennels were immediately set up, and unclaimed animals were quickly adopted by a sympathetic public.

Hachiko, a golden brown Akita who lived in Tokyo's Shibuya section between the two World Wars has been transformed into a virtual canine patron saint, as the very embodiment of Japan's highest virtues, loyalty, and punctuality. The pet of Professor Eisaburo Ueno of Tokyo University, Hachiko took it upon herself to escort the professor to and from the train station every day. Each afternoon she could be seen sitting patiently on the platform, waiting for her master's train to return, and other commuters came to know and respect her. After Dr. Ueno unexpectedly died at work, Hachiko continued her lonely vigil for ten more years, walking to the station each afternoon and waiting well past dark each night for a man who would never return. Upon her death at the age of thirteen, she was reunited with her beloved master in Tokyo's Aoyama Cemetery, and a memorial was installed in the train station (reminiscent of the 1872 tribute to Greyfriar's Bobby in Edinburgh, Scotland). Though it was removed and smelted for shipbuilding in World War II, a second memorial was installed in 1948. When the train station was being rebuilt, architects were instructed to design the new facility so as not to disturb the platform location of Hachiko's tribute. Today the very term "Hachiko" is used interchangeably with Shibuya to refer to this district, with phrases like *Hachiko mae de!* meaning "Let's meet at Hachiko!" and the memorial has become a fixture in romantic television dramas, often serving as the place where long-separated lovers reunite.

In 1994 on the sixtieth anniversary of Hachiko's death (which also happened to fall in the Year of the Dog), the Culture Broadcasting Network announced that it had obtained a never-before-documented recording of Hachiko. Broken into three pieces, the old vinyl record was repaired with a laser and broadcast to a national audience. A short but forceful *wan-wan,* the Japanese equivalent of bow-wow, was all Hachiko uttered, but that was enough to delight listeners who held to the traditional belief that a deep, robust bark is a sign of good health and karma.

In China, where free trade is just beginning to take hold after fifty years of communism and isolation, the idea of keeping pets who perform no real tasks—and are not intended to be eaten—is emerging in what is expected to become the world's largest consumer market. For decades Communist mandates discouraged the keeping of pets, although the use of dogs as an edible form of livestock (with none of the reverence of Native American custom) was acceptable. Since the late 1980s, the import and sale of pedigreed dogs, including Poodles, Pomeranians, and even Pekingeses, has become a thriving industry, with the animals fetching upward of two thousand dollars each. Finally in 1995, the growing popularity of pet dogs prompted Beijing's municipal government to enact a new set of draconian regulations and exorbitant licensing fees (seven hundred dollars, the equivalent of two years' wages for some citizens), in an effort to discourage the keeping of "luxury" animals. Even the times of day when the animals may be taken for walks is severely limited, as is the size of the dog itself. The law's proponents cite concern for public health and safety (the Beijing Police Bureau claimed there were fifty thousand dog-bite cases in 1994), but many suspect the repressive cultural agenda is aimed at slowing the "Westernization" of China.

In light of other societies' efforts to restrict dog ownership, the Beijing regulations probably will fail, and may even fuel interest in pets as symbols of affluence and status. For despite the laws, enterprising Russian breeders continue to reap vast profits from smuggling dogs across the northern border of China, and arranging their subsequent shipment to big-city flea markets.

Ten years ago Hong Kong activists for the International Fund for Animal Welfare initiated a letter-writing campaign to the ambassador of South Korea calling for an end to the eating of dogs and cats in that country, with little response. The presentation of an international petition containing three million signatures to Korean officials just in time for the 1988 Olympics was a national embarrassment, prompting promises that a new law would go into effect. But the bill was scrapped as soon as the Games ended and the international press had left. The situation improved after President Roh Tae Woo's visit to England in 1989, where he was hounded by animal rights protesters (when he dined with the Queen, the press advised her to "Lock up your Corgis, Ma'am"). Finally in 1991, media ridicule prompted the government to enact an unprecedented animal protection ordinance aimed at ending the torture of dogs and cats slated for human consumption. For the first time in that country's history, the traditional hanging or beating of dogs with lead pipes, or roasting them alive with blowtorches in the belief that this makes the meat taste better, is punishable by six months' imprisonment and a two-thousand-dollar fine. Also, a Korean Animal Protection Society now exists, dedicated to enforcing the new laws and implementing a national humane education program beginning in early childhood.

Even regions with long traditions of violent sociopolitical upheaval are not beyond the reach of an aspiring global humane ethic, as evidenced by recent events in Israel. With its continuing economic and political problems, this country never placed animal welfare on its list of priorities despite mounting evidence that violence to animals is linked to violence against humans. Both Arab and Jewish children act out violent episodes with animals and then, in later years, become so emotionally numb to animal (and human) suffering that it scarcely warrants a glance.

After more than a decade of pleading with apathetic Israeli authorities to abandon their practice of poisoning and shooting street dogs, and sanction the implementation of a national humane education program, Nina Natelson, founder of Concern for Helping Animals in Israel, made a major breakthrough in 1994, when CHAI coordinated one of the first international conferences in the Middle East dealing with the relationship between animal abuse and human violence. "The Ministry told [us] to expect an audience of 100 teachers and school psychology counselors," Natelson said, so it was a surprise when more than 1,200 Jewish and Arab educators asked to attend. Now a state-of-the-art animal shelter, the first of its kind in Israel, is under construction in Tel Aviv, thanks to a $250,000 bequest to the local SPCA by an anonymous benefactor. Also to be constructed on the shelter grounds is a humane education center named after the late Nobel laureate Isaac Bashevis Singer, one of the few places where children of both cultures can come together in a positive environment to share the experience of interacting with animals.

None of this is to say that the birth of a humane ethic in any society is an easy process. Those sufficiently Westernized to assume all the material trappings of modern life may still cling to archaic values, ultimately to the detriment of the dogs. Nowhere is this more apparent than in Puerto

Rico, where five hundred years after Becerrillo ruled by teeth and terror, the tables have been turned and it is dogdom that suffers at the hands of humanity. Machismo blended with fixations on racial/class purity have given birth to an exceptionally brutal canine culture. A protectorate of the United States, Puerto Rico enjoys a copious stream of American dollars from federal subsidies, tourists, restaurant franchises, textile and pharmaceutical industries, and in the material sense, is fully "Americanized." But like some nineteenth-century London street scene, satos (street dogs) are a fixture of daily life all over the island.

The demand for papered, purebred dogs in Puerto Rico is at an all-time high, and hand-scribbled personal ads cover community bulletin boards as islanders seek canine "boyfriends" or "girlfriends" for their pets. AKC registration papers are accepted as proof of "good family"—though the dogs need not be of the same breed. Puppies produced by these misguided attempts to provide dogs with love lives are like illegitimate children, worthless and unworthy of respect. Like so much trash, they are dumped by their owners alongside the road, far from home.

Bleeding and hairless from mange, the satos stand in stark contrast to the glittering facades of high-rise hotels, boutiques, and restaurants. Scav-

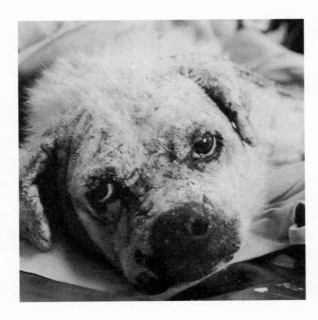

A dying Puerto Rican
street dog.
source: Author.

enging in hospital dumpsters or along trash-strewn beaches, their lives are slow deaths, caused by a combination of parasites, malnutrition, diseases, and injuries incurred in encounters with motor vehicles and sadistic humans, who beat, kick, stone, and poison them. Yet they continue to seek the companionship of people. And many still wear the tattered remains of collars.

Despite the crushed and mangled canine corpses littering highways and city thoroughfares, many Puerto Ricans maintain that life on the streets is perfectly suitable for dogs. Melanie Lenart, a columnist for the *San Juan Star*, even wrote in 1995 that Puerto Rico's dog-dumping tradition was actually a "morally superior system of live-and-let-live."

Though the clock of compassion is still set at an early hour in Puerto Rico, the seeds of a humane ethic are beginning to take hold. Rather than waiting for the government to act, a growing number of islanders have begun to operate their own, one-person rescue operations to provide immediate relief for the animals, or have formed grassroots organizations to establish small shelters. Armed with cartons of bottled water and bagged pet food, they venture out each evening to "make the rounds," catching and taking the dogs to vets whenever possible for shots or sterilization. Occasionally they are even able to find an adoptive home.

The Hands of the Clock Move Again

By 1993 more than 56 million American households owned dogs, many with more than one animal, and consumers spent $15 billion on veterinary care, dog food, toys, accessories, grooming, and funeral arrangements. Not only do more Americans own dogs, but an unprecedented number of animals are enjoying elevated status as full-fledged members of the family. In a recent survey of ten thousand households, almost 70 percent of respondents said they would risk their own lives to save their dogs, a number nearly equal to those who said they would seek emergency medical care for their pets before obtaining it for themselves. Three quarters of the respondents said they routinely give wrapped Christmas and birthday presents to their dogs, and almost half have photos of their pets in their purses, wallets, and offices.

But our love of pets is counterbalanced by the sobering fact that approximately twelve million dogs and cats are euthanized annually, according to the American Humane Association. Seven puppies and kittens are born for every human baby in the United States, making the task of finding homes for all of them an impossible challenge. (Most euthanized dogs are less than two years old, and 90 percent pass health and temperament criteria for adoptability.)

Experts attribute America's pet overpopulation to the indiscriminate breeding of owned dogs and cats, mixed and "pure," compounded by the persistent belief that surgical sterilization is detrimental to an animal's health and temperament—despite the many published clinical studies to the contrary. Five thousand puppy mills—backyard breeding factories that crank out half a million "papered" dogs for franchised pet stores, many of them horribly crippled by genetic disease—add to the tragedy by reducing the number of homes available to shelter animals. And contrary to popular belief, 15 to 25 percent of all dogs in shelters are pure breeds.

As more people have become emotionally attached to dogs, however, empathy for homeless animals appears to be growing. Archaic notions that shelter dogs are unattractive, diseased, or ill-tempered—the bottom of the canine barrel—have been pretty much dispelled, and the adoption of mixed-breed dogs is more and more viewed as a hallmark of an enlightened sense of social responsibility. In an effort to stem the growing tide of unwanted pets conceived and then reluctantly euthanized, California's San Mateo County passed a law requiring all citizens to sterilize their pets (those wishing to breed had to purchase a permit). The ordinance eventually was overturned, but not before the Peninsula Humane Society reported a reduction in incoming animals of more than 10 percent per year, and a decline in euthanasia of 15 percent.

In 1995, *Parade* magazine ran a feature on the pet overpopulation crisis in conjunction with the first annual "Spay Day USA," an event sponsored by the Doris Day Animal League. This nonprofit organization petitions veterinarians, humane societies, legislators, and celebrities to promote the spaying and neutering of all pets. And every autumn over two hundred communities across the country conduct "Candlelight Vigils" in public parks to remember and mourn the millions of animals put down in municipal shelters. As the sun sets, candles are lit, and after an extended moment of silent prayer, the crowd disperses in quiet, sometimes tearful contemplation, inspired to take a more active role in championing home-less animals.

Fall of an Empire

Western consumers exhibit growing disillusionment as both human and canine aristocracies crumble amid revelations that selective breeding does not necessarily make for superior people or superior dogs. A century after its creation, the American Kennel Club is struggling to defend the in-stitutionalized fancy against a growing onslaught of criticism, including accusations that their sanctioned dog shows are little more than "beauty pageants" and are counterproductive to the welfare of the canine race. Like a medieval dog gauge reduced to the diameter of a pinhole, a cen-tury of intensive genetic culling has so ravaged the purebred world that this practice, if it continues unchecked, threatens to undercut the genetic health of the entire species. Veterinarians, consumers, and a growing num-ber of breeders are concluding that the grand dream to elevate and enno-ble the canine race through the imposition of artificial breeding criteria is an inhumane, profit-driven mistake.

A forty-year gravy train of flattering articles and photo spreads for the AKC came to a halt in 1990 when the *Atlantic Monthly* ran a devastating in-vestigative piece by freelance writer Mark Derr. In "The Politics of Dogs," he concluded that breeding for beauty was destroying the health and in-born working talents of breeds, many dating back to the Middle Ages, while the AKC watched millions of dollars in registration fees roll into its coffers. "For sportsmen and faddists, the dog has become little more than equipment for a game [which] they justify in the name of freedom, argu-ing that no organization or governmental body has the right to even rec-ommend changes in their approach, and the AKC has endorsed their ideology through word and policy." Defenders of the AKC called Derr a mouthpiece for animal rights "extremists," who seek not only the extinc-tion of all dog breeds, but the abolition of all dog ownership.

"A great many legislators know little or nothing about pure bred dogs," reads one AKC pamphlet (*Canine Legislation: What Do You Mean, Lobby?*). "Invite them to shows, matches and trials. Ask them to present trophies, give dinner or lunch speeches or open festivities." The *AKC*

A show-quality German Shepherd in 1930.
source: Author.

Gazette even published a series of how-to articles on fancier activism, encouraging readers to "Attract the media by focusing on the rarest, the newest, the smallest, the biggest, the top-winning dogs in the show—and slip your message in along the way."

Roger Caras, author of dozens of dog books and eighteenth president of the American Society for the Prevention of Cruelty to Animals, espouses the view that it is advantageous to own a purebred dog over a "random-bred" canine because, "You will have some idea of what your are getting. . . . some people just like the feeling of having a superb example of anything around them." That rationale, even from someone as respected as Caras, now is being questioned by purebred dog owners who find themselves emotionally and financially devastated by crippling genetic diseases in their expensive animal investments. A flawless exterior is no guarantee of genetic health, as evidenced by the fact that hypothyroid disease affects 70 percent of the Akita population. Blindness plagues Collies, Dalmatians are notorious for deafness, and Pugs snort and gulp for air through de-

A prize-winning German Shepherd in 1995 exhibiting sloping hindquarters that have become a breed trademark in recent decades.
source: Isabelle Francais.

formed palates and nasal cavities. Once touted as the embodiment of canine vigor, German Shepherds exhibiting stylishly sloping hindquarters are so crippled by inherited hip socket disease that they often must undergo surgery costing thousands of dollars or be euthanized. The U.S. military has ceased using the breed due to this problem, opting instead for the Belgian Malinois (though it too is beginning to suffer the same condition). The Akita also is prone to hip and elbow dysplasia. In a sense, the breeds themselves—as they looked, behaved, and thrived for centuries—are in danger of becoming another aspect of lost canine history.

Five years after Derr's article, a second, even more damning story appeared in *Time* (December 12, 1994), picturing a weary, bloodshot-eyed Bulldog along with the headline, THE SHAME OF OVERBREEDING. Of the estimated twenty million purebred dogs living in the United States, according to the magazine, at least 25 percent now are afflicted with serious genetic dysfunction. And despite collecting $29 million in registration fees, the nonprofit AKC slashed its funding for education and genetic research from $1.6 million in 1992 to $575,000 in 1993. The organization does not require that dogs pass any health criteria in order to be registered.

Seven days after the *Time* article appeared, the AKC announced the establishment of a Canine Health Foundation to encourage genetic research. But as one breeder of Cavalier King Charles Spaniels put it, the AKC continues to avoid "the fundamental question of whether breeding to satisfy rigid, appearance-dominated is in the best interests of the dogs themselves."

But even here the hands of the clock appear to be moving again, with some British breeders calling for a total rebellion against the institutionalized fancy. Fancier David Hancock cites the "anatomical disaster" the English Bulldog has become, that nation's enduring emblem of stoicism and determination. He asserts that a century of breeding for the showring combined with endless, arbitrary revisions of the Bulldog standard have transformed what once was a canine capable of battling one-ton bulls into a waddling, wheezing parody. Not only were Bulldogs outcrossed with Pugs to alter their size and appearance, thereby "contaminating" the breed, but puppies now must be delivered by Caesarean section because of their unnaturally large heads. Some British breeders are turning their attentions to the American Staffordshire (Pitbull) Terrier, which more accurately represents the bull-baiting dogs as they looked for centuries, in the hope that their genes may help restore the Bulldog to its traditional vigor. In the meantime, England's Kennel Club has responded that it will review the breed standard—provided "conclusive, scientific proof" of harmful physical exaggeration can be shown. A similar rebellion appears to be building among American breeders of Border Collies, Cavalier King Charles Spaniels, Australian Shepherds, and Labrador Retrievers.

At the same time, the public's appreciation of and interest in mongrels is on the rise. The American Mixed Breed Obedience Registration (AMBOR) has made a conscious effort to "play a major role in changing the course of history," as has the Mixed Breed Dog Club of America, by conducting public obedience competitions to show off the talents of mongrel dogs. Such organizations, which welcome any and all animals regardless of lineage, have enjoyed a steady growth in membership. (In deference to the pet overpopulation crisis, these clubs require all member dogs to be surgically sterilized.)

The United Kennel Club (UKC), the largest working dog registry in the world, now welcomes the participation of AMBOR-registered mongrels in their Obedience Trials. "The UKC has long recognized the efforts that have been put forth by [AMBOR members] to rescue mixed breed dogs and give them and their respective owners the opportunity to participate in activities to recognize the abilities of their dogs, and the efforts of their owners to make them good canine citizens," says UKC President Fred Miller. Established in 1898, the Michigan-based organization operates under a "total dog" concept, stressing both the health and working talents of its member breeds. The registration papers of any animals produced through line breeding are stamped with the word INBRED. The UKC maintains an aggressive stance against the registration of dogs produced by puppy mills, and according to a 1992 brochure, "The majority of the dogs we register still perform the tasks the breeds were originally bred for. [Dogs] registered by the UKC in the early 1900s have the same temperament and instinctive qualities now as they did then."

Conscious Compassion

The ability to empathize with other creatures has been considered one of the unique hallmarks of the human species, requiring not only a sense of the self, but a capacity to recognize others as distinct and separate from the self—in essence, evidence of consciousness. As the culture of compassion continues to evolve, a growing body of anecdotal evidence and scientific observations has emerged to suggest that other animals also have the ability to express compassion equal to and in some cases, greater than that shown by people.

Nowhere is this more clearly revealed than in the growing number of households that choose to love and support dogs with permanent physical disabilities. In many cases the animals appear not only to be aware of their own disabilities, but of disabilities in their fellow creatures. Ron and Donna Sadjak of Massachusetts share their home with a dynamic Australian Shepherd duo named Sydney and Chelsea, both of whom are "differently-abled." Chelsea has microthalmia (eyes that are too small for their sockets) as well as cataracts, while Sydney sees clearly but has been totally deaf since birth. Australian Shepherds already are strongly driven by instinct, so it seemed only natural that Sydney would "round up the family cats, gently pushing them into a group to herd them about. They obey although they're obviously not fond of the idea," Sadjak says. Apparently realizing that there was something "different" about Chelsea, Sydney likewise volunteered to guide her about and shield her from obstacles with his own body. Both dogs are in excellent health despite such daunting physical conditions. "Most people are very supportive," the Sadjaks report, "but breeders aren't too fond of our keeping handicapped pets. They're quick to point out to us the genetic problems of our animals, and urge us to start over with new dogs—*their* dogs! I let them know we're responsible people who always sterilize our pets, not just because they're handicapped, but because of the pet overpopulation problem."

Today the scientific community is beginning to reevaluate its traditional assumptions about the intelligence of nonhuman animals, including dogs, and a growing number of experts believe that canines are anything but automatons. Love, in fact, appears to be the key to unlocking a flood of creative, emotional expression in dogs. The more intimate and interactive the relationship between human and dog—and the more enriched the dog's living environment—the more overt and complex canine behavior becomes.

Alan Beck, an animal ecologist at Purdue University, says that despite a lack of hard quantitative data, he and most of his colleagues accept the notion that dogs have an emotional and intellectual life, citing the relationship he enjoys with his own pet. "I am absolutely convinced, for example, that my dog feels guilty when he defecates on the rug. A blind observer could see it. He behaves the same way I would have if my mother had caught me doing it. If it looks the same as human behavior in the same situation, and is being used to solve the same problem, why shouldn't you be able to use words we use for human emotions to describe it?" he told *Time* magazine. Ethologist Marc Bekoff at the University of Colorado agrees. "I have no doubt that my dog Jethro experiences beliefs about the outcome of his actions, expectations about the future. He has goals. If he tries to solicit play and I don't play with him, he is surprised—and he looks it," Bekoff said. "It's just wrong to say dogs don't have thoughts and beliefs about their world just because these might be different from our beliefs."

In a sense, revelations that humans might not be all that different from other animals are nothing new, for in examining our shared history we find abundant evidence to suggest that the dogs have known all along that we are animals, too. It is simply that, with each succeeding century, a new set of "facts" has been used to justify an exploitive, one-sided relationship and to deny our greatest fear—that like the dogs, we too are vulnerable and mortal. If canines are indeed sentient, then it becomes all the more important for humans to take the necessary steps to preserve their history, not as a collection of assorted trivia pointing up our ability to manipulate them, and their willingness to serve us, but as a chronicle of their participation in the continuing spiritual evolution of humanity. The challenge is not so much to improve the canine race, but to improve ourselves, our relationship with dogdom, and ultimately, our relationship with the natural world at large.

"Our task must be to free ourselves by widening our circle of compassion to embrace all living creatures," Albert Einstein once said. Indeed, what might the future hold for our species if the culture of compassion continues to expand, blurring the class barrier between civilization and nature? Paradoxically, it may be the canine race that paves the way for the next great change in the human psyche, for as history has demonstrated time and time again, empathy for a single animal can evolve into empathy for an entire species.

Like Hermanubis, that benevolent celestial guardian of souls who stands between the greatest duality of all—life and death—it may be the mortal dog who bridges the gap between humanity and nature, to lead us back to paradise—the proverbial garden we left so long ago.

Glossary

Alaunt A large, Mastiff-like hound commonly employed as a hunting adjunct in medieval and Renaissance Europe. Such dogs were instrumental in the Spanish campaign to subjugate the natives of Latin America and the Caribbean in the sixteenth century.

anthropocentric regarding humankind as the central fact or final aim of the universe, or interpreting reality exclusively in terms of human values and experiences.

anthropology scientific study of the origin and the physical, cultural, social, and behavioral development of humankind.

anthropomorphism the attribution of human motivation, characteristics, or behavior to nonhuman animals, inanimate objects, or natural phenomena.

archaeology the recovery, study, and interpretation of material remains from human lives and cultures, notably those no longer in existence.

artifact an object produced, shaped, or altered by human workmanship.

automaton one who behaves in a mechanical fashion, void of intent or self-directed thought.

barbarian originally a foreigner, especially one not Greek or Roman, later used to identify people or tribes considered to have an inferior culture.

breed a group of domesticated animals cultivated by human beings to possess a uniform appearance and/or instinctive, specialized behavior that is inheritable and distinguishes it from other groups of animals within the same species.

canid members of the family Canidae, including wolves and dogs.

civilization a condition of human society marked by an advanced stage of development in the arts and sciences, and by corresponding social, political, and cultural complexity and stratification.

coprolite desiccated, frozen, or fossilized excrement.

culture a way of life; the totality of socially transmitted behavior patterns, arts, beliefs, and institutions, and all other products of work and thought characteristic of a community or population.

cur derivation of the medieval term "courtalt," referring to the practice of amputating the tails or toes of dogs belonging to the peasant class. In later centuries "cur" became a derogatory term for homeless or mixed-breed dogs.

cynotherapy the practice of healing by use of dogs.

domestication process by which successive generations of certain animals are isolated from their natural culture and selection process to facilitate their incorporation into human society.

empathy an understanding so intimate that the thoughts, feelings, or motives of one are readily comprehended by another.

ethology the scientific study of animal behavior.

euthanasia the action of inducing a painless death of a person or animal for reasons assumed to be merciful.

evolution the process by which a species may change over successive generations so that descendants physically or behaviorally differ from their ancestors.

fancy the recreational breeding and exhibition of domesticated animals, including dogs.

feudalism a political-economic system based on the relation of autocrat or aristocrat to vassal, as a result of land being held on condition of homage and services.

Forbidden City a walled settlement in central Peking (Beijing) containing the Imperial palaces and adjoining structures reserved for the Chinese monarchy until its fall in the twentieth century. Upheld as the center of the universe in Chinese tradition.

gene a functional hereditary unit occupying a fixed location on a chromosome that determines physical attributes carried from one generation to another.

heathen one who is regarded as irreligious, uncivilized, or unenlightened. Often used interchangeably with "pagan," meaning one who adheres to the religion of a tribe or nation that does not acknowledge the God of Judaism, Christianity, or Islam.

heresy an opinion or doctrine at variance with established beliefs, especially dissension from or denial of Roman Catholic dogma.

hominid primates in the family Hominidae, of which modern *Homo sapiens* is the only survivor.

humane the qualities of kindness, mercy, and compassion.

hybrid the offspring of genetically dissimilar parents or animal varieties.

hydrophobia an archaic term for rabies, literally a "fear of water."

Ice Age a series of cold periods marked by extensive glaciation alternating with periods of relative warmth, together constituting the Pleistocene era, which terminated between approximately fifteen thousand and eight thousand years ago.

ideology a body of ideas or beliefs reflecting the social needs and aspirations of an individual, group, class, or culture.

metamorphosis a marked transformation in appearance, character, or function of an organism.

Molossus Large, Mastiff-like canines employed by ancient Romans as sentries, bodyguards, and executioners.

mongrel a dog resulting from various or random interbreedings, the progeny of two or more breeds or varieties.

mummy a naturally desiccated or deliberately embalmed corpse, by application of chemicals and protective coverings to thwart decomposition.

mutation an unexpected genetic change in form or quality of an organism.

nature the physical world, including all living things. Also a primitive state of existence, untouched by civilization or artifice.

neoteny the retention of fetal or juvenile physical or behavioral traits into adulthood.

pedigree the recorded descent of an animal.

progenitor an originator of a line of descent.

race any population united or classified together on the basis of common history, nationality, geographical distribution, or genetically transferred physical characteristics.

sentient having an awareness of one's own existence, sensations, and thoughts, of one's distinctness from others, and of one's environment.

serf a member of the lowest feudal class in medieval Europe, bound to the land and owned by a lord.

society a distinct self-perpetuating group characterized by mutual interests, shared institutions, and/or a common culture.

species a group of actually or potentially interbreeding natural populations that are reproductively isolated from other groups; a taxonomic division subordinate to a genus.

tame brought from wildness into a tractable state by protracted contact with human beings. Not to be confused with domestication.

taxidermy the art of preserving and mounting animal skins for exhibition in a lifelike state.

taxonomy the science, laws, and principles of biological classification.

wild occurring, growing, or living in a natural state; not domesticated, cultivated, or tamed. Also means barbaric, ungovernable, turbulent, undisciplined, or chaotic.

zooarchaeology the documentation and study of animals in the archaeological record; also referred to as archaeozoology.

Recommended Reading

Ballard, Peter. *A Dog Is for Life. Celebrating the First 100 Years of the National Canine Defense League.* London: National Canine Defense League, 1990.

Bewick, Thomas. *A General History of Quadrupeds.* Newcastle: T. Bewick, 1824.

Burkett, Charles. *Our Domestic Animals.* Boston: Ginn and Co., 1907.

Caius, Johannes. *Of English Dogges; the Diversities, the Names, the Natures and the Properties.* (trans. Abraham Fleming) London: A. Bradley, 1880.

Clutton-Brock, Juliet. *Domesticated Animals from Early Times.* Austin: University of Texas Press (British Museum of Natural History), 1981.

Clutton-Brock, Juliet, and Kim Dennis-Bryan. *Dogs of the Last Hundred Years at the British Museum.* London: British Museum of Natural History, 1988.

Cohen, Barbara, and Louise Taylor. *Dogs and Their Women.* Boston: Little, Brown and Company, 1989.

Dale-Green, Patricia. *Dog.* London: Rupert Hart-Davis, 1966.

Derr, Mark. "The Politics of Dogs." *Atlantic Monthly* (March 1990): 49–72.

Dyer, Walter. *Pierrot, Dog of Belgium.* New York: Doubleday, 1918.

Fischer, Hank, *Wolf Wars: The Remarkable Inside Story of the Restoration of Wolves to Yellowstone.* Billings, Mont.: Falcon Press, 1995.

Godden, Rumer. *Butterfly Lions.* New York: Viking Press, 1978.

Goetzman, William. *The West of the Imagination.* New York: W. W. Norton, 1986.

Haddon, Celia. *Faithful to the End: An Illustrated Anthology of Dogs.* London: Headline, 1991.

Jackson, Thomas. *Our Dumb Companions.* London: S.W. Partridge, 1879.

Janssen, Rosalind. *Egyptian Household Animals.* Princes Risborough, Aylesbury, England: Shire Publications, 1989.

Kellert, Stephen. *The Value of Life: Biological Diversity and Human Society.* Washington, D.C.: Island Press, 1993.

Kellert, Stephen, and Edward Wilson. *The Biophilia Hypothesis.* Washington, D.C.: Island Press, 1993.

Kete, Kathleen. *The Beast in the Boudoir: Petkeeping in Nineteenth Century Paris.* Berkeley: University of California Press, 1994.

Lemish, Michael. *War Dogs: Canines in Combat.* McLean, Va.: Brassey's, 1996.

Lemonick, Michael. "A Terrible Beauty." *Time* (December 12, 1994): 64–70.

Lennie, Campbell. *Landseer. The Victorian Paragon.* London: Hamish Hamilton, 1976.

Linden, Eugene. "Can Animals Think?" *Time* (March 22, 1993): 54–61.

McCarthy, Susan, and Jeffrey Moussaleff Mason. *When Elephants Weep: The Emotional Lives of Animals.* New York: Delacorte Press, 1995.

Macaulay, James. *Plea for Mercy to Animals.* London: The Religious Tract Society, 1874.

McCaig, Donald. "Gone to the Dogs." *New York Times* (August 3, 1994): A15.

Olsen, Stanley. *Origins of the Domestic Dog: The Fossil Record.* Tucson: University of Arizona Press, 1985.

Patterson, Francine. *Koko's Kitten.* New York: Scholastic Books, 1985.

Pitcairn, Richard. *Dr. Pitcairn's Complete Guide to Natural Health for Dogs and Cats.* Emmaus, Pa.: Rodale Press, 1982.

Reed, Freddie. *A Friend in Need. A Portrait of Battersea Dog's Home.* London: William Collins, 1985.

Reitman, Judith. *Stolen for Profit: The True Story Behind the Disappearance of Millions of America's Beloved Pets.* New York: Kensington Books, 1992.

Rice, Berkeley. *The Other End of the Leash: The American Way with Pets.* Boston: Little, Brown and Co., 1968.

Ritvo, Harriet. *The Animal Estate: The English and Other Creatures in the Victorian Age.* Cambridge: Harvard University Press, 1987.

Sanborn, Kate. *Educated Dogs of Today.* Boston: McGrath-Sherril Press, 1916.

Sichel, Elaine. *Circles of Compassion: A Collection of Humane Words and Work.* Sebastapol, Calif.: Voice and Vision Publishing, 1995.

Sinrod, Barry. *Do You Do It When Your Pet's In the Room?* New York: Ballantine Books, 1993.

Index

A

afterlife: Egyptian, 31–32; Graeco–Roman, 61; Native American, 146–47, 158. *See also* Christianity; resurrection
Agent Orange, 197. *See also* Hayes, Howard
Ah Cum, 117, 119, 120. *See also* Pekingese
Alaunt, 69, 79, 174, 182, 285. *See also* Mastiff; Molossus
Alco. *See* Techichi
Alexander the Great, 46
Alpo, 239, 243. *See also* pet food, advertising
American Association of Zoological Parks and Aquariums, 21
American Kennel Club: breed standards of, 171; controversy surrounding, 277–78, 279–80; inception of, 111
American Mixed Breed Obedience Registration, 280
American Society for the Prevention of Cruelty to Animals, 134–35, 278
animal welfare: in Israel, 273; proponents of, 121, 127–28, 145, 257–58, 269; Puerto Rico, 275; United States military, 205–6; Victorian society, 127–30, 133–34;. *See also* cruelty to animals
Anubis: as guide to the afterlife, 31–33; forebear of Hermanubis, 59–60, 65; temples of, 33, 38. *See also* mummified dogs, Egyptian
Apollo, 54, 56
archaeology; code of ethics, 17; Egyptian, 34–35; paleoarchaeology, 16. *See also* history, destruction of; zooarchaeology
Argus, 46
aristocracy: canine, 98, 103–4; human, 105–6; medieval, 121. *See also* breeds, Victorian

Aristotle, 42
Asklepios, 55, 62. *See also* cynotherapy
Asnières Cemetery of Dogs, 259–60, 262–63, 256. *See also* cemeteries

B

barbarians: dogs, 69; as conquerors of Europe, 66–67; in the Roman Empire, 49–50, 51–52, 164
Battersea, the Dogs' Home, 130, 269
Becerillo, 85–88, 87, 174, 274. *See also* doggings
beef wars, 239–43. *See also* pet food, advertising
Belgian Malinois, 279
Belgische Rekel. *See* cart dogs
Bering Strait, 147, 157
Bewick, Thomas, 98, 123, 290
bloodhound, 76, 105, 175. *See also* Segusii
boutiques (for pets), 215–16, 222, 225
Boye, 90, 213
bread (for dogs), 94, 235–236
breeds: Chinese, 114–15; Egyptian, 29–30, 42; genetic flaws in, 111–13, 119–20, 170, 278–80; Graeco-Roman, 42, 52–53, 68; medieval, 68–69, 74; modern, 119–20, 144, 170–71, 277–80; Native American, 147, 171; prehistoric, 8–9, 14, 16; Renaissance, 69, 75–76, 100–101; Victorian, 94, 98–102, 105, 111–13, 119–20
Brehm, Alfred, 98, 140
Brisbin, I. Lehr, 21, 68
British Kennel Club, 111, 280
British Museum, 35, 152
British Museum of Natural History, 3, 99, 109, 120

Buffalo-Bird-Woman, 8. *See also* neoteny; women

Bulldog, 279–80

burial, Native American dog, 153, 163. *See also* cemeteries

Burkett, Charles, 105, 106, 113, 215, 234, 252

Byron, Lord, 251. *See also* cruelty to animals

C

Caesar, Harry I., 184, 190, 205. *See also* Dogs for Defense

Caius, Johannes, 77, 100, 122, 124, 212, 290

Canadian Kennel Club, 165, 167

cancer, 55–58, 196–97

Candlelight Vigil, 276–77. *See also* euthanasia

cannibalism (Spanish), 83

Canoe Dogs, 150–51

Cape Denbigh, 18. *See also* history; destruction of

Caras, Roger, 278. *See also* breeds, genetic flaws in

Carolina Dogs, 168–69

cart dogs, 96, 122, 124–25, 178–80; *A Dog of Flanders*, 141, 144, Dog Cart Nuisance Law, 133; in modern times, 144; *Pierrot, Dog of Belgium*, 137–38, 290; regulation of, 133–37

Çatal Hüyük, 12. *See also* Neolithic

Catherine the Great, 79

Catholicism, 67, 81, 84–85; policy regarding animals, 257–58. *See also* Christianity

Catlin, George, 159, 161–62

cats: in Battersea, 269, 270, Egypt, 35, 37; feeding of, 242; hairlessness in, 157; Graeco-Roman, 41–42; *Koko's Kitten*, 291; modern, 276, 282

Cavalier King Charles Spaniels, 91, 118, 280

cave canem, 50–51. *See also* Molossus

cemeteries (animal): in the Forbidden City, 264; memorial park style, 260–62; pri-vate, 252; public, 254; Victorian garden style, 260–62; war dogs, 204. *See also* funerals

cemeteries (human), 66, 79, 251, 257–58, 271. *See also* joint burial of people and pets

Charles I, 90–91, 94, 213

China (modern), 271–72

Christ, 62, 63

Christianity: emergence of, 62–65; institutionalization of, 67; in the New World, 81, 84–85; in the Renaissance, 88–90; policies regarding animals, 95, 98, 124, 251–52, 257–58

Christina , Queen, 79

Christopher, Saint, 64–65. *See also* Anubis; Hermanubis; resurrection

City of Dogs (Hardai), 31, 33, 36–38. *See also* Anubis; mummified dogs

clothing (for dogs). *See* boutiques

Clutton-Brock, Juliet, 3, 14–15, 30, 290. *See also* zooarchaeology

collars: African, 22; Egyptian, 25, 28; human, 211–12; as luxury items, 77; magical, 210; modern, 223–25, 227; Renaissance, 77, 211–12, 229–30; Roman, 51, 21; spiked, 210, 224–25; Victorian, 219–20, 259. *See also* Dog Collar Museum; dognapping; private collectors

Collies: preindustrial, 122; in war, 178, 185–86, 189

Columbus, Christopher, 81, 85. *See also* doggings

Comanche, 159. *See also* Native American

Concern for Helping Animals in Israel, 273

Conroy, J. Robert, 180, 181–83. *See also* Stubby

coprolites, 16, 286

cosmetic surgery (for dogs), 114–15, 125, 128

Coutts, Baroness Burdett, 130. *See also* animal welfare, in Victorian society

cowboy sport, 164. *See also* wolf, persecution of

cruelty to animals: among Native Americans, 161; in Israel, 273; Korea, 273; modern society, ix; prehistoric times, 22–23; Puerto Rico, 274–75; Victorian society, 121, 125–37, 145; World War II, 188

cult (animal): Egyptian psychology of, 32–33, 35

Cwn annwn (Dogs of Hell), 75. *See also* supernatural dogs

cynotherapy: Edwardian, 118, 181; Egyptian, 33; Graeco-Roman, 54–58; Latin American, 167; medieval, 77; modern, 57–58

D

Daniels, A.C., 234, 235–36. *See also* pet food, Victorian

Darwin, Charles, 98. *See also* evolution

Day, Doris, 248–49. *See also* sterilization; Spay Day U.S.A.

Demolition Wolf. *See* suicide dogs

Derr, Mark, 277, 279, 290. *See also* American Kennel Club, controversy surrounding

desmoiselles, 213–14

Dickens, Charles, 215, 264

Dingo, Australian, 10, 168, 227

Doberman Pinschers, 189; Devil Dogs, 190, 203, 208

dog-boys, 211. *See also* hunting

Dog Collar Museum, 229–30

dog food. *See* pet food

dog gauge, 71, 277. *See also* poaching

doggings: American Civil War, 175; American Revolution, 174–75; medieval, 79–80; Puerto Rican, 82; Roman, 49; Spanish, 81–88; in World War II, 188

dog handlers: American, 193–98; Celtic, 50; Egyptian, 28–29; Roman, 49; Vietnamese, 195–96; Women, 50, 207. *See also* war dogs

dognapping, 170, 220, 222

dogs (African), 12–13, 27, 28, 49, 227–28

dogs (disabled): medieval, 71; modern, 277–80, 281–82; Roman, 52

dogs (domestication of), 5–11, 15–16. *See also* neoteny

dogs (eating of): Egyptian, 33; Korean, 272–73; Native American, 161–62; in prehistoric times, 5, 8, 10, 13, 21; Spanish, 162

dogs (taxonomy of), 14–16, 18, 21, 29–30

Dogs for Defense, 184–88, 190–91, 200, 205. *See also* K-9 Corps

dog shows: modern American, 182, 277–78; Victorian, 106–7, 109–11, 117–18. *See also* breeds; Victorian

dog tax, 94

E

Einstein, Albert, 283

English Civil War, 90. *See also* Boye; Charles I; supernatural dogs, familiars

Epidaurus, 43, 55–56, 62. *See also* cynotherapy; hunting, Graeco-Roman

epitaphs (dog): Egyptian, 34; Graeco-Roman, 45; Victorian, 252, 260. *See also* cemeteries (animal)

ethoxyquin, 245–47. *See also* pet food

euthanasia: of American pets, 39, 275–77, 286; war dogs, 191, 196, 206

evolution: canid, 1, 3, 7–11, 15–16; human, 1–3, 11. *See also* Darwin, Charles; neoteny; wolf

execution (of dogs): in the French Revolution, 94–95; Middle Ages, 73; Rabies War, 218; Renaissance, 88–89; Russian Revolution, 94–95

extinction: cart dogs, 139; modern breeds, 279; Native American dogs, 151, 156, 162–63, 165–67, 169–70; Turnspits, 140–41

F

fairy spaniel, 79. *See also* lapdogs; supernatural dogs

fakers, 110. *See also* dog shows; Victorian fancy, 99, 171, 286 *See also* breeds: Victorian

feral dogs: Egyptian, 30–31, 38–39; medieval, 67; Native American, 164–165, 168. *See also* New Guinea Singing Dog; Dingo, Australian; homeless dogs; primitive dogs

fleas, 66, 77. *See also* plague

Food and Drug Administration, 245–46. *See also* ethoxyquin

Forbidden City, 115, 264–87. *See also* Pekingese

Frederick the Great, 92–93, 258

French Revolution, 94–96, 213

funerals (dog): Egyptian, 34; Renaissance, 251–52; Victorian, 259–60, 256–57, 266. *See also* cemeteries

G

Gaines, 238. *See also* pet food, advertising

Galen, 44

Gay, John, 145

gazehounds: Egyptian, 27, 29–30, 38; Graeco-Roman, 42; medieval, 69, 72–74; Renaissance, 76, 211; Victorian, 233; in World War I, 178

General History of Quadrupeds, A. See Bewick, Thomas

George (cancer-sniffing dog), 58. *See also* cynotherapy

German Shepherd: breed standard, 279; grooming of, 221; in war, 184–85, 194, 199, 202

ghost-dogs, 88. *See also* supernatural dogs

Gnostics, 62. *See also* Christianity; history, destruction of

Godden, Rumer, 111, 290

Greene, Gordon, 202–3. *See also* K-9 Corps

Greyfriar's Bobby, 271. *See also* Hachiko

Greyhound. *See* gazehounds

grooming: contests, 226; counterculture, 223–25, 230; dyed poodles, 222–23; in nature, 209; in Paris, 213–15; Renaissance, 211

H

Hachiko, 271. *See also* monuments

hairless dogs. *See* Xoloitzcuintli

Happa dog, 113 *See also* Pekingese

Hardai. *See* City of Dogs

Hartsdale Canine Cemetery, 202, 259–60, 263

Hayes, Howard, 196–97. *See also* cancer

healing dogs. *See* cynotherapy

heathens, 81, 102, 116, 160. *See also* Christianity

herding dogs: collars for, 210; disabled, 281–82; prehistoric, 11; preindustrial, 122

heresy, 67, 75, 95, 258. *See also* Christianity

Hermanubis, 59–61, 63, 146, 283. *See also* Anubis; Christopher, Saint

history, destruction of: Egyptian mummies, 34–35; Graeco-Roman temples 62; pet cemeteries, 263–65; prehistoric bones and sites, 4–5, 16–19; war dog documentation, 198–202. *See also* archaeology; extinction

Homeless dogs: Egyptian, 30–31, 33, 38–39; Graeco-Roman, 42–43; medieval, 67; Mexican, 167; modern, 39, 144, 274–77; Victorian, 218, 235. *See also* Battersea; euthanasia; mongrels

honors (for war dogs): Afghan War, 189; American Civil War, 177; Dickin Medal, 191, 201; Greek, 46, 47; Persian Gulf War, 206–7; U.S. policy on, 191, 202–4; World War I, 141, 143, 181–82; World War II, 190–91

horses: cruelty to, 127, 164; dead, 233; Graeco-Roman, 45; hairlessness in, 157; Native American, 158, 159, 164
Hound of St. Hubert. *See* Segusii
hunting: Celtic, 51–52; Egyptian, 26, 38; Graeco-Roman, 43–44; medieval, 68, 71–75, 79; Native American, 4, 151–52, 166; prehistoric, 3–4, 11, 13, 147; Renaissance, 211; Victorian, 101, 102, 103, 133. *See also* poaching
Hyde Park Dog Cemetery, 256–57, 260, 264–65
Hyksos, 28, 49

I

infantilism (dogs): in Chihuahuas, 8; Edwardian, 118; Renaissance, 77–79 *See also* neoteny; women
Inuit. *See* Native American
Italian Greyhound, 92. *See also* Frederick the Great

J

Jack, 176, 220
Japan: in World War II, 188; modern times, 270–71
Jarmo, 13
Jericho, 15
joint burial of people and pets: in *Dog of Flanders*, 144; Egypt, 34; Japan, 271; modern times 258; Renaissance, 79, 93–94, 258. *See also* cemeteries

K

Kane, Elisha, 147–48
kennel masters, 68, 234
kennels: Algernon, 117; Carolina Dog, 168; Egyptian, 27; Imperial, 114; Lackland Air Force Base, 192; medieval, 68, 70;

Renaissance, 75, 211; Victorian, 104–5, 107–9, 234
Kipling, Rudyard, 267
K-9 Corps, 184–92, 202
Korean dogs, 273
Korean War, 192
Krummerer, Bill, 189, 202. *See also* Memorial Day
Kunophontes, 43–44
Kynortion, 43. *See also* hunting, Graeco-Roman

L

Lackland Air Force Base (Working Dogs Agency), 192, 204, 206
Laconian, 42
La Grotte du Lazaret, 3, 14
Landseer, Sir Edwin, 116, 128–30, 222–23
lapdogs: collars for, 210; feeding of, 234; French, 94, 175; Renaissance, 76–78; Roaring Twenties, 221; Roman, 49, 113. *See also* women
Lascaux, 2, 5
Lee, Mrs. R., 140, 160
Lemish, Mike, 205, 290
Lennie, Campbell, 291. *See also* Landseer, Sir Edwin
Levrier. *See* gazehounds
lion-clip, 212–13
Lootie, 116. *See also* Pekingese
Louis XVI, King, 96
luxury dogs. *See* lapdogs
Lydney Park, 56. *See also* cynotherapy

M

Maltese, 113–14, 214
Manifest Destiny, 163
Marines, 190, 196
mascots: Afghan War, 177; American Civil War, 176, 220; British Civil War, 90;

Lydney Park, 57; World War I, 180–81

Mass of St. Hubert, 77. *See also* Christianity

Mastiff: collars for, 212, 229; Egyptian, 28–29, 38; Spanish, 210; at the Tower of London, 79; Victorian, 101, 133

Matîn. *See* cart dogs

matrilineal societies, 9. *See also* women

Memorial Day, 198, 202

men: humane education of, 130; Inuit, 7; prehistoric, 10; Renaissance, 77–79, 89–90, 94; Victorian, 102, 103, 113, 215

Mendez, Jesse, 193, 195, 198

messenger dogs, 179–80, 189

Mexican Kennel Club, 167, 170

mining dogs, 163

Mixed Breed Dog Club of America, 280

Molesworth Pet Cemetery, 257, 264

Molossus, 42, 46, 49–51, 69, 178, 288

mongrels: bias against, 102, 106, 139–40, 160; medieval, 71; modern, 144, 274–75, 280, 288; Native American, 171; popularity of, 223; in war, 183, 185, 190. *See also* homeless dogs

Monsanto Chemical Company, 246. *See also* ethoxyquin

monuments (dog): English, 271; Greek, 47; Japanese, 202, 271; war dogs, 202–4

mummified dogs: Egyptian, 34–35, 37; modern, 266; Native American, 154

murder (dog): 79, 111, 164, 258

muzzles, 219. *See also* rabies

N

names (dog): Egyptian, 24, 27, 29; Graeco-Roman, 46–47; Renaissance, 89–90

National Archives, 199

National Cancer Institute, 196

National Dog Groomers' Association, 226

National Federation for the Breeding of Draft Dogs, 135–36, 138–39

National Museum of American History, 200–201

Native American: dog varieties, 7–8, 147, 171; hunting, 4, 152, 156; mythology, 1, 23, 146–47, 173, 283; persecution of, 160–61; pet-keeping traditions, 6–8; rituals, 5, 158, 161–62

Neolithic: agriculture, 11, 13; archaeological sites, 12–13, 16; collar, 209; dogs, 13–14; livestock, 11, 13; pictorial art, 12–13

neoteny: 7–10, 15, 114, 288. *See also* women

New Guinea Singing Dog: breeding, 20, 23; genetics of, 19, 21; as pets, 21, 169. *See also* feral dogs; primitive dogs

Nigerian dogs, 227–28

Nixon, Richard, 206

O

Olsen, Stanley, 14–15, 18, 171, 291. *See also* zooarchaeology

Orote Point, 204. *See also* Memorials

P

pagans, 62, 64, 75, 88, 163. *See also* Christianity

Palegawra Cave, 15

Paleolithic: archaeological sites, 2–3, 5, 14, 16–19; canids, 3, 13–16, 18–19

Panati, Charles, 67

paratrooping dogs, 189, 193

pedigree, 106, 111, 113, 169–70, 224, 277–78. *See also* aristocracy

Pekingese: attempted murder of, 111; breed flaws, 121; *Butterfly Lions*, 290; cemetery for, 264; evolution of, 113–14; in modern China, 272; Victorian, 111, 233–35

performing dogs, 122, 185, 251, 259

Persian Gulf War, 16, 206

pet food: advertising, 239–40, 242–44; home-cooked, 239, 247–49; Graeco-Roman, 57; medieval, 233, military, 196; Native American, 147, 158; prescription,

244; table scraps, 232, 235; Victorian, 232–36

Pet Food Institute, 239, 243

Phoébus, Gaston, 68, 72, 100

Pitcairn, Richard, 247–49, 291. *See also* pet food: home-cooked

plague: bubonic, 30, 66–67, 114; in the New World, 162

Pliny the Elder, 52

Plutarch, 33, 34

poaching, 70–71. *See also* hunting

Pompadour, Madame de, 92

Poodle, 118, 212, 214–15, 222–23, 225–27; Boye, 90, 213; Masterpiece, 222

Post Traumatic Stress Disorder, 197–98

primitive dogs: breeding, 8–10, 11, 13, 20–21; skeletal remains of, 13–16, 18–19, 20; varieties of, 7, 10, 19–22, 168–69. *See also* feral dogs

private collectors: collars, 228–29; war dog memorabilia, 201–2. *See also* Dog Collar Museum

Puerto Rico, 85, 273–75

Pug, 92, 105

puppy: Egyptian, 28, 36, 38; prehistoric, 5. *See also* neoteny

puppy mills, 21, 276, 281

R

rabies (hydrophobia), 287; in Athens, 42; cart dogs, 133–34; China, 272; Egypt, 30, 33; London, 218–19

Ralston Purina, 240. *See also* pet food, advertising

Red Cross, 182, 200; dogs, 178–79

Reprobus, 64. *See also* Christopher, Saint

resurrection: of Anubis, 31–33; Hermanubis, 65; Lazarus, 62; in Native American mythology, 146–47

Roch, Saint, 63. *See also* cynotherapy

rock art 5, 13, 17, 152

Royal Society for the Prevention of Cruelty to Animals, 130, 133, 135

rubbing dogs. *See* cynotherapy; women

S

sacrifice (dog): Egyptian, 37; Graeco-Roman, 43–44; Native American, 158, 161–62

Sanborn, Kate, 137, 291

Sand Creek, Battle at, 164

satos, 274–75. *See also* homeless dogs; mongrels

scavenger dogs, 14, 67, 235

schools (war dog), 178–79, 184

Scott, Sir Walter, 253, 254

Segusii, 52, 76

sentience (dog), 282–83

sentry dogs: in Andersonville Prison, 175; Egyptian, 175; euthanasia of, 206; Graeco-Roman, 50, 58–59; modern, 207, 279; prehistoric, 13; at the Tower of London, 79; in Vietnam War, 192, 195, 199–200.

Shultheis, Oscar, 97, 221

sighthound. *See* gazehound

Smithsonian Institution, 200–201

socialization (human): of prehistoric dogs, 5, 7, 10; retired police dogs, 206; retired war dogs, 191, 206; wolves, 8

Spanish: conquistadors, 81–82, 158; dogs, 151, 162; in the Southwest, 154–55

Spay Day U.S.A., 276

Spratt, James, 235–36, 239. *See also* pet food, Victorian

sterilizaton (of pets), 280, 282; Native American dogs, 166–167; Spay Day U.S.A., 276; war dogs, 185

Stubby, 180–83, 201–2, 204

suicide dogs, 188

Summum, Incorporated. *See* mummified dogs

supernatural dogs: familiars, 88–91; Roman, 210; Wild Hunt, 74–75

T

Tahl Tan Bear Dog, 165–67
Tassili-n-Ajjer, 12, 13. *See also* Neolithic
taxidermied dogs, 116, 141, 199; at the British Museum of Natural History, 99–100, 152; National Museum of American History, 200–201; Rothschild Zoological Museum, 120
taxonomy (dog), 7, 13, 21, 29, 152, 160–61, 169–70
taxonomy (wolf), 11, 15–16
Techichi, 151–54, 160, 170
temple dogs, 33, 37, 56, 58–59, 62
territoriality (canid), 13
therapy dogs. *See* cynotherapy
Thief Dog, 74. *See also* poaching
trade in dogs, 41–42, 48, 69
travois dog, 158–59
toy dogs. *See* lapdogs
Turnspit, 122–24, 134–35, 139–41, 150. *See also* Mongrels: bias against
Tzu-tsi, Dowager Empress of China, 114, 232

U

United Animal Owners Alliance, 245, 246
United Kennel Club, 281. *See also* puppy mills

V

verderers, 71–74. *See also* hunting
vestigators, 52
veterinarians, 245, 277; Daniels, A.C., 235–36; Dodds, W. Jean, 246; Hayes, Howard, 196–97; Garbutt, Raymond, 236; Pitcairn, Richard, 247–48
Victoria, Queen, 128, 177; as humane advocate, 130; patron of Sir Edwin Landseer, 128; pets, 103–5, 252, 253–54; the royal kennels of, 234–35
Victorian bowel obsession, 233, 244
Viet Cong, 194, 195
Vietnam Dog Handlers Association, 198
Vietnam Memorial, 198
Vietnam War, 192–98
vivisection, 39–40, 44; *Stolen for Profit*, 291
Vlasac, 13

W

Walter Rothschild Zoological Museum of Tring, 120
War Dog Museum, 202
war dogs: commemorative stamp drive, 206; in the American Revolution, 174–75; American Civil War, 175–77; Egypt, 28–29; Gaul, 50; Greece, 46–47; Rome, 50; Spanish conquest, 79–88, 174; World War I, 136–39, 177–83; World War II, 184–92. *See also* sentry dogs; Vietnam War
weddings (dog), 220, 223
Wepwawet, 31, 64. *See also* Anubis; Christopher, Saint; Hermanubis; Resurrection
Wheeler, Sir Mortimer, 18. *See also* Lydney Park
White Dog Cave, 154
Wild Hunt, 74–75. *See also* supernatural dogs
Windsor Castle, 252, 263
witch-hunts. *See* supernatural dogs, familiars
wolf: Asiatic, 11, 147; behavior of, 3, 5; hybrid, 9–8, 18; North American, 11, 147; persecution of, 160, 164; as progenitor of the dog, 3, 7, 18; ritualization of, 4, 6; tamed, 4, 6, 8–9, 11, 16, 147; timber, 11;

Wolf Wars, 290. *See also* cowboy sport
women: *Dogs and Their Women,* 290; effect
on canine fashions, 210, 214–15, 221–22;
Egyptian, 25, 27, 34; medieval, 75, 77–79;
Native American, 6–9, 146, 150, 159; prehistoric, 5, 7–10; Renaissance, 89; Victorian, 102, 111, 118, 175, 236–37; as war dog
handlers, 50, 207
Wood, J.G., 140, 150, 215
wool dogs, 155–56
World War I, 177–83

World War II, 183–92
Wounded Knee, 164

X

Xoloitzcuintli, 156–58, 161–62, 167, 170

Z

zooarchaeology, 3, 5, 18–19, 30, 35, 289